PRAISE FOR *EVERYDAY ILLEGAL*

"*Everyday Illegal* is a pioneering study of the effects of immigration law status on the lives of undocumented immigrants, their families, and their communities. Dreby paints an intimate portrait of the undocumented that is at once vivid and nuanced, while also poignant and heartbreaking. A combination of keen observation, analytical rigor, and compelling narrative, this remarkable book is essential reading—rich with indispensable lessons about the costs that the US immigration system imposes, every day, on some of the most vulnerable members of our society."

Hiroshi Motomura, author of *Immigration Outside the Law*

"*Everyday Illegal* is an urgent call to reframe immigrant illegality and reform a system that produces the very un-American reality of different classes of citizens."

Luis Argueta, director and producer of the immigration trilogy *abUSed: The Postville Raid* (2010), *ABRAZOS* (2014), and *The U-Turn* (2015)

"This beautifully written study forces us to recognize the impact of our inhumane policy and is a must-read for understanding the underbelly consequences of an immigration system that demands mass deportation and the criminalization of immigrants who want to work and provide a better life for their f

Mary Ro   *tside*
the Amer

Everyday Illegal

Everyday Illegal

WHEN POLICIES UNDERMINE IMMIGRANT FAMILIES

Joanna Dreby

UNIVERSITY OF CALIFORNIA PRESS

University of California Press, one of the most distinguished university presses in the United States, enriches lives around the world by advancing scholarship in the humanities, social sciences, and natural sciences. Its activities are supported by the UC Press Foundation and by philanthropic contributions from individuals and institutions. For more information, visit www.ucpress.edu.

University of California Press
Oakland, California

Library of Congress Cataloging-in-Publication Data

Dreby, Joanna, 1976– author.
    Everyday illegal : when policies undermine immigrant families / Joanna Dreby.
        pages   cm
    Includes bibliographical references and index.
    ISBN 978-0-520-28339-8 (cloth) — ISBN 978-0-520-28340-4 (pbk. : alk. paper) — ISBN 978-0-520-95927-9 (ebook)
    1. Illegal aliens—United States—Case studies.   2. Immigrants—Family relationships—United States—Case studies.   3. Children of immigrants—United States—Case studies.   4. United States—Emigration and immigration—Social aspects.   I. Title.
    JV6483.D74   2015
    305.9′06912—dc23

                                                              2014038846

Manufactured in the United States of America

24   23   22   21   20   19   18   17   16
10   9   8   7   6   5   4   3   2

In keeping with a commitment to support environmentally responsible and sustainable printing practices, UC Press has printed this book on Natures Natural, a fiber that contains 30% post-consumer waste and meets the minimum requirements of ANSI/NISO Z39.48–1992 (R 1997) (*Permanence of Paper*).

For

Christian Cuauhtemoc Mariscal-Dreby

and

Dylan Tonahuac Mariscal-Dreby

Contents

Prologue

For more than 200 years, our tradition of welcoming immigrants from around the world has given us a tremendous advantage over other nations. It's kept us youthful, dynamic, and entrepreneurial. It has shaped our character as a people with limitless possibilities—people not trapped by our past, but able to remake ourselves as we choose.

But today, our immigration system is broken—and everybody knows it.

President Obama, "Remarks by the President in Address to the Nation on Immigration," November 20, 2014

As this book was being prepared for publication, the Obama administration announced an executive order changing some of the policies it will use in dealing with unauthorized immigrants. How the order will play out in the deeply partisan political system, whether it will in fact be implemented, and what the effects of its implementation will be, are unclear. The actions, if executed, are unlikely to undo the damage done to families by the current restrictive immigration system. But the announcement does offer some hope.

Symbolically, the announcement acknowledges that far too many individuals—people who have lived and worked in this country for years, who have raised their US citizen children here, and who pay taxes and contribute to their local communities—have been blocked from legalization and targeted for deportation. They are a part of this society but lack legal recognition and the rights that come with it. Historically, most immigrants to the United States have eventually been able to legalize; we are, after all, a country of immigrants. Today, however, for many people there is no pathway to legalization, no line to join. The system is, indeed, broken.

The executive order proposes a few patches to this broken system. First, it increases the number of young people who can apply for DACA (or Deferred Action for Childhood Arrivals), which gives the unauthorized raised in the United States and educated in US schools temporary work authorization and a reprieve from deportation. By removing age caps, providing a three-year work authorization period, and adjusting the cutoff date for arrival to the country (from 2007 to 2010), it makes more young people eligible for the program. The possibility of expanded work and educational opportunities is an important gesture. The current restrictive immigration system has instituted a rigid pecking order among children based on their legal status. Increased opportunities for young unauthorized immigrants can help to ease some of the inequalities that result from this system.

Second, the executive order provides a similar reprieve for the parents of US citizen children; that is, some parents will be eligible for temporary work authorization and protection from deportation through the newly dubbed DAPA program (or Deferred Action for Parental Accountability). For families with unauthorized members, this change is likely to have a huge impact. Knowing that their parents will not be targeted should bring relief to those young children who experience fear and stress at the possibility of their parents' removal. That some parents will receive work authorization opens the door to improved economic security for the US citizen children living in these families.

Third, the executive order allows some of those who are currently detained or in the process of being deported to apply for DAPA. It also slightly broadens eligibility for provisional waivers in cases of extreme hardship so that some families can avoid the existing bars to reentry. (I explain these bars in the book.) Theoretically, these measures promise to keep immigrant families together, avoiding tragic stories of lengthy family separations.

Fourth, with this executive order, the Secure Communities program will be discontinued and replaced by a program that outlines priority categories for the identification and removal of immigrants deemed to be undesirable—those categorized as threats to national security or public safety. Under Secure Communities, the net used to identify "undesirable" and "criminal" immigrants had been cast far too wide, catching many whom we consider to be valuable members of their communities, so this is a welcome change.

It is too early to tell how important these changes, taken together, will be for families. In practice, individual families' situations are quite complex. One gray area, for example, is the concept of "extreme hardship." Can an unauthorized husband who is threatened with deportation apply for an extreme hardship waiver because he supports his wife in graduate school? Will immigration officials measure her emotional distress at his leaving or her potential for economic solvency if he is deported? This college-educated wife could clearly find work, yet she might not then be able to continue her education, while her emotional distress is likely related to the nature of the marital relationship. Is it not beyond the purview of immigration officials to make judgments about the intensity of emotional bonds in marriages? Ambiguities in the application of immigration policies to real-life scenarios mean that while some families may be able to avoid separations with this executive order, others will undoubtedly not.

And how far will DACA and DAPA go toward repairing codified injustices? Although DAPA has not yet been implemented, we can extrapolate based on experiences with DACA, in place now for two years. We know, for example, that many eligible young people have not signed up for DACA. Possibly this is because DACA is temporary and can be rescinded in the future, leaving recipients especially vulnerable once they have been documented and entered into the system. Or perhaps varied access to the program in different local communities, and limitations on the benefits derived from the DACA status specified by some local jurisdictions, explain the gap between eligibility and application rates. Moreover, youth who have received DACA report varying outcomes, as the accumulated years living with an unauthorized status appear to have had a cascading and longstanding impact on many people's lives.

I imagine that what we have learned from the DACA experience will also be applicable to DAPA. That is, we can expect fewer parents to apply than are eligible. We can expect the impacts to vary across communities nationwide, and that parents who receive DAPA in more welcoming local contexts will have much better experiences that those living in places where opposition to immigration is high. In fact, twenty states have recently signed onto a lawsuit against the Obama administration, challenging the executive order. This action shows that if the measures are executed, implementation strategies will likely vary widely across the country. We can also anticipate that DAPA will not fix all the problems experienced by families whose members have different legal statuses. While some family members will be able to obtain relief, others will invariably be left out. And, perhaps more importantly, the impacts of the years living out of status will linger even for those who benefit from the executive order. The impacts on families of the restrictive immigration system cannot be erased nearly so easily.

As for enforcement priorities and practices, while Secure Communities seems to have been a particularly bad policy for families, those I interviewed also experienced negative impacts in places where Secure Communities had not been implemented. The continued relentless insistence by the administration to identify and eliminate all criminal and undesirable immigrants from this country promises much of the same. In fact, the executive order initiates a new Southern Border and Approaches Campaign that will distribute even more resources to the US-Mexico border, making unauthorized crossing ever more treacherous, all in the attempt to keep more of the foreign born out. And yet structural factors such as unequal trade policies, the US economy's dependence on informal labor, and the US-backed war on drugs in Mexico and Central and South America—and the increasing violence associated with street gangs and drug cartels—will continue to uproot families, generating even more need for emigration.

Herein lies the problem with the current framing of the social problem of unauthorized immigration. Unauthorized immigrants today are viewed as criminals who break the law, precisely *because* the law does not provide sufficient mechanisms for those who need and want to live and work in the United States to do so legally. Thus policy debates are stuck in a framework in which the only solution appears to be one in which we must decide who are worthy immigrants and who are not, who should be punished for breaking our laws and who should be pardoned. Such a framing inevitably codifies social inequalities based on legal status.

When policies become particularly restrictive, as they have over the past few decades, such framing undermines families. I describe in this book the specific ways they are undermined: by the threat of enforcement and the fears that result, by the webs of dependency that develop between family members when some have status and others do not, by the differential pathways available for children with varying legal status, and by the reinforcement of stigma related to immigration.

And I suggest that our society would do better if we were to implement family-friendly immigration policies. But family-friendly policies must operate from an alternative framework, one that views unauthorized migration in a different light.

I invite you, the reader, to consider the following as you read this book. Start with the assumption that unauthorized migration is unavoidable. If there is immigration, and we are a country of immigrants, then there will always be some proportion of the population that is unauthorized. Global economic policies both generate and depend on unauthorized labor. The pertinent questions then become, how do we treat members of this unauthorized population? And how does our treatment of this group impact both families with unauthorized members and our society as a whole?

This book tells the stories of families living in the United States during a particularly restrictive time in which unauthorized immigrants are primarily viewed as criminals despite their unquestionable, integral role in the fabric of this society. I ask you to consider the possibility, as you read what follows, that the blame ought to fall on the laws that are unjust, not on the people who are affected by them. And if the laws are what bring injustice, should we not reframe them to better support immigrant families who live, everyday, among us?

Acknowledgments

Moses Nagel pressed me. Under the fluorescent lighting of the Flying Chicken restaurant, after a few rounds of pinball, I found the idea captivating. "When else would you tell your story?" he said. Scared and excited, I had to do it, or at least try. The next few months I reread the manuscript, edited it, and inserted myself so that the readers would not only notice my presence as a researcher but also know something of how my own character fits into the story. It is how it should be. Thank you.

Moses along with Leisy Abrego, Katie Dole, Ed Dreby, Arturo Erasmo, Tanya Golash-Boza, Amy Gottlieb, Aaron Major, Margaret Mansfield, Helen Marrow, Cecilia Menjívar, Eva Nagel, Rich Ocejo, Kevin Roy, Leah Schmalzbauer, Mary Valentis, and anonymous reviewers read different pieces of the manuscript and provided extremely useful feedback. Vanessa Colon, Erynn De Masi Cassanova, Pawan Dhingra, Zachary Dye, Nancy Foner, Roberto Gonzales, Phil Kasinitz, Tamara Mose, Hiroshi Motomura, Maria Silvia Navarro, Richard Serpe, Rob Smith, Clare Stacey, Roger Waldinger, Julia Wrigley, and Min Zhou listened to either early renditions of the project or later formal and informal presentations of findings. Their personal reactions and professional advice helped shape this book. Editorial encouragement, especially from Naomi Schneider, pushed it forward into final publication, as did the valuable support of the production team at the University of California Press, especially Dore Brown and Elisabeth Magnus. Thank you.

The Foundation for Child Development generously supported this project, along with Kent State University and the University at Albany-SUNY. The research would not have been possible without this support.

Research assistance made data collection and analysis possible and kept me sane from the very beginnings of the project to the final edits. Timothy Adkins, Gladys Apaestegui, Alison Drinkard, Gowoon Jung, Daniela Pila, Lina Rincón, Mariana Romero, Lindsay Stutz, and Rachel Sullivan deserve much thanks. I am grateful to Bob Anderson for his generosity and for the photographs that accompany this book.

Many people offered their selfless trust to enable this project. I have decided to keep the details of the places where I did fieldwork and collected interviews confidential, so I will not name them here. To those that allowed me to interview them, recommended me to others, endorsed the project, put in a good word on my behalf, allowed me into their schools and school districts, and welcomed me into their homes time and time again, thank you so very much.

To Raúl, thank you for your unwavering faith in allowing me to draw on details of our life together.

To the children upon whose experiences this book focuses, and their parents, thank you.

Temo and Dylan live with me, put up with me, every day. We are family, and they are my starting point. More than this, I relied on them for many aspects of this project. During data collection I depended on them to hang out with children they did not know. They moved with me, leaving friends and family behind, to set up a solid comparative project. I asked their advice when I did not understand something I had learned from another child. I read them passages of this book, which they approved even though they may not have fully understood. Thank you, boys, for all of your help. Thank you for pushing me and for your advice: "Don't stress." I love you.

Manual de Detenidos de

ICE

Lucas

Fecha Efectiva y Primera Distribucion

Fecha Efectiva: Diciembre 2011

Revisado: May 2012

Revisado:

1 Introduction

LEGAL STATUS IN FAMILY CONTEXTS

Surmounting legal barriers, for many of the forty million foreign-born individuals who live in the United States, marks the first step on the yellow brick road toward the American dream.[1] To achieve legal status, immigrants have typically had to meet certain requisites. Today, however, we face an emerging social problem: the complete elimination of pathways to legalization for many US immigrants. This book focuses on the fallout, exploring what it means to have or not have a legal status under restrictive policy conditions. Accounts from children and parents in Mexican immigrant households show that illegality—the term I use for the awareness of needing a legal status and the negotiations around lacking a legal status—generates social inequality in the contemporary United States.[2] Mexicans certainly are not the only immigrant population facing the impacts of illegality,[3] but US immigration policy has made legalization especially onerous for Mexicans.[4] Demographers estimate that of the 11.7 million unauthorized persons in the United States in 2012, approximately 58 percent were Mexican.[5] Mexican families' experiences

Opposite: Photograph by Bob Anderson

demonstrate the divisive impact of stagnant public policy on the everyday lives of families.

This book is also a sequel.

Fifteen years ago, I lived and worked in one of the new and flourishing Mexican immigrant communities in central New Jersey. Many parents I knew had left their children in the care of others to come work in the United States, so I began a study of the meaning separation had for parents and children (and their caregivers) living apart.[6] The militarization of the US-Mexican border and the tightening of the US immigration system, efforts that began in earnest during the 1980s, created the conditions under which families' prolonged separations unfolded a decade later.[7] Prior to this period, Mexican men commonly migrated north as labor migrants, periodically returning to visit their families—wives and children—who typically remained in Mexico.[8] Family separation involved men's temporary absences from the family unit. Yet as circular migration became ever more difficult for men to accomplish, many young married couples rejected the stress of long-term spousal separation.[9] Employment north of the border attracted women, many of whom, discontent with long-distance marriages, reunited with their husbands.[10] It also lured unmarried mothers who saw migration as their only means out of poverty.[11] With a marked increase in deaths on the border families regarded women's migration north, crossing the increasingly militarized border, as risky.[12] But they viewed it as even riskier for children.

So women set forth without their children. They considered these heart-wrenching separations to be difficult but temporary—as the absences of husbands had previously been. They deemed them worthwhile since they represented a step toward either family reunification or survival, a necessary sacrifice for the family to get ahead.[13] A decade after the Immigration Reform and Control Act of 1986 (IRCA), the last major immigration policy reform that combined legalization with increased penalties for unauthorized migration, temporary separations of parents and children for Mexican families made sense. Men could not return to Mexico as frequently as in times past. So women too came to the United States to work alongside men. Children waited with grandparents until parents had carved out enough of a foothold to send for their children. Families hoped that either with or without legalization programs they would eventually be able to reunite.

This logical strategy generated many a tragic experience. Unintended consequences ensued. Parents, especially mothers, grappled with guilt. The children I met felt resentful. Expectations parents had for their children, and children of their parents, often went unmet. Separation transformed power dynamics within families. I wrote *Divided by Borders* about how mothers, fathers, children, and caregivers made sense of these separations.

ADMINISTRATIVE TRAP

Over the course of the next fifteen years, US immigration and enforcement laws further solidified and restrictions increased. The Department of Homeland Security subsumed all operations of what had previously been the INS, or Immigration and Naturalization Services, and parceled out operatives to two agencies, one to deal with processing immigration applications (US Citizen and Immigration Services, USCIS) and one to enforce immigration laws (US Immigration and Customs Enforcement, ICE).[14] On both ends, families found themselves stuck. Post-IRCA, small changes to immigration policy rendered most of the unauthorized living in the United States ineligible to regularize their status through the USCIS if they had entered the country without inspection, as most Mexicans do when crossing the southern border. Even those who were married to US citizens and parents to US citizen children faced these restrictions. So unauthorized family members became vulnerable to the enforcement practices of ICE, which considerably intensified efforts to identify and remove unauthorized foreign-born residents often cooperating with local law enforcement agencies located thousands of miles from the US-Mexican border.[15]

During the 1990s, the tightening of our US immigration system meant that families considered undergoing temporary separations and living divided by borders. But by the start of the twenty-first century, the system had crystallized and become so strict and far-reaching that legal status had begun to divide even families residing together in the United States.

Such an unforgiving system paralyzes families as well as the debates over immigration reform. Formerly, immigration policy debates often remained outside the realm of partisan politics, uniting coalitions of strange bedfellows: business owners and humanitarians for more leniency; environmentalists, unions, and xenophobes for more restrictions.[16] When the right combinations of groups came together, amendments to the laws, however small, passed.[17] But in the early 2000s partisan politics engulfed the issue, blocking both comprehensive immigration reform and the passing of more modest measures, like the DREAM Act, which would provide conditional permanent residency for undocumented youth educated in US primary and secondary schools.[18] Bipartisan consensus exists over only one issue: enforcement.[19] Funding for border control has dramatically increased, from $1.2 billion in 1986 to $17.9 billion in 2012 (adjusted to 2012 dollars).[20] And the Obama administration (2009–present) has stepped up deportations, conducting them more frequently than at any other point in US history, surpassing estimates of the massive repatriation of Mexicans in the 1920s and 1930s.[21] Congressional discussions over immigration reform propose to maintain and increase existing border security measures as a precondition to any pathway toward legal permanent residence.[22]

Under this policy climate, Mexican migrant families have hunkered down. Border crossings for Mexicans, more costly than in times past, have become especially perilous as violent Mexican drug cartels expanded into smuggling operations.[23] Seasonal returns to Mexico have become ever more difficult to arrange and thus less common.[24] The net inflow of Mexicans to the United States had risen significantly between 1995 and 2000, right before I began research on *Divided by Borders*. Between 2000 and 2005, some estimates suggested that the inflow had come to a complete standstill.[25] Now more and more Mexican immigrants have their children in the United States and raise them here,[26] afraid that if they leave they will never be able to come back.

Pathways to legalization for the estimated 11.1 million unauthorized immigrants living in the United States do not exist.[27] No person is or can be illegal, but today's policies cast the everyday, commonplace activities of many people as "illegal." In the 1980s, Leo Chavez described the undocumented as living "shadowed lives" on the fringes of American society.[28] In the twenty-first century, those without "papers"—*sin papeles*—live among us as the parents, siblings, aunts, uncles, and children of US legal permanent residents and citizens. They may be our family members, friends, neighbors, fellow students, coworkers, or acquaintances. In 2010, 16.6 million people lived in a mixed-status family, that is, a family in which at least one member was unauthorized.[29] To put this into perspective, 4.5 million US citizen children had at least one undocumented parent.[30] Compare this to 4.1 million children living with a biological mother and a stepfather.[31] Numerically speaking, today you are about as likely to know a child living with a stepfather as you are to know a child living with an unauthorized parent.

This book takes up the story where *Divided by Borders* left off. It charts what happens when an unforgiving immigration system divides families internally while they are living together. The stories derive from four years of ethnographic research with Mexican families in two communities, one in Ohio and one in New Jersey. I conducted formal interviews with 201 family members: 91 parents and 110 children. I also visited twelve families periodically at their homes, sharing family meals and weekday afternoon routines and at times attending weekend family excursions. I followed twelve first, second, and third graders in these families into their school classrooms to better understand how children and their families navigated settings outside the home.[32] I draw on both formal and informal conversations and observations; some were with the teachers, administrators, and social workers whom Mexican immigrant families interface with regularly. Most were with Mexican community members, whether study participants, acquaintances, or, in many cases, those I consider to be my friends. *Everyday Illegal* documents how, under restrictive immigration policy, illegality is more than a legal status: it is a social one.

THE JOURNEY

In the true spirit of a sequel, this book—like *Divided by Borders*—reflects some of my personal journey. In 2007, I got a job, so I uprooted my family—me and my sons Temo and Dylan—from the bilingual, bicultural community where we had lived in New Jersey and moved across Pennsylvania to northeastern Ohio. Four hundred miles is not much compared to the thousands of miles families I have interviewed have migrated, but the cultural gulf felt tremendous. Temo had stood out as one of the whitest kids in his bilingual preschool classroom in New Jersey. Suddenly he became a student of color, with his tan skin and dark features, in a kindergarten class of children with blond hair and hazel or blue eyes. The new job demanded much of my time. I could not rely on the support of friends and family who had helped me through graduate school in New Jersey; single motherhood hit me head on. Every day I juggled the routes between work, school, and the Turkish babysitter who watched eighteen-month-old Dylan. Latino families did not live in my neighborhood. We stopped speaking Spanish at home, and Dylan began asking for *karpuz* instead of *sandia* or watermelon.

Something had gone missing from our lives. I learned of a nearby church that ran a youth program to support Latino children's Spanish-language skills and culture in a place where little else did. I signed up.

Over the next three years, members of a vibrant and diverse, though rather invisible, Latino community rescued me. One of the few groups helping new immigrants in the area, they were used to newcomers. Not all I met warmly welcomed me; I felt an outsider, with my newly obtained professor status differentiating me from working families in the community. But new friends helped me recover a sense of home and belonging. Invited to dinners and parties, I ate the foods I had learned to love in New Jersey and in Mexico. I met former farmworkers, migrants from some of the places I had been to in Mexico, as well as professional immigrants who had come on work visas to some of the area's largest employers. Quite a few—mostly men, but also some women—had intermarried. Particularly drawn to these families, I imagined their experiences to most approximate mine. I had lived with my now ex, Raúl, a Mexican immigrant, for five years. As I learned about others' lives, I gained perspective on my own.

For me and my family, though, the simple contours of daily life in Ohio had the largest impact. In the New Jersey city where we had previously lived, the Mexican community had a visible presence; walk down any street in the city and you could see dozens of handmade signs in Spanish alongside those of more formal restaurants, bodegas, and bakeries. In 2010, half of the city residents identified as Hispanic or Latino, and a quarter as Mexicans.[33] We regularly ate Mexican cheese and sweet bread, which I purchased at the Dominican bodega down the block. We listened to music on the multiple Spanish-language radio stations based out of New York City. We danced salsa, *cumbia,* and *bachata* at parties with friends. We lived within walking distance of many people I interviewed for *Divided by Borders.*

In Ohio, the only Spanish-language radio was an hourlong program broadcast on Sunday mornings. Stores selling Spanish food products peppered seemingly random strip malls rather than being concentrated in any one area of the city. I found no bakeries; Mexican bread came shipped in from Chicago, and families bought Mexican food products at Walmart. The families I met lived in diverse neighborhoods, typically far from each other, and from me. I drove everywhere. Less than 2 percent of the population in the city where I met most families identified as Latino or Hispanic, and less than 1 percent identified as Mexican.[34] A few Mexican families rented and owned homes in the university town where I lived; I eventually met them all. In Ohio, distance made the Latino community much more intentional.

When I started formal research I hoped to compare the experiences of children growing up in these two vastly different local communities. After two years of fieldwork in Ohio (2009–10), I returned in 2011 to New Jersey, where I had previously lived and worked, to match the interviews and observations I had done with families in Ohio. I intentionally included those of many different legal statuses, reflecting the diversity in the types of immigrants I had met in Ohio. How much had illegality affected families in which one parent was foreign born and the other a US-born citizen? What about families in which parents and children—or siblings—did not share a legal status? In what ways did children with different legal statuses navigate their lives in these two very different types of communities?

I expected to write a book about the variations at the local level that altered children's experiences. But a different story emerged. Mexican parents and children in Ohio and New Jersey described surprisingly similar experiences with illegality. Being unauthorized—even in the relatively protective community in New Jersey—was very different from what it had been like in 2003 when I had begun research for *Divided by Borders,* and earlier when I had first met Raúl. Living "hyperaware" of the law children were cognizant of either their own legal status or that of their parents even before social structures made legal status prohibitive, before they sought jobs, filled out applications for educational loans or college scholarships, or applied for drivers' licenses.[35] Illegality powerfully shaped children's lives and those of their family members, and their relationships with each other, even when no one in the family had actually been deported.[36] It affected families regardless of where they lived.[37] In a restrictive policy environment, illegality matters regardless of each individual family member's legal status. It begins to affect us all.

My family's experiences inspired this research, but *Everyday Illegal* is not our story. I include myself and my children in some of what follows because it feels impossible not to. My own experiences frame the relationships I had with many families. Often those I interviewed asked for details on my own life; my disclosures seemed only fair to those who divulged what, at times, seemed so private.[38] So I decided that the only way to respectfully tell others' stories was to do so along with my own; this type of quid pro quo developed in my conversations with families, and often I felt it was expected. Parents I interviewed asked me about how I had met Raúl and about what it had been like for me to be married to a once unauthorized Mexican. They wondered about my boys' relationship with their father, a topic that I at times found discomfiting, much as some of my questions surely disquieted them. Of course, legal status produced absolute differences between me and most of the study participants. My children and I are US-born citizens. We have the rights that come with this status, the ability to travel, drive, work, and go to college that so many I interviewed did not.

Yet my own experiences illustrate the creeping consequences of illegality, even for those of us who enjoy the rights of US citizenship. This is a trend I found true in the experience of every person I met and interviewed, even families in which all members had legalized their status. I pause to give one example. Raúl and I have been divorced for quite some time. While we were married, he obtained his legal permanent residency via a spousal petition, through his marriage to me. A few years ago, he called from his lawyer's office; in readying his citizenship application, they had detected a problem in the paperwork that presented a red flag, making it look as if our marriage might not be a legitimate one. Raúl's immigration lawyer recommended he not apply for citizenship. The USCIS had begun scrutinizing citizen applications; if Raúl submitted the paperwork uncovering the mistake, even if I preemptively supplied an affidavit of support explaining the error, our family circumstances would look suspicious. He could be stripped of his legal permanent residency and deported. We squabbled for a few weeks over whose fault the mistake was; it is too bad immigration court doesn't accept this as evidence of a bona fide marriage. Raúl is stuck in what Cecilia Menjívar has termed a state of "liminal legality."[39] Even my two children cannot escape the threat of the deportation of their father.

THE STORIES

Everyday Illegal, much like *Divided by Borders,* documents the nexus between the public sphere of immigration policy and the private lives of families. With the exception of me and my boys and one family whom I interviewed in both studies, all of the characters here are new. They could, however, be one and the same; many parents I interviewed had experienced a separation from their children or from their own parents when they were children because of international migration. The plot also differs. In *Divided by Borders* I relate the conflicts inherent in separations from the perspective of different stakeholders—parents, children, and caregivers— bringing these three perspectives together when I tell the stories of three families. *Everyday Illegal* explores families' experiences thematically.

In chapter 2 I describe the culture of fear that current enforcement policies promote, outlining the ways these fears rise to a level of public health concern. For some, like Inés, whose story I refer to throughout the chapter, fears manifest in physical symptoms. Women, especially, may experience anxiety about the impacts of enforcement actions on their families. Indeed, because deportation efforts target men, women risk becoming what I describe as "suddenly single mothers." For the families I met who had, in the past, experienced the detention of a partner, significant hardships ensued, including problems with housing, food security, child care, and more, all without the emergency support services often available to other types of families who suddenly lose a spouse, such as Social Security benefits. When an incident ends in deportation, fathers in Mexico face significant financial barriers to maintaining a relationship with their children in the United States. For others, current enforcement policies reinforce ongoing low levels of anxiety related to legal status, making them highly aware of illegality.[40] Even very young children have an acute fear of family splits due to deportation; they fear that their peers may judge them if the legal statuses of any family members are revealed. And children have begun to equate immigration with illegality, depending on media coverage to understand the threat that immigration enforcement poses to their families. Chapter 2, "*Nervios,*" demonstrates the myriad ways that gendered enforcement policies put families on edge.

I then turn to within-family experiences. When restrictive laws vastly increase the number of unauthorized residents in the United States, intricate webs of dependency emerge. Chapter 3, "Stuck," describes power negotiations between spouses and between parents and children for members of what we now so often call "mixed-status families." As with the impacts of enforcement efforts, gender matters greatly, with illegality intersecting with existing gender and generational negotiations. Particularly acute for couples experiencing conflict, legal status places women like Isabel, whose story the chapter follows, in an especially vulnerable situation in which they may feel stuck not only with manipulative partners, but also in relationships with the sympathetic individuals they encounter to help them navigate their way out of abusive relationships. Women living in intact relationships also experience increased burdens because of legal status. Women do more household labor when they are unauthorized and dependent on the income of a legal-status partner. Surprisingly, despite working outside the home, women with legal status also get stuck with more housework when they live with an unauthorized partner. Gender patterns also exist in the division of household labor between parents and children, including what scholars at times describe as brokering activities, with girls performing more tasks than boys. Again, legal status matters, with unauthorized boys reporting more household work than US-born boys and unauthorized girls getting stuck with the most household tasks. These patterns suggest significant intersections between gender, generation, and illegality in power negotiations within families.

Chapter 4, "It's Not Fair," extends the theme of the intersections between generation and illegality by considering what happens when legal status differentiates children. An overt pecking order arises under restrictive immigration policy, extending different opportunities to US-born and unauthorized children in different families and siblings in the same families, like that of US-born Camilo and his unauthorized sister and brother, whose story the chapter follows. While one might expect that legal status would matter for children once they entered the workforce, or sought higher education families' accounts show that illegality also marks differences in younger children's daily routines.[41] US-born children and unauthorized children differ in their day-to-day activities, including the opportunities they have access to outside the home, affecting their contributions to household labor within the family. US-born and unauthorized children also have different relationships to the family migration project, with the former often experiencing periods of separation from their parents. The impacts of these separations bleed into children's school performance and access to opportunities outside the home. Legal status even shapes children's identity formation, with the unauthorized feeling excluded from the United States but also from Mexico, a place they cannot visit. Inequalities between children in different families, and among children living in the same family, characterize restrictive immigration policies. Over time, illegality—just like race and class disadvantages—is likely to have unexpected long-term consequences for children's social mobility.

As it turns out, children appear to be well aware of these differences. Chapter 5, "Stigma," looks at how legal status shapes children's peer relationships outside the home. While families' stories of the culture of fear, dependency in relationships, and children's prospects for social mobility did not differ across the two communities, the contours of peer relationships varied considerably by where children lived. Children in Ohio surrounded by few children like themselves described many experiences of isolation, as well as incidents in which their racial or ethnic differences from peers mattered significantly. In a place where the Mexican immigrant community is invisible as a social group, children like Kevin—one of the children the chapter focuses on—attempted to blend in. Proud of their heritage, children in Ohio did not keep their racial or ethnic differences a secret, but they often deemphasized them. Legal status mattered less in interactions with peers.

In contrast, children in New Jersey lived among peers just like themselves, in a community with many other children of immigrants and many other low-income Mexican families. Although also quite proud of their Mexican heritage, children in New Jersey drew symbolic boundaries with other children along the lines of legal status, much as children in other settings differentiated along the lines of race, class, and gender. They viewed legal status as a stigma, information that was private, and a secret to be kept from their friends. They might stigmatize children like Preciliano, a child whom I describe in the chapter as encompassing traits associated with the Mexican foreign born, a group the children identified with unauthorized migration. Comparing children's peer group experiences across Ohio and New Jersey suggests that while national immigration policy has immediate impacts for all families, some of the long-term consequences of illegality for children may vary by where they live.

Chapters 2 to 5 draw directly from the accounts of families I interviewed. In the concluding chapter, I summarize the evidence as to why, for children and families, legal status has begun to accrue the power of social status distinctions. Under restrictive immigration policies, the social consequences of legal status intensify, especially for children and for families, calling for a reframing of our understanding of illegality. Rather than an administrative category that one must wait in line to achieve, legal status is a source of social inequality. Restrictive policy environments heighten the social consequences of legal-status differences, so that children and families experience these differences much as they experience the effects of race, class, and gender. Immigration policy that hopes to moderate these social consequences for children and families must seek to deemphasize enforcement, decriminalize immigration violations, offer pathways to regularization for unauthorized migrants, and provide speedy mechanisms for regularization.

A NOTE ON METHODS

The policy backdrop, as well as the method, makes *Everyday Illegal* a continuation of the stories in *Divided by Borders*. What happens to Mexican migrant families who have decided to raise their families in the United States when the restrictions of US immigration policy become fixed and feel permanent? To answer this question I use the approach of "domestic ethnography, focusing on features of family life as opposed to the community emphasis of traditional ethnographies.[42] Yet in the ethnographic tradition I link macro processes to micro interactions, exploring "how contemporary global migration patterns both strain and intensify the most intimate relationships of people's lives—the bonds between family members."[43] This book focuses specifically on the unexpected consequences of US immigration policy for the everyday lives of families.

The research design incorporates the perspectives of various family members but explicitly focuses on children's lives. I relied on community contacts in New Jersey and Ohio to help identify potential families for interviews and then selected a small group of six families with different legal-status combinations in each site (twelve in total) who agreed to have me hang around a bit more to better understand their children's experiences. Interviews, as I describe in the Appendix in more detail, offer only glimpses into children's experiences, so I sought to place these accounts in context: the contexts of parents' migratory stories, the family's daily routines, the typical school day, and the contours of the broader community. I met with and formally and informally interviewed community members, mapped the demographic data of the census tracts where children lived, and compiled the school report card data from the schools they attended. I attended twelve children's schools, sitting in the back of the classrooms and following them to classes like art, music, and ESL and to the lunchroom and recess, gaining permission from parents and then from the schools (and in some cases the superintendent), in order to observe each child for an entire three days. I visited these twelve children in their homes as well, spending time mostly with their mothers, cooking or conversing, watching children do their homework or play with my own children, who often came with me on visits. Contact with families in home settings varied; some agreed just to the six visits I proposed, others I visited much more often, and a couple families in New Jersey I visited less because of time constraints.[44] In these families, I also formally interviewed each of the children twice, once when we first met and once again a year later. I alone collected all the data, but I had others help to transcribe tape-recoded interviews, which I had conducted in Spanish, English, or a combination of both.

Although repeated contact with families mostly occurred with these twelve families, I occasionally visited with, or ran into, members of the larger group of families I interviewed—I saw children in schools on my visits, for example, and spent time with other families at various events—giving me further insight into families' experiences within their broader communities. With a few, I have had longer-term contact, both prior to and since our formal interview.

I wanted to understand the specific details of the smaller group of families as they related to patterns among the larger group of interviews I did with eighty-one families, so I coded information gathered in those interviews (with the help of a number of research assistants) into SPSS.[45] This had the added benefit of allowing me to include information, like legal status and contributions to housework, on spouses, children, or siblings I did not interview. In the end I gathered information on a wide range of family types: eighteen families (and 84 individuals) in which all members had legal status; nine families (and 34 individuals) in which all members lacked a legal status; and fifty-four families (264 individuals) living in various types of mixed-status households.

In narrating families' stories, I weave between the experiences of an individual, or a group of individuals, and the overarching patterns I found across the families I met. I do so not to glamourize or dramatize but to humanize. I change identifying details often, as it is necessary to protect those I met; except in chapter 5, I purposively omit the state where the focal family in each chapter lives—in order to protect their identities. None of the names here are real, except for those of my own family members. I tell the stories that follow as richly as possible out of respect for the intricacies of family life. Of course, oversimplification is inevitable when the goal is describing social patterns rather than personal biography. And lives change: I lay out only the stories as told to me, and as I observed and interpreted them, at a given period in time.

Social science research often aims to identify generalizable findings. I cannot make such claims. My approach looks at the meanings legal status had for the individual children and families I interviewed in two sites, and no further. The reader should remember throughout that although I refer to families as living either in Ohio or in New Jersey, they do not represent the experiences of all Mexicans in either state or any site.

To complete in-depth interviews with unauthorized migrants, the only viable sampling technique is through informal networks.[46] I worked diligently to find families from several sources, informed by conversations with teachers and other community leaders and by my long-term involvement at each site. I gathered the most varied perspectives possible. For example, I sought interviewees who attended evangelical and Mormon churches; I did so in both sites, although this was especially important in Ohio, as I originally met many families through a Catholic church. I also looked for families without strong ties with the local Mexican community; this meant interviewing some families in New Jersey outside the focal city where I did most interviews. I spoke with some college graduates, a few with master's degrees and one with a PhD, alongside those who had less than six years of formal schooling. In New Jersey most educated migrants experienced a drop in class status after migration because they had migrated without a visa. In Ohio, however, I was able to interview quite a few professional migrants.[47] The stories I tell exhibit the complexity and diversity of families' experiences, yet I highlight those that capture commonalities with others I met.

Exploring the meaning of legal status for individuals' lives calls for this type of method: survey questionnaires cannot capture the nuances of family life, nor can such analyses elucidate the combinations of factors that make legal status salient for individual family members.[48] Even when demographers usefully describe overarching patterns, many large-scale studies have not included information on legal status, further limiting the type of information we have about the daily lives of the unauthorized.[49] Small-scale studies like this one help identify important themes, especially when they consistently arise among different types of families and across two very different communities.

I selected the sites in Ohio and New Jersey because I knew these places well, but also for the deliberate contrast. In both places the Mexican immigrant community grew in the mid- to late 1990s. These are the stories of new Mexican immigrants, distinct from the stories of those in places where Mexican immigrant settlement is much more long-standing.[50] In northeastern Ohio the community developed without a geographic center, a type of population typically not represented in the literature on the new destinations of immigration. In central New Jersey, the Mexican immigrant community congregated in a specific physical site, a pattern also notable in other parts of New Jersey. How family members come to terms with illegality in their everyday lives across these different locales may not occur everywhere. But because settlement patterns similar to those in northeastern Ohio and central New Jersey have occurred in other US states, they might.[51]

LEGAL STATUS IN FAMILY CONTEXTS

Legal status has widespread repercussions for children and families regardless of where they live. Of course, legal status continues to be an administrative status that either allows or denies access to services in the United States. But more than this, under a restrictive policy environment, illegality follows individuals as they navigate life in the United States. In *Everyday Illegal*, I advocate for a shift from a legal to a social framing. When the immigration system emphasizes enforcement over legalization, legal status becomes the basis for social distinction in ways much like the effects of race, class, gender, and generation on the lives of children and families. As proof, I examine the processes by which illegality shapes family relationships, exacerbating existing inequalities between members while also creating new ones. Differences in opportunities reorder gendered relationships between spouses, creating new sources of dependency. Dynamics between parents and children mutate, with US-born children gaining power in certain cases over their undocumented parents. And children experience illegality differently depending on their own migratory history. Even when children attend the same schools and live in the same families, legal status puts children on different pathways that shape their lives as young people and also, potentially, in the future.

Consequences go well beyond those of the relationships between family members. When laws frame the everyday activities of individuals as illegal, there are trickle-down effects. Unauthorized migrants may feel stuck and fear authorities, but so do legal members of their families and communities. Their children, despite their own legal status, have begun to associate a stigma with immigration and to disassociate from their immigrant past. Children's understandings of illegality do not have meaning only in family settings. In peer group interactions, legal status wields influence. For children living in certain communities, it may become a managed identity and status differentiation may become a salient feature of peer group culture.

In an immigration system that emphasizes enforcement and offers extremely few pathways toward regularization, illegality engenders social consequences for families and for children and their peers well beyond the paperwork that proves legal residence or US citizenship. *Everyday Illegal* tells the story of how under a restrictive immigration system illegality becomes an urgent social problem with unexpected outcomes not only for immigrant families but for us all.

2 *Nervios*

ON THE THREAT OF DEPORTATION

Inés doesn't look nervous. The fifty-two-inch TV in her apartment immediately ensnares my two boys, along with Inés's seven-year-old, Lesly, who is watching a Disney Channel soap opera. The show fills the living room of this one-bedroom apartment, which is furnished with a dark blue velvet love seat and sofa, secondhand, and a glass coffee table decorated with white and pink crocheted doilies. Inés phones her husband, Adrián, from the walk-in kitchen. He isn't working today at his construction job, again, because of the poor weather. I wait, admiring the red and blue betta fish Inés has mated in her thirty-gallon tank: she posted photos of the tiny baby on Facebook, a proud surrogate mother. Inés learns that her husband has not yet picked up her medicine at Walmart. She tells him I will take her on our way to visit *los primos.*

Younger and taller than I am, Inés is heavyset with the light-colored clear complexion of TV commercials and dreamy black eyes. Generous and fun, she lightens most conversations, smiling often, constantly giggling and tossing out jokes. When one goes over my head, a fairly frequent event, she always notices and backs up to explain. Today she appears, at first, to

Opposite: Photograph by Bob Anderson

be her usual self, giving me her winning smile and hug in greeting. My only hint that something is off is that the apartment is not immaculately clean, and Inés wears dingy pink sweatpants and a thin white sweatshirt dotted with fuzzies; she has not carefully lined her eyebrows and wears no makeup. She looks, for the first time, like a normal harried mother.

We leave. I drive the familiar route, finding parking easily on this Friday morning. We split up—Inés and Lesly to the pharmacy line, Temo and Dylan to the bathroom, and me in search of cold medicine for Temo and various types of ibuprofen for my chronic headaches that have flared. We meet at the checkout, but Inés has already gone through the line so I cannot pay for the bag of bagels, the My Essentials cream cheese, and the caramel Coffee-mate she picks up for our visit to her cousins. Back in the car, Inés directs me. She has become what ethnographers call a key informant,[1] introducing me to over a half-dozen women to interview and taking me, in person, to meet more, including *los primos*. I have already visited once with Inés but do not remember the way.

"It's that I haven't had the medicine now for a few days," Inés explains as I slow down for a red light. "Now I am starting to feel funny." I wonder what this medicine is. "Last night we came to get it, but it was too long a wait, a whole hour, so we left."

A few minutes of silence pass. "I was in the hospital last week."

Oh. I don't say anything. Inés keeps talking.

"Turn to the right up there, at the gas station."

She goes on. "I stopped eating well and haven't been sleeping for like a month. They said it must have all just built up."

Again, a moment of silence passes before she adds, "You see, I couldn't stop worrying about what would happen if Adrián is deported. I couldn't stop thinking about it—What would I do?"

It is November 2011. In early October Inés called me one day, desperate, asking me to return a phone call that had come up on her caller ID. "I am worried it is Immigration." I called, quickly learning that the number belonged to a local home security company, and reported back. "It's that two plainclothes police officers came knocking on the door yesterday asking for Adrián," she explained uneasily over the phone.

Adrián's boss had reported some of his equipment missing and had identified Adrián as a suspect. The police searched Inés's apartment and

Adrián's car for the stolen items, and, finding nothing, they took Adrián in for questioning. After his release, a few hours later, Inés could not sleep. Adrián had been stopped earlier in the month for driving with an out-of-state license, and she feared what might happen when he went in to pay the ticket. At the time I referred Inés to a lawyer, and a few weeks later she texted that the lawyer had called the police to check on the case. Adrián had done nothing wrong, the lawyer reassured. I thought the matter settled.

Now Inés pulls up the sleeve of her matted, white sweatshirt.

"See all these marks on my arms, I don't remember doing them." Her long fingernails painted white with black flower spirals stroke a dozen light scars, healed a week later. "Maybe I really did scratch myself with my nails. Or maybe it was my bracelet. I have a thick metal bracelet I sometimes wear. It was all the worry; I don't even know what happened."

Initially, the emergency room would not release Inés because of the unexplained bruises and deep scratches on her forearms. When she was admitted to the hospital for two nights, they prohibited Adrián from seeing her in case he had caused her injuries. The hospital then transferred Inés to a behavioral health clinic. They released her a day after she started antianxiety medication.

"The medicine ran out, so I haven't taken any for two days. At first I felt fine, but now I started to feel the tightness in my throat again. So that is why I wanted to be sure to get the medicine today."

It seemed a classic case of *un ataque de nervios*,[2] an anxiety attack.

THE THREAT OF DEPORTATION

Scholars have begun to define the fears that seemed to engulf Inés as resulting from the threat of deportation ravaging immigrant communities ever since the Department of Homeland Security drastically increased enforcement efforts.[3] Inés's fears were neither irrational nor unfounded; in communities where the police cooperate regularly with ICE, her husband Adrián might have ended up detained, and potentially deported, as a result of this incident.[4]

What are the social effects enforcement has had on families, particularly women and children and their relationships with men and fathers?

Inés's experiences illustrate that deportation tactics have had wide-ranging impacts. They affect each family member slightly differently, as the culture of fear is gendered. Women experience anxiety and stress, as they fear becoming suddenly single mothers and facing severe unanticipated economic hardships if ICE detains or deports their husbands. Deported fathers in Mexico struggle to maintain ties with their wives and children remaining in the United States and may disappear from children's lives if the family cannot orchestrate a reunion. Children fear the separation of their families and begin to equate immigration with illegality. Significantly, enforcement practices affect the lives of US citizens—like Inés's daughter Lesly—alongside the unauthorized, like Inés and her husband Adrián, whether or not an actual deportation takes place.

These are some of the consequences of making enforcement a primary feature of US immigration policy. Previously, the most extensive deportation campaign in US history, conducted between 1929 and 1939, forcibly removed approximately four hundred thousand US citizen and noncitizen Mexicans from the United States over a nine-year period.[5] Since 2009, however, approximately four hundred thousand individuals have been deported *every year*. This represents more than double the 189,000 who were deported in 2001.[6] Deportation and removal characterized US policy toward the foreign born at the start of the twenty-first century and reached an all-time high by the end of the decade (figures 1 and 2). (The term *alien* in these figures is the official term used by the Department of Homeland Security in compiling the number of foreign born removed from the United States. Its use to describe the unauthorized population denotes the US government's perjorative stance toward this population.)[7]

Deportations especially threaten Mexicans living in the United States.[8] Mexicans make up approximately 30 percent of the foreign born and 58 percent of the unauthorized population.[9] In 2010, 83 percent of the detained, 73 percent of those forcibly removed, and 77 percent of voluntary departures were Mexican.[10]

Deportations also target men, like Inés's husband Adrián. While the Department of Homeland Security has not publicly released data on the gender composition of deportees and does not assert any official practice, evidence suggests that in most cases men are the ones who are arrested,

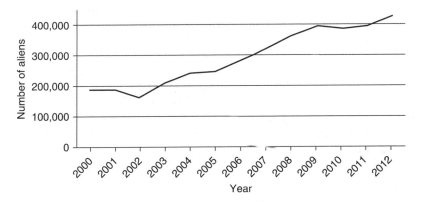

Figure 1. Aliens removed from the United States, 2000–2012. Source: US
Department of Homeland Security (2014). See also Simanski and Sapp (2012);
US Department of Homeland Security (2011a, 2011b).

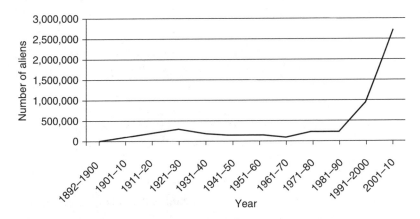

Figure 2. Aliens removed from the United States, 1892–2010. Source: US
Department of Homeland Security (2014). See also Simanski and Sapp (2012),
US Department of Homeland Security (2011a, 2011b).

Table 1 Percentage of Husbands in Sample Who Had Ever Been Arrested, Detained, or Deported

	Ohio	New Jersey	Total (n = 81)
Ever arrested	30.2	24.3	27.5
Ever detained	23.3	13.5	18.8
Ever deported	11.6	8.1	10.0

detained, and deported. A recent report on Secure Communities found that men constituted 93 percent of detainees, even though only 57 percent of the unauthorized population is male.[11] One study found that among those in short-term US Border Control custody on the US-Mexican border, 76.56 percent of interviewees were male.[12] Eighty-four percent of Dominican deportees interviewed by David Brotherton and Luís Barrios were male,[13] and statistics collected on the US-Mexican border found that 89.2 percent of repatriated Mexicans in 2010 were male, up from 81.6 percent in 2000.[14] Tanya Golash-Boza and Pierrette Hondagneu-Sotelo argue that current deportation practices constitute a "gendered racial removal program."[15]

Increases in enforcement efforts directly affected those I interviewed in both New Jersey and Ohio. Of the eighty-one families, one in five reported that an extended family member had been deported. Fewer (10 percent; see table 1) had actually experienced a deportation. However, a significant number of the husbands of the women I met—nearly one in three in Ohio and one in four in New Jersey—had had confrontations with the police.

In more and more communities across the United States, local police departments have aligned their efforts with those of the Department of Homeland Security.[16] Some have signed 287(g) agreements with the Department of Homeland Security deputizing their police officers to act as immigration agents.[17] Secure Communities programs, which systematically check the immigration status of anyone arrested or booked into a county jail have gained favor,[18] although the program had not yet been implemented locally at the time of Adrián's run-in with the police.

Families described highly unpredictable interactions with police. I asked one woman in Ohio, for example, about her experiences with the police. "They have been very friendly. They have stopped me and they've asked me for my papers and I show them my license from Mexico, and they haven't said anything. . . . They have also stopped my husband, and they gave him a ticket for running a red light, supposedly, and another for not stopping [at a stop sign], but that is it, and we have never had to go to court."

But for another woman in Ohio, a police officer brought about the deportation of her husband. Vanessa's husband had been driving home from his night shift at a restaurant when a patrol car stopped him. He showed the officers his Mexican driver's license; one officer returned to the patrol car and the other stayed with her husband, telling him that his partner was a "bad seed." The partner returned and cuffed Vanessa's husband with plastic restraints. He then concocted a ticket for running a yellow light. This happened early on a Sunday morning. On Monday Vanessa's husband paid his ticket at the courthouse and the judge ordered him free to go. But the police did not release him; the arresting officer had already called ICE, who put a hold on him. The next day ICE came and took him to a detention facility. Two weeks later he was deported to Mexico.

In Inés's case, Adrián had not even been arrested; he did not face deportation or even risk deportation when he went on later that month to pay his traffic ticket without incident. Yet the possibility of deportation haunted Inés, culminating in her hospital admission. As Nicholas De Genova argues, it is a migrant's deportability—not a deportation act itself——that has the greatest impact: "The disciplinary operation of an apparatus for the everyday production of migrant 'illegality' is never simply intended to achieve the putative goal of deportation. It is deportability, and not deportation per se, that has historically rendered unauthorized migrant labor a distinctly disposable commodity."[19]

THE RIPPLING EFFECTS OF ENFORCEMENT POLICIES

As enforcement efforts intensify, the threat of deportation creates a culture of fear among immigrants.[20] In some communities, for example, the unauthorized withdraw from community events because of their fears of deportation, with some reporting that they have stopped eating out at restaurants and prefer to spend nonworking hours at home to avoid detection.[21] Some suggest they do not utilize social services, even those they may be eligible for through their US citizen children.[22] Street-level bureaucrats, such as child welfare workers, perceive that fears of deportation among unauthorized clients have inhibited their abilities to effectively assist families.[23] Latino immigrants, regardless of their own legal status, become increasingly cognizant of legality.[24] Illustrating the extent of the effects of such fears on both the documented and the unauthorized, a Pew Hispanic Center survey in 2008 found that a full 68 percent of Latino respondents worried that they, a family member, or a close friend might be deported.[25] Another study found that Latinos, documented and undocumented alike, experienced a decrease in the quality of life and less confidence about the future because of public attention to immigration issues.[26]

Such fears may profoundly affect individuals' psychological well-being, as they did for Inés, provoking her *ataque de nervios*. One study finds documentation status to be a significant predictor of self-reported negative emotional and health states.[27] Another shows deportation to constitute a specific source of acculturative stress for both unauthorized and legal migrants.[28] Vanessa in Ohio, whose husband's deportation I described above, explained the aftermath of the incident even after the couple was reunited. "My husband won't drive; he was left traumatized by what happened." As for herself, "I don't feel safe talking to the police. . . . Sometimes I want to dye my hair blonde and have blue eyes." Her comments signify the perceived racialization of undocumented status.[29]

All of this stress, the anxiety surrounding illegality that deeply affected Inés, seems to be relatively new. Of course, some communities of unauthorized migrants have experienced this threat during previous periods.[30] In central New Jersey, however, this was not my experience just a decade earlier.

ENCOUNTERING LUÍS

When I first met Raúl in 1998, risks existed, but not the fear. Back then, Raúl was Luís. We met at volunteer ESL classes that a group of us organized, some recent college graduates, others immigrant community members. I taught a lower-level class; Raúl started out as a student in a higher-level course, going on to teach introductory English classes over the next few years. Raúl, or Luís, introduced himself to me, not at the school, but when we crossed paths at the Hispanic Riverfront Festival, under the bright lights of the Ferris wheel, awkwardly encountering each other next to the "games of chance."

"Do you have children?" Luís asked, smiling brightly, his four silver-plated front teeth shining.

Dumfounded—I was twenty-one and had just graduated from college, of course I didn't have children—"Um, no."

But surely he was just making conversation; I tried for a polite response, "Do you?"

"Yes, I have two, a two-year-old and a four-year-old, back in Mexico." I could not hide my shock. "Oh. You look so young."

Giggling again, dimples appearing, Luís responded, "I'm actually twenty-six."

Weeks later, Luís confessed that his real name was Raúl. Like many others, he used Luís, an alternate name, for work: the clearly fake pink green card ("green cards" were not green) superimposed a picture of Raúl as Luís with a false Social Security number. The ID served as a formality. The boss at the landscaping company where he worked cutting grass, staining all his oversized secondhand jeans bright green, knew it wasn't real. And I, who knew so little about immigration at that time, recognized a fake when I saw it.

Over the next year I got to know Raúl and the system of the fake IDs so many used for work. I had other Mexican friends, other unauthorized friends, before Raúl, and after, but I learned much from him as our relationship developed. Raúl told me how he had first come to the United States, riding the trains with Central Americans who had come through the small town in Veracruz where he grew up. Once he nearly starved but was saved by the youngest traveling with them; Yohann—probably no more than eleven years old—had hidden enough tortillas to feed everyone, pulling them out of his knapsack when least expected, when the group were stranded in the disconnected railway car they had been riding in. Raúl had been to Texas before coming to New Jersey in the late 1990s, following a friend who spoke of ample employment opportunities and offered him a place to stay until he got settled.

Raúl had been married to Rosa, who lived near his hometown in Mexico. When he came to New Jersey, the marriage faltered, although it had always been one of long distance. But he continued to send money regularly, calling home weekly. Raúl carried the photos of his children in his wallet; he proudly pulled them out to show me under the lights of the Ferris wheel. Later, when a new 8 by 10 photo arrived of Christian, his oldest, dressed in bright white pants and shirt for his kindergarten graduation, I helped pick out a plastic silver frame at the dollar store.

Raúl's stories intrigued me, his life intrigued me, as did the world he showed me, something I had not seen so plainly before we met. We were so different, but too young to be scared; I took the chance. For four years I felt safe with Raúl, not afraid.

During that time his illegality did not alarm me. Sure, we knew a few people who had trouble with Immigration, but usually they had other problems with the courts. There was a friend who had accidently gone into the wrong home when drunk one night and was charged with breaking and entering in a nightmarelike case that ended in his deportation. Another more distant acquaintance, a gang member, was arrested and needed the recommendation to a lawyer. We sporadically heard rumors of routine traffic stops, outside the city, and warnings to stay off certain routes. Occasionally I worried, but I do not remember the palpable kind of fear described by those I interviewed. Raúl worked hard and did nothing illegal, admonishing me when I forgot to pay my parking tickets on time. Was I simply naive? I call Raúl on his cell phone now to ask if my memory has simply blanked it out. "No, no. Well, back then they weren't deporting people, not like now," he confirms. After all, in 1998, when Raúl and I met, deportations numbered half of what they did ten years later, when Inés had her *ataque de nervios*. Perhaps equally important, at that time the local police departments in New Jersey where we lived did not cooperate with federal immigration officials. New Jersey quietly implemented Secure Communities across the state in 2012.[31]

Legal status mattered, but mostly because of the inconvenience. Originally Raúl insured his own silver and blue Dodge pickup, but when the insurance lapsed I added him to my policy. The first few times I went to Mexico, to meet his family, I traveled alone. When we moved in together, I signed the paperwork for the credit check, and the electric bill was listed my name. We married in 2001, giving us equal legal footing in the relationship, and then had Temo in 2002.[32] It never occurred to me to worry about Raúl's legal status. I never really thought seriously that he might get sent back, not until the day years after our divorce when, as he was trying to apply for citizenship, the potential for deportation came up.

THE ECONOMICS OF DEPORTATION

Deportability now affects so many families, straining the relationships between husbands and wives, and at times between parents and children. The dread of family separation lies at the surface, the obvious culprit.[33] Underlying the fear, however, is economic distress combined with the gendered contours of relationships that, in Inés's case, spurred her *ataque de nervios*.

Economic concerns preoccupy Inés. The majority of the women I interviewed worked full time (six out of ten), although most relied heavily on their partners' income, since their earnings, as immigrant women, were low compared to those of men.[34] Inés depends completely on her husband's income. Her typical weekday routine consists of "waking up between 7:00 and 7:30 to get Lesly ready and take her to school." Lesly takes her breakfast at home, usually cereal with milk or yogurt and granola, sometimes waffles or pancakes. Inés doesn't pack lunches: Lesly qualifies for the free lunch program. Inés then walks her daughter twenty minutes to the nearby school. Inés knows how to drive, and the couple's vehicle is at her disposal; her husband drives a company car to work. But she worries about making the five-minute ride without a driver's license, so they walk unless rain or snow prevents it. "After that, I come home. Sometimes I [hang out] with Carmen or one of the others [mothers]; there is always someone to see. 'Come have a coffee at my house' or 'Why don't you come here.' If there is nothing to do, or no one to invite for a coffee, I come home to clean. And I spend the day at the house. Then I go pick up Lesly. And when I get back I cook if I haven't cooked before I pick her up. And she eats."

Inés and her husband pay $936 a month for their apartment. Two-thirds of the families in New Jersey, and one-third in Ohio, shared their apartments or homes with other families to save on the rent. Inés and her husband do not want to share, although she often thinks about trying to move into a two-bedroom and rent the other room to help with expenses. They lived with others in the past, which led to problems. When Inés first came to the United States seven years before, she and Adrián moved in with her brother:

> We lasted there one year. There Lesly was born. But we started to have some problems there, with my brother. Because we lived in an apartment together with my brother and his wife, two other men, and me and my husband. So I didn't have a good experience living with other people—it was so hard. When I was pregnant with Lesly, you know how one can get really depressed. I cried over every little thing. Because I cleaned everything there. It was me who woke up early. I picked up, I cleaned the bathroom, the kitchen, the living room. And she [brother's wife] would get up somewhere around ten. And would you believe it that she would go ahead and do everything that I had just done! I didn't say anything; I just closed myself up in my room and I would cry and cry. It was bad. If I made food, they wouldn't eat what I made. And if I didn't cook, she would tell my brother that I hadn't cooked. So whatever I did, she wasn't happy. And I was there all alone. We didn't have a car, we didn't have anything. She would go out and come back with McDonalds and sodas. And I was pregnant—with all those cravings! And they didn't invite me to eat with them.

Without sharing, the cost of the one-bedroom apartment, electric bill, car insurance, phone, and Internet stretches the family budget beyond Adrián's salary when he does not work six or seven days a week. When I first meet Inés in February of 2011, she explains, "In the summer, we are okay; thank God, it isn't so hard to pay the rent. Because my husband works in construction all seven days. He earns well. But now, starting right before Christmas, he doesn't work regularly. From the little bit we saved from the summer we paid January's rent. And the rent that we just paid [for February], my brother had to lend us the money." Inés wants to work herself, to help, but Adrián has traditional feelings about work and marriage. "He says to me, 'Why do you want to work? We are fine.' He says, 'Who is going to look after Lesly?' Right now I've said to him, 'Maybe I had better go work,' and he says, 'Don't you worry. Hopefully work will come soon.' But I get upset because I think about the rent, the food . . ."

Inés has started selling Mary Kay to her rather extensive network of friends. Adrián drives her to deliver the products; her direct selling does not undercut his beliefs about gendered divisions of labor.[35] Inés also visits the Salvation Army to request help; they give her bags of food to help during the winter months.[36] I do my part, buying two eyeliner pencils, a smoky black and chestnut brown that last a few months. Inés earns little from the venture. She has to front the money when friends—whose husbands also don't work in the winter—cannot pay in a timely manner. By the time we take our second trip to *los primos,* Inés has stopped selling.

Despite her chipper demeanor, economic hardships constantly worry Inés and put her over the edge when she feels threatened by the mere thought of Adrián's detention or deportation. The experiences of women whose husbands have been detained or deported justify Inés's concerns.

SUDDENLY SINGLE MOTHERS

One of the most devastating impacts of deportation is the creation of female-headed single-parent households.[37] Because ICE targets men for deportation, with some districts going so far as to regularly release detained women and deport detained men, women become what I term *suddenly single mothers,* scrambling to be the sole providers for their US-born children with no preparation for single parenthood.[38] Wives of deportees, most of whom are unauthorized migrants themselves, cannot rely on support services designed as a stopgap for families who suddenly lose a working spouse, programs like unemployment, workers' compensation, or Social Security. Because many are unauthorized, they cannot apply for welfare or food stamps for themselves, something that families of the incarcerated may rely on during periods of family separation.[39] Although US citizen children are eligible for social service benefits, unauthorized parents underutilize social services available to their children because of their fears of disclosing their legal status in the application process.[40] This results in far lower enrollment rates in programs such as child care or food stamps that can help their children's early cognitive development.[41]

Prior to a detention or deportation, families like Inés's struggle to make ends meet. After a deportation or detention, they easily slip further into poverty. Of the eighty-one families I interviewed, sixteen had either directly experienced a deportation or detailed the deportation experiences of a close family member or friend. Every one identified economic hardship as a result. Mothers scrambled to find enough work and arrange for child care. "However it turns out, one suffers so, so much," explained one mother whose husband had been deported twice.

A related financial impact is housing insecurity. A mother in New Jersey, for example, relocated eight times with her two children in the three years after her husband's deportation. One in Ohio had to move in with her sister: after her husband was deported she could no longer afford their two-bedroom condo on her salary as a restaurant hostess alone. Sofia, also in Ohio, was detained with her husband who was deported; she was eventually released, with the help of a lawyer, to her US citizen children. When she returned home with an ankle monitor locked to her leg, her cousins—who shared the home—moved out because they did not want to risk ICE finding them there. She fell behind on the rent, unable to afford the four-bedroom house alone.

Most of the families I interviewed sought family reunification as quickly as possible. Yet it is costly, and stressful, for mothers to orchestrate reunifications. One struggled for months to save enough money for her four children's passports in order to be able to take them back to Mexico to live with her husband who had been deported. Another wanted to stay in the United States with her three US citizen children, but the hours at her factory job had been cut back, and she was not able to make ends meet. She decided that the best recourse was to return to Mexico. Still, she did not have enough money saved. She explained, "It's just that right now I cannot leave because they don't have their passports, and then . . . the baby . . . he doesn't have his Social Security number yet. You see, I have to get the Social Security card in order to apply for his passport. You see the problem?" Although the financial consequences are the most striking, as these cases illustrate, mothers also face a tremendous amount of emotional stress figuring out how to reunify and support the family financially during a husband's absence.

EMOTIONAL CONSEQUENCES

Inés worries about the effect of a deportation on her financial situation. But she also panics at the unfathomable thought that a deportation may permanently destroy the family she has worked so hard to maintain. Inés and Adrián have just one daughter, but Inés is trying to get pregnant and has miscarried twice. She takes folic acid supplements daily; the successful mating of her betta fish is a fertile omen.

Inés's determination to have another baby stands despite challenges in her relationship with Adrián. I observe great inequalities in her marriage, which involves a rigid division of household labor in her family; she cooks, cleans, does the laundry, and takes her daughter to school, something that Inés is not entirely happy about. "Sometimes, when he is here, he helps. But when he works, no. I do it all." Inés views her husband's jealousy as the greatest problem. It is the reason behind his refusal to let her work. During one period, Adrián became so threatening that Inés almost left him. "How can I explain it? He was very bad to me. He wouldn't let me talk on the phone, he wouldn't give me money to buy phone cards to call my mother— if he saw me talking on the phone, he would ask who I was talking to."

"Has he always been like this?" I ask. Inés clarifies that he has since stopped.

"How about in Mexico?"

"In Mexico, not really. But we only lived together for two months. When he brought me here—Oh my God—Once I was going to have one of my brothers come for me because I couldn't stand it anymore. I had to be talking on the phone at the window so that when he arrived I could hang up."

"What happened?"

"I think he got scared, the fear," Inés reflects. "I told him that he better change or I was going to leave. I told him I could not stand it anymore."

These details demonstrate that Inés's dread of Adrián's possible deportation does not arise from the fear of being alone, although she certainly does not want to be alone. She wants to live with Adrián. She wants another baby with him and strives to make her marriage work. But Inés has contemplated leaving him in the past, when the relationship was difficult. Her anxiety about Adrián's possible deportation seems to arise primarily from the fear that a sudden separation will be forced on her family, a possibility she cannot control.

DEPORTED FATHERS

When deportations permanently separate families, they create a very specific type of single-parent household in which men's involvement in their families suffers immensely. Single-parent households that result from divorce are often characterized by ongoing involvement from both parents and joint custody agreements.[42] Women whose partners are imprisoned, while in some ways similar to those whose partners are detained or deported, may choose to maintain ongoing ties with their partners, sharing with their partners as best they can during visits, "doing time together."[43] While some of the families I interviewed had managed to stay together even after a deportation, for a smaller group the detention or deportation led to a lasting change in the household structure, one in which men completely withdrew from their families.

For example, Gladys's husband was deported after being arrested for involvement in illicit business activities. The relationship had been abusive, but Gladys did not experience relief with his arrest. Rather, she felt it turned her life upside down. Before he was deported, she had been a stay-at-home mother. At one point, because of his abuse, they had separated temporarily; Gladys's husband had supported her financially throughout. Tellingly, while separated, Gladys moved to Arizona near her sisters while her husband remained in New Jersey, sending money to her from afar. In contrast, after his arrest, Gladys's husband disappeared from her life. She began to work an afternoon shift. When I interviewed the family three years later, Gladys saw her children, ages fourteen and seven, only a few hours per day during the week. Her ex-husband occasionally called every other month from Mexico, but fourteen-year-old Marjorie had little to say about her father: "I don't really have much contact with him." Her seven-year-old brother said, "I just say hi and pass [the phone] to my sister."

Another woman, Carolina, told a similar story of her brother's three-year incarceration and subsequent deportation: "It is very sad, the story of these kids, because they know that their dad was deported and had to go to Mexico, but his wife already has another man, so their story is very sad because they say, 'Where is my dad,' and the woman, she gives them a different father." Carolina still visited her nephews, but she felt uncomfortable about the relationship the children had with their stepfather—one in which her brother had been replaced because he was unable to facilitate a relationship with his children after his deportation. Carolina's brother does not intend to return to the United States, feeling that he was falsely imprisoned. "He has been very affected about what happened here in the United States—he is afraid that they will catch him again, that they will send him to jail again, for something that he didn't do." The separation of father and children would be permanent.

Perla's husband also remained supportive during both his incarceration and their resulting separation. And, while he remained in the United States, his family offered Perla support in raising their two daughters without him. But after he was deported, both he and his family ceased contact with Perla, who subsequently struggled as a single mother, working two jobs, one at a gas station in the mornings and another cleaning at night. She would not have been able to afford her one-room apartment if her younger brother had not moved in with her. She also depended on him for child care. Perla felt angry that his family had stopped supporting her after his deportation. "Only once did his brother come and take the girls out to eat." Her ex-husband had no communication with his daughters. The only time he called from Mexico, she explained, he didn't seem to know what to say and hung up quickly, apparently overwrought with emotion.

While my interviews in New Jersey and Ohio did not shed light on men's experiences after deportation, for a separate project I interviewed a father in Mexico who described the disadvantaged position he found himself in after his incarceration and subsequent deportation. He was unable to find regular employment in Mexico; he also had no regular communication with his ex-wife, who lived with a new partner and child, along with his two US citizen children from their marriage. When first deported he decided to go back: "I thought I could fix things with my wife and then maybe have an arrangement to see my kids on the weekends, you know, something like that." But since a failed attempt at an unauthorized reentry, he had been back in Mexico for over a year. During that time he had spoken with his children just once, on the previous Father's Day, when his ex-wife called and said, "I have a present for you" and passed the phone to his oldest.

"I haven't told anyone about this, but how that broke my heart to hear his voice," he explained. Even worse, though, was when his son said he would pass the phone on to his younger brother, "and I heard him say no, I don't want to talk to him. Man, that even broke my heart worse."

Fathers separated from their children under certain circumstances provide economic support for their children. And, if successful providers, they may maintain long-lasting emotional ties with the children they do not live with. For example, fathers in transnational families often use frequent phone calls, gifts, and remittances to stay connected to their children.[44] They believe they have made a worthwhile sacrifice by leaving their children if they can fulfill their roles as economic providers for their families via migration. For example, one father I interviewed in 2004 in New Jersey who had three children back in Mexico told me, "No, [I don't feel guilty]. I think I would feel bad if I knew the children were suffering, and that they wouldn't suffer if I was there with them. But they aren't, so I don't." Similarly, divorced fathers who are invested in their children's upbringing, and who provide financially for their children, may be regularly involved in their lives.[45]

Deportees, however, cannot earn enough money in their home countries to support their children living in the United States. From this disadvantaged position, they struggle to sustain emotional bonds from a distance. In this sense, deportation disarms men, robbing them of the ability to fulfill their roles as family providers.[46] Women described the devastating effect of deportations on their partner's self-esteem. Vanessa, for example, explained how hard it was after her husband was deported. "You see, in your country, when you go back, everyone adores you. But he arrived and everything was bad, and he was ashamed. He almost never went out of the house. He felt awful. He didn't have money." María felt angry when her Honduran husband acted defeated after he was deported to Mexico. The day of his arrival, he was robbed and had his Mexican ID stolen.

They were going to deport him all the way to Honduras, and I said to him, "Here; I have some copies of the IDs," and I said, "I will send you the papers."

And he said, "What for?" I told him, "I sent a copy to my father so that he can go and get you wherever you are, or give me a fax number, something where I can send some proof, the children's birth certificates that prove you are their father or our wedding certificate. That way they can let you go." He said, "No, don't do anything."

Deportees face high levels of stigma upon their returns; they may be viewed as failed migrants and often criminals, even if the deportation had nothing to do with a criminal offense.[47] Deportees have trouble finding stable work; they are also demoralized. In the absence of an economic tie to their children, fathers' emotional connection also falters. Deportations permanently interrupt their bonds with their children.

This is the scenario that may have put Inés over the edge.

"Sometimes I dream that I go get Lesly at the school and there I find all the other mothers who tell me, 'Don't go back to the apartments.' . . . Or sometimes I dream that my husband gets arrested by the police at work; they call me and tell me that he is in jail."

"Do you two ever talk about what you would do if that ever happened?" I ask.

"Actually, no, never—he just says to me, 'Ay! You and your dreams.'"

IN LIMBO

Dreams of detention haunt Inés for good reason. She has seen its effects, up close. Inés arranges our visit to Teresa, whose husband is in jail. Lonely and isolated, Teresa needs her friends, calling Inés almost every day. She lives a fifteen-minute car ride from Inés. Inés has gotten a few women together to visit Teresa before, chipping in for a taxi. But the taxi is expensive. I have a car and a driver's license.

I meet them at Inés's apartment. Amalia brings her infant baby, snuggled in a car seat. It is early in March, and the bright blue sky betrays the crisp cold still in the air. Clara carries plastic bags full of sweet bread and coffee creamer. Inés sits in the front, directing me. Inés has told Teresa about me. Teresa did not want to sit for a formal interview, but she said I could visit, with the others, to chat informally, a more comfortable setting for her to tell her story. Later that afternoon Clara refers jokingly to the lot of them as *las intimas chismosas,* the intimate gossips. "Listening to us she is probably going to write a book called *las intimas chismosas.*" Amalia cannot stop giggling at the thought. The rest of us laugh; it seems a fitting end to the day.

In the morning we have not yet forged the gossip bonds. We arrive at the small house, me stomach jittery and nervous. Teresa greets with a smile, guarded, inviting us to sit at the kitchen table. The first floor has two rooms, the kitchen and a living room stuffed with plastic children's toys and furniture. Two bedrooms lie up the stairs; the house is large compared to Inés's cramped apartment.

The women bustle to make coffee and break open the package of sweet Honduran cornmeal bread, passing around pieces to all. We circulate the bottle of creamer and a ceramic jar painted with grapes and apples and containing white sugar. Inés chatters about the changes in her clothing sizes since she came from Mexico. Amalia, nursing, heartily takes another piece of the bread. "I'm eating for two," she adds, not worried about her currently solid figure. Teresa, confident as well, laughs describing the rolls around her midsection: "But I never get bigger in my legs or bottom, so I can still wear my same jeans." Teresa has two children, a third grader, currently at school, and a two-year-old sleeping in the other room. Inés—tall and heavyset—and Clara—short and heavyset—each with seven-year-olds, talk of starting an exercise class at the girls' school. Suddenly losing appetite for what's in front of me, I look up to see the others have stopped eating as well. Inés quips to break our guilty expressions, "Well, I am going to have another piece to give me strength for my new exercise regimen." We laugh as she reaches for a new piece. Amalia, I learn, is thirty-three, Teresa and I are thirty-four, and Clara is thirty-one. Inés says she is the oldest, at thirty-five, causing the others to laugh and clue me in: really Inés is twenty-seven, the baby in the group.

Female bonding over food now in motion, the women begin to discuss Teresa's predicament. Teresa doesn't drive. She manages because the school bus stops in front of the house. Her older son goes to CCD class on Friday nights,[48] but a friend from church drives him. As for shopping, her husband's coworkers from the restaurant alternate taking her out once a week.

Teresa's husband has been in jail since October, six months. He had been caught twice before for driving without a license but had always paid the fine and been released. This time police stopped him for speeding. "He had the children in the car with him, so they are counting it as more severe. He showed them his license from Mexico, but they didn't accept it and arrested him."

"Six months is a long time," I say. "I am surprised that he wasn't released on bail."

Teresa explains they cannot post bail because it is too much. They have decided to wait it out and let him to do his time. His court date is a month away, in April. The lawyer warned Teresa he will probably be reported to ICE and deported once released.

It is hard to be alone. Inés pays close attention as Teresa explains, "It's that you rely on your husband to pay the bills and to do everything, so you just don't know how to do it. I have had to learn a lot of things." Amalia asks what she does about the rent. "The landlord knows us and is someone my husband used to work for. He told me I don't have to pay the rent. He knows the situation and that when he is released he knows he will be good for the money." This keeps her afloat. "The other bills I am trying to pay and keep on top of."

Teresa tried to apply for assistance, but they required a green card, which she doesn't have. She is unauthorized. She did apply for help via her youngest child, who is a US-born citizen, but could not for the older boy, as he was born in Mexico. The food stamps she receives "just for the little one. As for me and my older son, they don't care. We can just starve."

The toddler wakes and begins to wander around the kitchen as we chat. He must know we are talking about his father, because he grabs a photograph off a refrigerator clip magnet and waves it around, clutching it with stubby fingers. In it, the boy sits in a church on the lap of a man with a chiseled thin face, a deep brown mustache, and dark hair; he wears cowboy boots, jeans, and a collared shirt. Teresa's son keeps pointing at the picture saying "Papa." We don't know what to say. "*Si, tu papa,*" Clara answers first, smiling at him. Following her lead, we each nod at him as he walks around, insisting. A subdued mood sets in. Teresa says her older son has been having a hard time at school and has been very distracted. The teacher contacted her wondering what had caused his change in behavior. Deportation and detention negatively affect children's performance in school.[49]

Inés looks out the window. "Is that your boss's house?" she asks. Teresa affirms; she started working two days a week cleaning the house of her husband's employer. "I didn't realize she lives right over there."

"What do you do with your son?" This is Clara.

"I take him with me, and the woman there watches him while I clean."

We stay in the kitchen the entire morning. After a bit, we make sandwiches for lunch: tomato, mozzarella, mayonnaise, and jalapeno peppers on wheat. We work in assembly line fashion; I add the *chiles* at the end of the line.

The sandwiches hit the spot. The mood perks up, and we begin complaining about husbands—or, in my case, exes. Teresa grills me about my divorce. In the spotlight, I shift in the plastic chair, mentioning the cultural differences, something like "It's that we were so different. We did not really realize it until Temo was born; the cultures are so different. But we get along pretty well now."

"Did he ever hit you?" she asks.

"No, nothing like that. We fought, but, no, because of the cultural differences, maybe, it was easier to split before things got really bad."

And so we talk about *machista* Mexican men. All complain, but superficially. No one expresses too much discontent with her partner, not in this setting. We also talk babies, admiring Amalia's daughter, who has woken up. Amalia nurses and passes her around while she prepares a bottle of formula. Inés and Clara contently describe clothes shopping with their girls. Inés is silent on her efforts to get pregnant.

We evaluate Teresa's living arrangement. Would any of us be afraid to be alone in the house Teresa lives in, so isolated, out in the country? Inés tells stories of her hometown in a small rancho in Michoacán, Mexico, suggesting Teresa do what her mother used to do while her father was away working in the United States for long stretches. "You go outside dressed as a man, with a big hat, and boots, a couple of times a week. You can wear your husband's clothes. You walk around the property so no one knows you are here alone."

That was in March 2011. On our ride out to *los primos* in November of the same year I ask after Teresa to take the focus off Inés's recent *ataque de nervios*.

"She is all right. Her husband was released and is back home with her now. They are still waiting to find out what will happen with the deportation."

LOS PRIMOS

I worry about Inés during the thirty-minute car ride. We arrive at the sixties-style blue and white split-level home, awkwardly set at the bottom of a grassy hill in farm country. We bustle inside, greeted at the door by one of the subjects of my visit: ten-year-old Moisés, wearing a black knit hat low over his eyes. Three families share the three-bedroom house, now out of date and showing signs of disrepair: three brothers, their wives, and seven children. I interviewed the mothers on our prior visit. Inés brings me now so I can talk to the children.

I introduce Temo and Dylan to Moisés, who takes them back to his bedroom to play video games. Inés deposits her offerings in the kitchen, greets each of the women with a kiss, and sinks into the brown micro-suede sofa with daughter Lesly. The others have already had breakfast, but they prepare the coffee and two bagged Thomas New York–style bagels for Inés and me. We move to the glass-topped dining room table, Inés eating a half a bagel piled with cream cheese before swallowing her pills with a glass of Tropicana. When I finish my coffee, interviews start. The women decide I will use the downstairs bedroom, with each mother bringing the five older children down, one at a time. Three hours later when I come upstairs, Inés is asleep on the sofa.

Glancing in her direction, one of the cousins comments, "She really needs a lot of sleep right now." They know what has happened and worry about her too.

Now my head pounds. I did not expect this today. Inés concerns me, sleeping away her anxiety with the help of the pills that have made her drowsy. And the interviews with the children weigh heavily. Stephanie, ten, and Alex, eight, do not talk much about immigration. But conversations with Andrés, twelve, Homero, fifteen, and Moisés, ten, have caused, unconsciously, my shoulders to tighten, my neck to strain, and my head to ache even more.

Andrés was born in the United States, son of a Salvadoran mother and a Mexican father. I ask Andrés, as I ask all the children I interview, if he knows what an immigrant is.

"It's a person that lives in Mexico or Guatemala or something and they travel here illegally."

I do not correct him but ask what he thinks it is like to be an immigrant.

"Scary, because you never know if they'll want your passport. They catch you out of nowhere. They come and put you in a truck and send you back to Mexico."

Andrés tells me that some of his family members are immigrants. "Would you want people or your friends at school to know that people in your family are immigrants? Or do you prefer they don't know?"

"Some of them know. Like my Spanish friends. They are immigrants."

"Do they talk to you about being scared?" I ask.

"Sometimes."

Andrés admits he doesn't know anyone who's been asked for a passport and been taken away. "Then how do you know they do that?" I wonder out loud.

"They want to know if you're from this country," he explains.

I push, "Have you seen that happen to anybody?"

"No, I've heard of it."

"Who did you hear that from?"

"My mom. They called her and said there was this Walmart in the city where there were people that were taking immigrants."

I ask Andrés if he is scared since some of his family members are immigrants.

"Not really. Well—yes. 'Cause if everyone leaves, it's only going to be me and my sister, my little cousin that you were just talking to and my little sister and my little cousin." Four of the seven cousins in his household, and none of the adults, are US citizens.

"Do you really think they might leave you all alone here?"

"Well, almost all my family is immigrant."

Andrés says that he has talked with his mother about his fears but that she tells him not to worry. The family has not set up a plan, at least not one they have communicated to Andrés, about what they will do if someone is detained or deported.

"Do you ever feel proud that in your family there are immigrants?" I ask.

"Yes. I'm proud that they had to go through all this trouble just to get here."

"Yeah, I think it's something to be proud of. Have you ever heard people being teased for being immigrants?"

"It happens frequently at school," he explains, "where kids will say to each other, 'Oh. You're illegal. Call the cops.'"

Homero, Andrés's older cousin, came across the border at age eight and remembers how he struggled to learn English in his bilingual classes. While we start the interview in Spanish, in the middle he switches over to English.

He tells me, too, that all in his family are immigrants. Unlike his younger cousin, he understands that some immigrants have papers and others are illegal. It doesn't bother him that people know he is Mexican or know that he comes from another country. Still, he explains, "I am not going to go around saying, 'I'm an immigrant.'"

I ask, "Do you ever feel scared that you're immigrants?"

"Yes."

"Why?"

"Immigration. We don't have the papers."

"Have you known anyone who's had problems with Immigration before?" I ask.

He nods yes.

"Can you tell me what happened?"

"They got sent back."

Moisés, like Homero, was born in Mexico; he was just four when he came with his mother to be reunited with his father, living here. For this ten-year-old more than the others, legal status issues are troubling; he brings it up less than five minutes into the interview.

"Do the kids at your school know that your parents are from Mexico?" I ask.

"Only one. There's a lady, Elizabeth. She's a teacher from my school. She is the only one who knows that we are from Mexico."

"So you don't tell the other kids. How come you don't want them to know?"

"Since we are not born here and we don't have the papers . . . Probably they are going to send us to Mexico. I won't see my friends."

He goes on to tell me about how he plays soccer every Monday and Friday evenings, likes to go to church and take communion, and loves to sleep late until 1:00 p.m. when he is allowed. Moisés feels like he has everything he needs, "except for a PS3." He feels happy he is Mexican because "I get to eat Mexican food. There's two things in Mexican food that I really like: tacos and tamales."

"Do you feel proud to be Mexican?" I question.

"Kind of. We have a lot of money here, but in Mexico we don't have any money: we're poor. My mom lives like in the woods. There's a lot of people that lives in the woods because they don't have any money. My dad wants a second chance and wants me to go to college and get money."

Toward the end of our interview I ask, as of the others, "What do you think it is like to be an immigrant?"

"Dumb, scary," he rattles off. He seems to have thought about this before.

"Why is it scary?"

"Because, what happens if some cops come to our house and they want to see our papers? We don't have it. And my little brother and my four cousins have it. And we have to go. That's what's scary about it."

Moisés does not know anyone this has happened to. The police have never come to his house. Once his father was stopped while driving with Moisés in the car. "He needed to show his license. He still had it. They didn't say, 'Let me see the papers.' They just said, 'Let me see the license' . . . He was lucky!"

"It sounds like you're worried about this. Why are you worried about it? Why do you think that will happen?"

"I don't know. Maybe I have a feeling it will happen. Perhaps it won't."

"Do you ever talk to your parents about it? What do they tell you when you tell them you're scared?"

"That's how life is. That's how life is when someone doesn't have the papers; you have to go to the country you were born in. And you never go back to America." Moisés explains that they don't have many things in that house in the woods in Mexico where he used to live.

"Do you think it will be really hard if you had to go back? What would happen to your brother if you went back?"

"He'll just have to take care of himself. Maybe they'll adopt him." Moisés's younger brother is a US citizen.

"It sounds kind of scary to be an immigrant. That sounds like a lot of worries for a ten-year-old. Don't you think? Do you tell your parents that you're worried? What do they tell you?"

"They just say, 'If we see a cop, don't tell them we were born in Mexico or they will take us away.'"

"Do you ever talk to your cousins about it?"

"Yes."

"Do you guys have a plan?"

"Yes. Run away."

CHILDREN'S FEARS OF SEPARATION

Fears of family separation not only affected women like Inés, but also clearly troubled children. Andrés, Homero, and Moisés were among the last I interviewed; their comments are typical of the types of fears articulated by children I met of all ages, all legal statuses, and both genders in Ohio and New Jersey.

Parents told me they avoided talking to their children about legal status issues. For some it was just too complicated. One mother insisted that her two US-born children did not know that she was unauthorized: "No, no, they don't know . . . but they do ask about it. My son asks me why I don't have a license. And I tell him that I don't have a Social Security number but, no . . . I think about them and I don't want to tell them because it's a lot, it's long to explain, it's too complicated." Other parents wanted to protect their children from adult worries. One mother of an eight-year-old explained, "No . . . I have never talked to her about it . . . I have not put any of these ideas in my daughter's head. I have never told her because her mind is, right now, with her childhood, with playing . . . with her life as a girl."

In just a few cases, parents who had personally experienced an incident with the police or the deportation of someone they knew well decided to talk to their children about it. One mother told me why she had explained her situation to her three US-born children.

It was here [at the store where she worked] just two weeks ago, and I was on my way home but then some clients arrived. In the time I went back to open the store—because I told the children, "Wait here in the car, I'll be right back."—I came to open up, and when I got back out I saw that there were a bunch of police all around my car. They said someone had called to report that the children were in the car too long. I told the children this, after this happened: that if it happens again they are going to send me to Mexico or something. . . . I told them, "And you guys will stay here." . . . I got very scared. I talked a lot with the children. I said, "If the police send me to Mexico, you guys will have to stay here. Maybe your father will take you. The important thing is that you will be here with him." Let's hope it never happens.

Another couple I met had carefully prepared for deportation; this was after a close friend was deported suddenly after a traffic stop, leaving behind his wife with an eight-month old son who lived with them until she could make arrangements to return to Mexico. The mother, a university-educated public accountant prior to migration, explained, "After that experience that happened to us, well, we have taken some precautionary steps. One never knows."

I asked what plans they had made. "The plan is for the security of our children. We have friends who are citizens, also from our town, from Oaxaca. We have written letters to leave the children safe."

"In case they detain us," her husband added.

They also had the children's passports ready. I asked if the children knew about the plan. "Yes. We are in a situation in which we have to speak to them with the truth. So that they know what can happen and how we can solve the problem."

Most parents, however, treated the topic as off limits, avoiding direct conversations with their children about it. When I asked if his kids knew about immigration issues, a father who had already been naturalized explained, "I don't think they're aware of it. Not like in families, like my sister, and they're from Houston and on her husband's side, the one in the picture, his family . . . They had to cross illegally, his brothers. That's sort of a taboo conversation to have, not talk about it . . . But it's kind of like everyone knows." Indeed, in interviews children seemed well aware of the implications illegality had for their lives, as Moisés had clearly articulated.

Unauthorized children I interviewed understood that they needed to be careful around the police. One nine-year-old recounted the story of his border crossing, with his younger brother, two years earlier: "When we came here, the first time the police fined us, the second time they sent us back to Mexico, the third they let us go, and the fourth time they let us go too." Noticeably, he did not distinguish between the police and immigration officials in the retelling. In Ohio, the boys continued to view police as synonymous with trouble, as their mother explained: "They know [about their legal status], and sometimes when I see a patrol car, I say, 'Police in sight,' and they know that they have to sit up straight . . . then they see that it has gone by and the danger is gone, then they relax." Another mother said of her nine-year-old son, "He is conscious [of the family's legal status] because when we are in the van he puts on his seat belt and he checks on the other [US-born, four-year-old brother] in his car seat . . . or he sees a police and he says [to his brother], here comes the police, sit good." Anita, a legal permanent resident who had been unable to legalize the status of four of her five children, explained that her eleven-year-old "has a great fear of the police. She was afraid that they would send her back to Mexico." At school "her biggest worry is this [her legal status]. She used to evade people so they would not ask her questions because she was afraid that they would ask her for a Social Security number. . . . She started biting her nails out of worry."

US citizen children, like Andrés, also expressed fears of deportation disrupting their families. I asked a six-year-old if she ever felt scared that her parents were immigrants. She said yes, "Because if I am here and my mom goes to Mexico I am going to be sad because I would miss her." A ten-year-old US citizen whose mother had severe kidney disease and received dialysis biweekly thought her family would have to go back to Mexico someday, "[be]cause the *policiales* are looking for people that don't have papers to be here." A twelve-year-old was scared his parents were immigrants because "we might be apart."

Some of these children had had a friend or extended family member detained by immigration officials. Most had never known anyone who had been detained or deported, but they talked about the possibility of being separated from their parents. Often they had seen news coverage about the increase in enforcement tactics nationwide. A ten-year-old told me when I asked her if she had ever seen someone have their parents taken away, "Yes, I've seen it on TV." A twelve-year-old said she was scared that the members of her family were immigrants "because when that happened on the news that a lot of people were getting like catched, like um, came on the door random and just took them. Yeah, I got really scared that time." When I asked a nine-year-old about what she thought it was like to be an immigrant, she answered, "Sad." "Why?" I wondered. "I saw a video of people and they are immigrants, and one time they were going back to Mexico and the policeman caught them and they took them. And they had a daughter and they left the daughter in the car."

Remarkably, children without any unauthorized family members expressed fears of deportation. Shannon, a US-born citizen whose Mexican husband had been a legal permanent resident for the thirty years he had lived in the United States, explained, "Not that long ago, my husband misread his green card. [He said] 'I haven't gotten anything in the mail. My green card is gonna expire. I have to renew it.' Brandon [son] was concerned about it: 'What happens if you don't? Are you gonna get in trouble? Are you gonna get sent back to Mexico?' He hears about all these laws tightening and immigrants and their status and whatnot. We later found out that my husband is not getting any mail because his green card expires a year from now."

Similarly, Elena's entire family had migrated legally when her husband, an engineer, came to Ohio on a professional work visa twelve years prior. The couple's two children, ages fourteen and twelve, had both been born in Mexico but had been living in the United States with their parents and recently had become US citizens. Elena explained: "With my daughter it is curious. When she got her citizenship two years ago she said to me, 'Oh Mommy, if only you had your citizenship [too]. I don't want them to remove you.' The two [children] began to talk about it, and my son said, 'If Mom's residency expires she can't stay here.' She was ten then, and so she worried about me. I told her that as long as I have my papers, the residency, I won't have any problem, plus I behave myself. But her worry was that they would remove me."

Elena's children lived in a suburban middle-class neighborhood. The whole family had immigrated legally. However, they knew other Mexican families through their church that had faced problems with immigration and been deported. This had instilled the fear in the ten-year-old that her family, too, was at risk. Clearly, enforcement practices not only affect unauthorized children and US citizens with unauthorized family members but potentially instill legal uncertainty among all children of immigrants.

(MIS)UNDERSTANDINGS OF IMMIGRATION

Ten-year-old Andrea told me that an immigrant "is when someone is illegal in this country and police-ICE come to look for them to send them back to their country." Her eyes started to water when she then told me her parents were immigrants. I asked if she was proud that her parents were immigrants. She said, "No." "Do you ever feel scared that they are immigrants?" I continued. "Yeah," she said, her chin quivering. "What scares you?" I asked. "When the police-ICE come they will take them." Andrea confused being an immigrant with being illegal. "What do you think it is like to be an immigrant?" I asked. "I think it is hard because you have to, like, try not to be caught by police-ICE, and you would like to stay in this country to like have jobs and children to be legal in this country."

Like Andrea, a number of children born in both Ohio and New Jersey equated immigration with illegality. A twelve-year-old boy who was a US citizen told me when I asked him what he thought it was like to be an immigrant: "Like they must be like scared when like they, if they catch them, then they have to go back to their country." A ten-year old said that most of his family were immigrants and that he thought it would be "weird" to be an immigrant. "What's weird about it?" I asked him. "I think that like the people that are not from here, they are not supposed to be here." When I asked a ten-year-old what an immigrant was, he explained, "It's when say someone from Mexico came across the border, he's in the United States right now. He is an immigrant now 'cause he wasn't born here, he was born in Mexico and when he crosses the border, he's an immigrant." Children responded this way even after I gave them a definition for an immigrant as simply being someone who was born in one country and then moved to another country to live.

Children who were immigrants themselves also made this mistake. I asked thirteen-year-old Cristina, who was a legal migrant, what she thought it was like to be an immigrant. She answered, "Well, I think it is very difficult because you can't . . . like if you leave and then they ask you for your papers and you don't have them, they will call Immigration." The only children who did not make such a conflation were those US-born children I interviewed who had one parent who was also a US citizen. The unquestioned citizenship of both parent and child may mean they better understood variations in immigration statuses, although it did not safeguard them from fears of family separation.

Children of different ages, of course, may understand legal status differently.[50] Older unauthorized children, for example, were able to explain more coherently the way legal status negatively affected their lives. One fourteen-year-girl told me: "[It's] kind of unfair for us because, for example, I want to become a doctor. But I probably can't do college here because first of all, it's so expensive and you need to like have papers." Younger unauthorized children were not nearly as articulate. Often they seemed confused about legality. This was true for Belen, Margarita, and Gregorio, all age six. In separate interviews, each said he or she was born in Mexico. When I then gave them a definition of an immigrant (as someone born in one country who moved to another country to live) and asked if they knew anyone who was an immigrant, they surprised me by saying no. These cases perhaps confirmed parents' assertions that children did not really understand immigration.

Although it is true that very young children may not understand the concept of immigration, they do seem to be aware that there are social differences based on legal status even if this is difficult for them to articulate. For example, seven-year-old Kevin said that he had been born in Mexico and that he loved Mexican food but that he did not know anyone in his family who was an immigrant, giving the same response as Belen, Margarita, and Gregorio did. This was after I had given him a definition of an immigrant. But when I later asked him point blank, "Are you an immigrant?" he admitted, "Yes." "Would you want your friends to know that you are an immigrant?" I asked. "No," he answered. "Why?" "Because

I would be ashamed." Many young children like Kevin had negative associations with the word *immigrant* while simultaneously relating positively to the word *Mexican*. Being culturally different was not a problem, but the political definition connoting exclusion was.

According to Roberto Gonzales, children's awareness of illegality is not fully realized until they confront external, structural discrimination.[51] This helps explains the differences between the older and younger children I interviewed. Older unauthorized children have begun to face more constraints due to their status, so they may understand the intricacies of this legal definition more clearly. Yet younger children know there are status differences related to immigration. Although perhaps they cannot always articulate it clearly, legal status, for them, is a private family matter, not to be shared with others. Twelve-year-old Osvelia—a US citizen—wavered when I asked if she wanted people to know about her parents' unauthorized status: "I really don't—like, um, I want some people to know." "So which people would you feel okay knowing?" I asked her. "My friends that I feel like keep secrets well."

Children expressed a great deal of misunderstanding about immigration, equating all immigration with legal exclusion. More importantly, they frequently associated stigma with immigration. In fact, while 81 children of 110 told me they felt proud that they or their parents were Mexican (or Latino or Hispanic), only 27 of 110 said they felt proud that they or their parents were immigrants. The conflation that children make between immigration and illegality is potentially devastating for children's sense of self as they grow up the children of immigrants in the United States.

DEPORTABILITY AND FAMILY LIFE

I sit on the sofa next to Inés, still sleeping, watching the Disney Channel and putting off Temo and Dylan, who keep asking when we are leaving. ("In a little bit," I whisper into Dylan's ear. To Temo I give the "Be polite" stare.) First we eat tacos, served by the mothers. Inés is too drowsy to join us. Eventually I tell Inés I really must go, feeling guilty as she seems happier to sleep on the sofa. By now my headache turns my stomach. Inés, groggy, agrees when I mention that I do not want to keep Temo out too late because of his cold. Back at her apartment, she invites me in; I think she probably does not want to be alone. But I cannot stay. We text in the morning, Inés asking after Temo. I tell her he's feeling better. *"Hay k bueno, bendito sea Dios k pudo dormir bn :) ps yo ayer llegue a dormir otravez jejeje, me dormi como a las 6 y ya desperate a las 9, pero todo bn."* Translation: "Oh that's great, thank god that he could sleep well. Well. yesterday I got home and slept again, ha ha ha, I slept at like six and woke up at nine, but all is well."

Apparently Inés has recovered and her nerves have settled down. Adrián has had no further trouble with the police. Teresa's husband has not yet been deported. Although Inés's daughter Lesly surely knows that something has happened to her mother, she keeps it to herself, continuing to be a model student at school. Inés's fears may linger, but good news counteracts them: Inés is pregnant and delivers a healthy baby boy later in the year.

Families, of course, grow, regardless of immigration legislation. Relationships develop, tire, get strained, and improve. Fears come and go. Yet the daily lives of individual families, of women like Inés and children like Moisés and Andrés among so many others, are increasingly affected by legal status. The threat of deportation has very real impacts not only on immigrant communities but on the daily lives of individual men, women, and children in families. Deportability causes anxiety—and *nervios*—for all, compromising families' sense of well-being. Yet deportability also affects each member of the family in different ways.[52]

For women, a culture of fear disrupts a sense of well-being in the family but also—significantly—women's sense of self-determination, autonomy, and control over their families. Deportations risk transforming women into suddenly single mothers, and not of their own choosing, as in the case of Teresa living in limbo for more than six months. The resulting economic instability can be devastating, as women have no time to prepare for such changes to their families, and little to no social support, informal or formal, to rely on. The simple fear of such consequences can have severe repercussions, as when Inés ended up in the hospital because of an anxiety attack. For Inés, as for others, single motherhood was not as scary as the feeling of powerlessness that resulted from knowing that the government could, at any time, invade their family, disregarding their own choices about those with whom they lived. Existing enforcement policies significantly reduce the power of women in their families, women who already experience inequalities at home vis-à-vis the men in their lives.[53]

For men, state action via enforcement policies undermines fatherhood. Men's relationships with their children center often on their ability to provide for them. Economic provision especially marks the lives of immigrant men, who frequently move to a new country in order to better support their families. Enforcement activities remove men, more than any other family members, from the family, terminating their role as the primary head of the household. Ironically, immigration enforcement weakens men's roles in families at a time when other governmental policies seek to promote marriage, crack down on "deadbeat" fathers, and encourage more active roles of men in their families.[54] Deportation policies create single-parent households, crippling men's ability to have active roles in their children's lives.

For children, deportability disrupts their sense of stability. Research on divorce shows that financial and emotional instability has devastating consequences for children's lives.[55] Additionally, the passage of localized enforcement policies may have impacts on children's psychological well-being, with research documenting an association between middle school students' awareness of S.B. 1070 legislation in Arizona and their sense of belonging as Americans.[56] When national-level policies emphasize enforcement over integration, children fear their own potential deportations and those of their parents. Parents do not want to worry their children over something that they themselves, as parents, have no control over. Thus most avoid talking extensively with their children about deportation. Yet children learn that they must hide aspects of their experiences from others or be "careful" in their interactions so as not to get asked too many questions that might reveal their status. Though few of the children I interviewed and spent time with in Ohio and New Jersey had had direct experiences with immigration officials, many described fears that such policies would separate their families. Children seemed quite aware that legal status, to some extent, differentiated themselves from either their peers or the other members of their families. However, children also often misunderstood the details of immigration. Most notably, they often equated police with ICE and immigration with illegality. They associated stigma with immigration.[57]

These are the consequences of national policies that emphasize immigration enforcement, and the consequences of the threat of deportation on families. In the late 1990s, when Raúl was illegal, enforcement efforts concentrated on the US-Mexican border. Unauthorized migrants living in communities far from the border, in northeastern Ohio or central New Jersey, faced many administrative hurdles. Being illegal created everyday inconveniences, often leading to exploitative situations, especially at work. But previously illegality did not instill fears like those tormenting Inés and causing her *ataque de nervios,* or those voiced by children like Moisés when he described his plan to run away if Immigration ever came to arrest his parents. This is something different.

3 Stuck

DEPENDENCE IN INTIMATE RELATIONSHIPS

Thirty-nine-year-old Isabel—dressed in a matching eggplant-colored sweatsuit—prepares a varied breakfast of eggs, quesadillas, sausages, and French toast in her newly updated kitchen. I perch on a stool facing the black and tan marbled countertop jutting out from the wall. Not sure how to help, I listen. Isabel, a good head shorter than me, hair dyed golden and face carefully made up for 11:00 a.m. on a Sunday, takes her time with breakfast, slowly grating cheese and deliberately breaking eggs, enjoying the ritual and explaining her stalled efforts to move on.

Isabel relocated here only a few weeks ago but seems settled. The kitchen opens into an equally small dining room, where a glass-top table stands, and then into another room, crowded by faux-leather sectional, glass coffee table, and large, flat-screen TV, which her three children, ages seven, five, and three, watch alongside mine. For a woman recently separated from a husband who turned violent and mean, the renovations provide at least a semblance of security.

Opposite: Photograph by Bob Anderson

The median household income in this neighborhood is just $28,500; a third of the residents live under the poverty line and just 2.8 percent have attended college.[1] The neighborhood is among the poorer ones in this small city. Isabel had a friend install a wire fence along the entire inner edge of the sidewalk before she moved in. She unlocks the gate every time she comes in and out of the driveway.

Though her physical needs are met, emotionally Isabel remains on edge. Later, after pulling out a photo of her ex, a tall blond man, grinning, in a faded yellow American Eagle jersey, his arm draped over a petite woman in a white pantsuit who looks like his mother, she says, "But I love this man still. If this man said, 'Come back with me,' I would go back. For my children, because I love him. It's that he is my *güero* [white boy]."

Isabel fell in love with her native-born husband, seven years younger, in 2005. They met at her job on the line at a factory where he worked in quality control. "At the beginning he said it didn't matter. The language. Different languages, different religions, and age, very different. At the beginning, he loved me. None of it mattered to him." They dated for three months, and then, with Isabel pregnant, they married back in Mexico. "We made all the arrangements from here, so that all I did was go back to get married there. I wanted to be with my family. It was the first time I ever got married."

I am not sure how Isabel managed that trip. Isabel did not have legal permission to reenter the United States because she had first crossed the border in 2000 as an unauthorized migrant. Originally she aspired to migrate legally; from Mexico she applied for a visa three times. "In Mexico I was a professional. I taught yoga. I saw all my colleagues in the United States taking classes. I said, 'I want to go too . . . for the next course, I want to go.' But they all had visas, and I didn't." By the time she was twenty-eight, repeatedly denied, she took a visa for Canada instead and then crossed into Washington State to live with her mother's cousins.

At age thirty, Isabel got pregnant with her first child, Alexa; the boyfriend left before she gave birth. Family members on her father's side encouraged her to move east, with them, where the cost of living was lower, so they could help with the baby. She agreed. But working and providing for her daughter proved difficult; she sent the baby to live with a sister in Mexico. Then, Isabel met *el güero*. In total, they lived together for four years, raising their own two children alongside Alexa, whom they brought back from Mexico after the wedding.

This was before the relationship turned sour. "I was to the point of suicide. When *el güero* said to me, 'I don't love you anymore,' I used to say to myself, 'What meaning does my life have here?' I was on the edge . . . In that moment you see everything so tragically, horribly, as if your life is worth nothing. . . . You cannot beg for love. You cannot beg someone who is telling you, 'I don't love you. I don't feel anything for you. Everything about you bothers me.'"

Despite her conflicting emotions, I feel sure Isabel is better off in this newly renovated home, as abuse marks her relationship with *el güero*. When they fight, which still happens often, especially when she picks up the children at his apartment, he threatens her physically and emotionally. Once instead of hitting her he kicked the television, breaking it to pieces. Since she is unauthorized and he is a US citizen, *el güero* brings up her legal status to wield power in arguments. "At any moment he arrives, he grabs the Yellow Pages and he says, 'I am going to call Immigration right now, the police.' I say, 'Call them. What are they going to do to me? Absolutely nothing.' So he doesn't call. But it is always the same. [she switches to English] 'I'll call Immigration. Then I'll get my kids. And you'll go like this' [snapping her fingers]."

Isabel feels stuck with her US citizen husband; she still loves him and depends on him for the everyday activities necessary to raise their children. She is also stuck legally, a fact that increases her dependence on her husband even while they are living apart.[2]

Webs of dependency like these extend beyond intimate partner relationships. When legal status differentiates family members, spouses feel stuck, unauthorized parents feel their legitimacy as parents is undermined, and children seem to feel they grow up ahead of schedule. This in turn affects the division of labor in family relationships. Unauthorized members may lose power vis-à-vis those who have legal status, much as children experience less power in their families because of their age and women because of their gender.[3] Illegality challenges and recreates divisions of power in families.

LEGAL STATUS IN FAMILY RELATIONSHIPS

If an increase in enforcement fuels a threat of deportation, the lack of pathways to legalization produces a situation in which family members do not share the same legal statuses. At the end of the first decade of the twenty-first century, an estimated 16.6 million people lived in mixed-status families in the United States.[4] Status differences mark parent-child relationships, like those between Isabel and her three US citizen children: 73 percent of children born to the unauthorized in 2009 were native-born US citizens.[5] These differences also create great inequalities between spouses who do not share legal statuses, like Isabel and *el güero*, altering the negotiation of gender roles.[6] Because legal status fractures families, with some enjoying all the benefits of citizenship and others not, to understand the effects of illegality on children and families we must look not only across families but also within them.[7]

How is it that so many family members of US citizens remain unauthorized, and that so many today live in mixed-status families? US immigration policy offers two principal pathways toward regularization: employment-based petitions and family sponsorship. Few families I interviewed came to the United States with employment visas. When families do, spouses and children typically travel together and share many rights and privileges. However, dependent spouses of H1B visa holders cannot work in the United States; thus they experience inequalities like those of mixed-status families. Elena, for example, had a dental practice in Mexico that she gave up to join her engineer husband working in Ohio. "In Mexico it was run, run, the patients, the food, the career, homework, tests, and I came here and nothing. . . . I didn't get bored, but it was strange. . . . It was difficult, it was a complete change in my life." Since emigrating, Elena had not worked outside the home. Research shows heightened tensions and conflict in marital relationships due to visa category inequalities between spouses, dynamics that also occur among mixed-status spouses.[8]

Ironically, most mixed-status families result from family sponsorship procedures, as family schisms are built into the application process. As Deborah Boehm explains, "Regulations further separate . . . families by focusing on each member of a family rather than on family units."[9] In other words, because one family member must apply for another, staggered applications leave family members in limbo waiting for their cases to process. Theoretically, the time gap is minimal. Practically, huge backlogs in application times for family sponsorship applications, especially for those from Mexico, leave some members in indeterminate status and in the worst cases, separate families. US-born Betty and her Mexican-born husband, for example, met in 1997, before the laws changed dramatically, making legalization via marriage much more difficult. Still, when they filed for his visa at the Mexican consulate, "They denied it!" At the time, their son was just two months old. "I came back to [live] with my sister and family, to help me with the baby." Her husband remained in Mexico awaiting the visa approval, which came eleven months later. The couple spent the first year of their son's life living apart.

The length of time during which legal disparities divide spouses, and at times parents and children, varies with the efficiency of the application process. In ideal cases the lag of status between family members is short; in worst-case scenarios it drags on as different family members wait for visas to be approved. The inequalities family members experience in these cases result from an administrative problem. And they fluctuate depending on specific policies. Allow dependents of H1b visas to work, and that power dynamic between spouses disappears. Reduce the wait time in immigration application processing, and status differences become temporary and less significant.

To give one more example: in the 1990s many unauthorized people in abusive relationships were unable to legalize unless their legal-status partners submitted the application on their behalf. Abusers often refused to do so, leaving unauthorized partners in an especially vulnerable situation. To remedy this codified injustice, community advocates pushed for legislation through the Violence Against Women Act (VAWA) allowing victims of domestic violence to petition for immigration statuses on their own, without the cooperation of abusive spouses.[10] This small change in policy has had a large impact, with women (and some men) gaining independence from abusive relationships during the processing of immigration cases, although critics point to problems.[11]

Of course, the bar to prove domestic violence remains high, so that when Isabel sought legal advice about her situation, the immigration lawyer advised that she did not have a viable case. *El güero* controlled his violent outbursts to the point that Isabel had not had to seek treatment for injuries in a hospital. She never resorted to a domestic violence shelter and had only spoken informally to a social worker through her church about the abuse. One of *el güero's* sisters offered to testify, but it didn't matter because when Isabel went back to Mexico to get married and then returned again to the United States, entering a second time, she committed what immigration policy considered an unpardonable offense. "The best lawyer said no. I would lose the case . . . In my case, I know I committed a federal offense. But it was because I needed to be with my husband and bring my daughter here."

At the start of the twenty-first century, a lack of pathways to legalization for many unauthorized migrants—and especially Mexicans, who often entered the United States without inspection—triggered the dramatic rise of mixed-status families. And so legal-status inequalities between family members have evolved from being a temporary (although at times lengthy) administrative problem to being a fixed source of family-based inequality. In 2010, most unauthorized Mexicans—and those I interviewed like Isabel—were ineligible to regularize their status even when married to a US citizen or a legal permanent resident.

Changes implemented with the Immigration Reform and Control Act (IRCA) in 1986 along with legislation passed in 1996 (appropriately named the Illegal Immigration Reform and Immigrant Responsibility Act) set the stage for the rapid growth in mixed-status families.[12] IRCA legalized 2.7 million people who had arrived prior to 1982; however, it also effectively cut off access to legalization for those who did not qualify.[13] Furthermore, starting in 1997, unauthorized migrants who entered without inspection (EWIs)—that is, those who entered by walking across the border—faced either a three- or a ten-year bar to readmission, depending on the length of time they had resided in the United States without status (for periods less than one year the three-year bar applies). So when Isabel married *el güero*, she would have had to return to Mexico and wait ten years for a visa in order to return to live with him. Isabel, however, went back to Mexico to get her daughter Alexa and then reentered the United States without permission. In 2010, repeat EWIs like Isabel faced permanent bars to readmission.[14] This is why the lawyer would not take her case. Only during removal proceedings can the unauthorized who meet certain

criteria obtain a waiver to these bars, and such waivers can be quite difficult to obtain.

Until 2001, the provision 245(i) gave mixed-status spouses a way
around this conundrum, allowing unauthorized family members to avoid
bars to readmission by paying a $1,000 fine to adjust their status within
the United States.[15] In some of the families I interviewed, spouses had met
and legalized their status during this period without having to spend years
living in Mexico or living apart. In others, legalization came via family-
based petitions filed prior to the changes in the law. Sharon, an Ohio-born
mother of three, explained: "Right at the beginning, when I met him, he
actually came over here illegal. At the beginning, he didn't want to tell me.
It was something he said he was working on. I didn't know or understand
a whole lot about it. . . . I think it was in 2000 or 2001 that laws changed.
You can't just marry an American person to get papers."

Fortunately, her husband's father had filed a petition for him in the
1990s. "[The children] don't know all the things that we had to go through
to get him to this point." Since 2001, unauthorized spouses of US citizens
can no longer legalize their status through marriage without facing bars to
admission.[16] Unauthorized Lily in New Jersey explained, "[My Mexican-
born husband] is a citizen now. He is going to apply for me. But it will take
ten years. . . . We didn't get to put in an application for the 245(i). So we
are blocked. We can only pray to God."

Although most commonly affecting spouses, the combination of bars to
readmission and the removal of provision 245(i) leaves the parents and
children of US citizens also ineligible for legalization, as in the case of
Anita's family. Anita's husband came to work in the United States in 1992
as an unauthorized immigrant. In 1995 he received legal permanent residency (a green card) through his employer, and subsequently he submitted applications for Anita, who was living in Mexico, and their only daughter at the time. During the ten years that elapsed between application and
approval, he returned periodically to the couple's rural home to spend
time with his family, so Anita and her husband had four more children,
but "since we didn't know all the rules, we didn't put in for the other ones."
When Anita's visa was finally approved, she and her oldest daughter were
eligible to migrate, but the four younger ones were not. Anita went to the
United States without them, leaving them with her mother. But she could

not bear the separation. Within a few months, the younger children crossed the border to live with their parents, who later were able to naturalize. However, the four younger children cannot apply for residency, despite their parents' citizenship, because they entered without inspection. If not for the bars to readmission and lack of the provision 245(i), these four minor children would be able to adjust their statuses on the basis of the citizenship of their parents.

Had Isabel been able to apply for citizenship immediately after her marriage to *el güero*, things might be different. *El güero* still might call on his US citizenship in power struggles during their fights; couples experiencing conflict during a divorce often leverage power from a former partner's vulnerabilities. But the legal-status differences would disappear once Isabel's immigration status processed, and that source of inequality would not carry weight. Isabel would not be quite so stuck. In a system in which legalization is not possible, the law codifies legal-status dependencies in relationships between partners and parents and children.

DOMESTIC ABUSE

Illegality puts those in abusive relationships in overtly vulnerable situations.[17] The unauthorized may not seek help because of their precarious legal situation,[18] while abusers use legal-status differences to control the actions and activities of their partners.[19] Often manipulative, abusers threaten to use their citizenship status to gain custody of children and to disempower their spouses.[20] Of course, abusers may initially be attracted to unauthorized partners because of this power differential.[21] Regardless, the psychological impacts are devastating.

Isabel hardly acts the victim when challenging *el güero* to go ahead and call the police. She recognizes his abuse, so she seeks independence even though she continues to feel emotionally attached. Yet if not for Isabel's successful mobilization of her networks, she would not be in this house serving plates full of breakfast food to the children, who barely make a dent in it before running off to play again. Now Isabel pulls out new Tupperware containers of different sizes, carefully lining up the prepackaged sausage links into one and French toast made of Country White into another. She serves more coffee. I sip while eating a few strips of the luke-warm flour quesadillas with thinly sliced ham cooked in the toaster oven. Isabel puts a piece of toast on her plate but doesn't eat; she mindlessly packages her breakfast into one of the plastic containers with the other leftovers. "Did you buy this house all on your own?" I ask.

"This house, I fixed it up alone. My boss bought the house for me."

Shortly after meeting *el güero*, Isabel left her factory job and began working as a housekeeper for an older couple. At first, she lived in their home. After she gave birth to her and *el güero*'s child, and brought her daughter Alexa back from Mexico, she moved into a house *el güero* had purchased. "He worked in a big company that distributes all the merchandise to the stores . . . he loaded at night. At that time, he earned really good . . . he drove a car of the year. When he and I decided to move in together we said, 'Okay, great, let's get a house.'" Proud Isabel extols the neighborhood where she once lived, one of the best in the area, and the school her children previously attended.

But then *el güero* lost his job and stopped paying the mortgage. This was around the time their relationship fell apart. "He let the house go. He never paid anything. I loaned him money, to save the house. I don't know what he spent the money on, who knows . . ." The house went into foreclosure; he moved out. Isabel came to this neighborhood where she gates her car at night. "My boss bought this house for me when he saw all these problems that I was having," she explains.

At the time, Isabel had not told him about her legal situation, only her personal dilemmas. When he agreed to help and requested some paperwork, she realized she had to tell.

> I gathered my courage and I said, "Sir, I need to speak with you about something very important. You know what? I am illegal. What you are asking me for [paperwork for the purchase of the home] I cannot give you." He asked me to explain. I explained. "Whatever you decide, I accept. If you want to dismiss me, I will still thank you with all of my heart." "What are you talking about? My wife adores you." He made me laugh. "My wife loves you more than me." Thank God I told him the truth. I told him absolutely everything.

Unwavering support buoys Isabel. "He said, 'Don't worry. We will get you the best lawyer.' But the best lawyer wouldn't take the case."

Isabel also depends on her in-laws. One of *el güero*'s sisters likes Isabel, and puts the home's bills in her name, since Isabel cannot set up the utilities without a Social Security number. A friend insures Isabel's car, which Isabel drives to work without a license out of necessity. Isabel manages a functional living arrangement. The fragile support system hinges heavily on her employer's benevolence, the goodwill of her in-laws, and the reluctant cooperation of *el güero*, who watches the children every day after school until she finishes work.

Still, Isabel struggles to provide for her children from the $320 she earns a week cleaning her wealthy employers' home. "My husband has never given me even a dollar. Not when we were married, and now even less. He used to say that he wouldn't ever give money to any woman." Isabel switches to English to mimic him: "He would say, 'I'm not giving money to any woman. I don't care who she is.'" Then in Spanish she adds, "Y yo le decía, 'Pero yo soy tu esposa' [I'd say, 'But I am your wife']. [He'd answer,] 'I don't care.'"

Even after moving in with a new girlfriend, *el güero* continues to call on his unquestioned citizenship to pressure Isabel. This preoccupies her. "I cannot imagine the people that have to be separated from their children. Better to be thankful that the children are here. Because, as an illegal, one has to think. You have to be conscious of the reality." While not preventing Isabel from exiting the difficult relationship, legal-status differences between her and *el güero* do stop her from severing her ties completely. And every time he threatens Isabel, it reinforces her dependency on him, and his family, to survive as a single mother, as an "illegal."

Allusions to child custody issues sting most because they play on fears of deportation. In a different case, a mother told of her angry ex-husband, a legal permanent resident, who constantly tried to use her lack of status to gain custody of their children, to no avail. At the time fighting a deportation order with the help of a lawyer, this mother felt infuriated when her ex-husband tried to take her oldest son with Down syndrome, even though he contributed only irregularly to his care.

> There was this one time we went to court but didn't get the divorce. The children remained like they could be for either of us. Nobody had custody. He then went to the school to pick up the oldest and sent his girlfriend to

pick up the younger two, they went to Head Start. My best friend called me: "I think he is going to do something. He is going to try to take the kids." First I flew to my son's school, and he was already there. He called the police, saying that he had the right to take the children. The police came and he showed them his papers: "Look, here are my legal papers. She doesn't have papers, ask her for her papers."

The school principal intervened, saying that she would not allow him to take the children without a court order. "The police went on her [the principal's] side. He said, 'I cannot do that.'" Another time when the couple was in family court something she said made him so mad that "he began to shout that I was an illegal, that he had papers . . . and the judge told him, 'If what you are trying to do is to get me to call Immigration to deport her, I am not going to do it.'"

This mother, like Isabel, did not evade law enforcement; she sought help with domestic disputes. In a sense, her ex-husband, like *el güero*, unsuccessfully attempted to use legal status for gains at the personal level. Yet whether women in this situation rely on a sister-in-law, a boss, a judge, a police officer, or a school principal who refused to report their status to the police, they depend on cultivating heterogeneous networks and sympathetic individuals to face manipulative and abusive husbands.[22] As De Genova suggests, the power of deportation is in the threat, not the outcome;[23] that the men called attention to their legal-status difference left a psychological imprint on both women, who increased their dependence on others to deal with the unequal balance of power in their relationships.

I visit Isabel ten months after our first interview, when Isabel recounts the extent to which she continues in a legal limbo, still stuck in a relationship of dependency with *el güero*.

Last week I was over there because the kids wanted to play in his backyard. So I went to pick them up and was sitting on the step. And he started to get abusive. So I called the police. The police asked for my ID—my license— because my car was there in the driveway. And *el güero* said, "Oh, she doesn't have a license," just to get me in trouble. The police officer was nice and just said that I had better get a license before I start driving the car all around. But he keeps trying to get me in trouble. He wants custody of the kids. He is saying that since I have no papers he should get custody of the kids so they won't be abandoned if I ever get deported.

This is not an empty threat: custody rights do not extend across borders. A 2011 report estimated that more than 5,100 children may be in the US foster care system and cannot be reunited with their parents because of a parent's detention or deportation.[24]

Legal status augments the imbalance of power already existing between partners, which is especially overt in cases of domestic violence.[25] Abusers with legal status, like *el güero,* may seek relationships with women without status. They may find that legal status further legitimizes their privileged status as men, and they may act out physically when they feel threatened by female partners. Abusers without legal status may feel their masculinity threatened by the power implied by the legal status of their spouses, an inversion of gender roles, and may act out violently to express and reassert their masculinity.[26]

Although cases of domestic violence are especially telling, most of the women I interviewed did not experience—or talk about—violent relationships with partners (seventeen of eighty-one did). Still, illegality may arise in disputes. Explained the sister of a US-born mother married to an unauthorized Mexican from whom she had temporarily separated in the past, "Because my sister and her husband are so [annoyed] back and forth with each other, all the time. So my sister would sometimes make comments about her husband's legal status." Such tensions suggest deep connections between legality and power inequities in marriages.

ILLEGALITY AND THE DIVISION OF HOUSEHOLD LABOR

Scholars often use the division of household labor as an indicator of gender inequality.[27] Women's greater contributions to the household mark their disadvantaged position in larger society and also in the family.[28] This is true for Isabel, who complains that *el güero,* currently unemployed, watches the children but really "doesn't do absolutely *any-thing*" for them. I asked in interviews how often each family member contributed to certain chores and cross-checked the accounts from parents and children.[29] Most women interviewed—seventy-four of the eighty-one—lived with male partners.[30] And the majority of these women reported always taking charge in all categories of household work, including decision-making tasks, household labor (cooking, cleaning, laundry, shopping), contact with outside services (translation, filling out paperwork), and child care; few men always helped out with these tasks. And while very few mothers never contributed to these tasks, the majority of men never participated in everyday household activities.[31] Women's greater contributions to household labor are consistent with findings in research with immigrant and nonimmigrant families.[32]

How does legal status affect gendered negotiations of these tasks? I compared the reported contributions of unauthorized, legal-status, and US citizen mothers and fathers in these different categories of family housework. Unauthorized women did child care and made child care decisions more often than other mothers; unauthorized fathers also contributed to child care more often than other fathers. Cooperation in child care tasks suggests flexibility in some gender roles due to the constraints of low-wage labor and/or having an unauthorized status. Lower-income fathers in Mexican immigrant families have been found to contribute more to household tasks,[33] and the unauthorized experience high levels of poverty.[34] Since unauthorized parents often both work full time, they may be more willing to share in tasks like child care to avoid paying for child care.

Among legalized parents, the story is more complex. Legal-status mothers always reported doing the cleaning, cooking, and laundry slightly more often than unauthorized and US-born mothers. This may be because legalized women less frequently worked outside the home. Fathers with legal status more often always contributed to the family tasks related to decision making and those linking families to services—more than US-born fathers and unauthorized men. Legal-status men's clear position as economic breadwinners via migration may explain their more robust roles in tasks related to being the heads of household and their delegation of daily household tasks to their legal migrant wives.

More tellingly, US-born mothers more often reported always doing the tasks that linked families to services and transporting children than other mothers, perhaps owing to their greater familiarity with US infrastructure and their legal right to drive. Yet none of the US-born fathers—all of whose partners did not share their legal status in my sample—reported always contributing to any household tasks.

Indeed, while mothers in all family categories contributed more to household tasks than men, table 2 shows that women in mixed-status families reported *more* household work than women not living in mixed-status families. This was true both when women were the unauthorized *and* when women were US-born citizens.

The sample is small and thus only suggestive. Yet the stories from the eighteen families I interviewed in which partners either currently (fourteen) or previously (four) had a mixed legal status suggest high levels of dependency of unauthorized spouses on their partners.

Of course, gender norms and expectations between individual couples emerge strongly in narratives about household labor negotiations. Yet race, class, and other cultural differences between spouses have been found to shape gendered negotiations between partners.[35] Accounts from mixed-status families suggest that legal-status differences may further complicate gendered negotiations within families among those of varying class and educational backgrounds.[36] In eleven of these families, the fathers were, or had been, unauthorized migrants and the mothers were US citizens, and in seven families the mothers were, or had been, unauthorized and the fathers were US citizens. For unauthorized women, increased dependency translated into more contributions to household work. For unauthorized men, dependency increased the workload of their female partners with status.

UNAUTHORIZED WOMEN STUCK AT HOME

Like Isabel, unauthorized women struggled to insure their own cars, find work, or even put bills in their own names. Unauthorized women who were partnered with unauthorized men shared this experience of disadvantage with their spouses. More than half of the unauthorized women in my study were formally employed like their partners: thirty-two of fifty-one worked full time outside the home and an additional four worked part time. This created more of an equal footing in terms of scheduling, with partners alternating tasks depending on who was home. One unauthorized father whose partner was also unauthorized, for example, explained the family's weekday schedule, "She comes home and begins to cook. When I arrive I

Table 2   Percentage of Mothers Who *Always* Completed the Following Domestic Tasks

	Unauthorized Mothers		Legal-Status Mothers	
	MIXED-STATUS SPOUSE (N = 8)	SAME-STATUS SPOUSE (N = 51)	MIXED-STATUS SPOUSE (N = 6)	SAME-STATUS SPOUSE (N = 16)
Decision-Making Tasks				
Making family decisions	50	58	100	57
Making child decisions	88	80	100	57
Coordinating schedule	88	75	100	43
Common Household Responsibilities				
Laundry	100	86	100	86
Shopping	100	82	100	57
Cooking	88	82	100	57
Cleaning	100	80	100	57
Yard work	0	4	50	14
Outdoor maintenance	0	2	50	0
Indoor maintenance	13	10	50	0
Tasks Linking Family to Services				
Making appointments	86	70	100	86
Interacting with gov't agencies	86	62	100	71
Translating	13	14	75	14
Child-Rearing Duties				
Child care	88	84	100	57
Help with homework	13	8	50	27
Transporting children	75	60	100	72

help, whether by washing dishes or cutting stuff up. That way she isn't doing it all evening." Both had worked in low-wage jobs ever since arriving as teenagers to the United States. Similarly, Leticia, previously a law student in Mexico but now an unauthorized mother of a ten-year-old and an infant, had a full-time job at a hotel during the day and went to another part-time job in the evening at a pharmacy. We had trouble scheduling our interview and finally met on a day Leticia had off when her husband was out at a job clearing snow. A high school graduate in Mexico, he worked in landscaping and earned money in the winter only after snowstorms, which didn't happen often in the mild winters of New Jersey. So usually it was Leticia's partner who was home with the baby and Leticia who was at work. "You see, my partner isn't working. It is the winter and there is no work for him. Times are tough. So it is my turn to work now."

In contrast, unauthorized women who were partnered with legal-status spouses less frequently worked outside the home; with half describing themselves as full-time homemakers. Regardless of women's own class or educational backgrounds, when they lived without status and with men whose legal, full-time employment economically sustained the family, unauthorized women contributed more to domestic tasks.[37]

Dalia, mother of three, spent her days at home with her four-year-old son. "I do my housework . . . (laughs) . . . the food . . . watch TV with my [four-year-old] son . . . I make [food] so that when my older two arrive from school at three in the afternoon, and then, with the schedule—right now—for seven I have food ready too, because that is when they [husband and brother-in-law living with them] arrive from work." Dalia's husband, out all day working in construction, contributed more to domestic tasks than many men. He did all the yard work and took care of indoor and outdoor maintenance of the home on weekends. He also always did the weekly food shopping together with Dalia. He made most decisions about the family's schedule and the children's schooling. Dalia did all the child care, laundry, cleaning, and cooking.

Dalia's husband had first come to the United States from the rural town where they both lived when the couple's older two children were ages five and two on a temporary employment visa he had obtained despite having less than six years of formal education. Dalia—who also had not finished primary school—migrated, with her two children, across the border three years later to join him, "because our children were growing up and he didn't want us to be apart. He wanted our children to grow up with the both of us, together." At the time of our interview he had papers: "He does, he is fixing them through his employer. . . . Not until he has everything fixed, then he can do something for us."

"Are there things you don't like about the United States?" I asked her later in our conversation.

"No . . . Everything I like." She started to say something and then stopped herself.

"Yes?"

"Yes . . . I want to . . . I would like to work . . . but . . ."

The division of labor made sense given the couple's schedule, with Dalia at home and her husband at work. And Dalia could not work without the papers that her husband had. But she wanted to. The legal difference between Dalia and her husband instilled a division of labor in the home that she was not entirely happy with.

Similarly, Saraí was the unauthorized wife of a legal permanent resident who worked a grueling restaurant schedule: he was gone from 10:00 a.m. to 11:00 p.m. six days a week. Saraí worked, but only part time on the weekends as a hostess at a restaurant that paid her under the table. Because her husband worked all the time, he did virtually nothing in the home, except at times helping to schedule appointments, since his English was better than Saraí's, even though both had graduated high school in Mexico.

Even Tania, an unauthorized mother who worked full time managing the family store, had many more responsibilities in the home than her legal-status husband, who worked at a restaurant. Tania did not describe her husband, who had lived in the United States since he was a teenager, as terribly traditional; he willingly helped out at home when he was there. However, he rarely was home because of his work schedule. On a daily basis Tania took charge of both the household and all the decisions about their three children, ages eight, five, and two. During the summer she took the children with her to work. "Sometimes we can't with these three. We need to give them more time. . . . It is hard when one works, and even harder with three children."

"My husband has his papers. He just got his citizenship two years ago," Tania explained. She had migrated to the United States after graduating from high school in Mexico and had joined her parents and younger siblings, all of whom had already naturalized. Because Tania was technically an adult when she migrated, her parents did not submit an application for her as they had done for her younger siblings. At the time of our interview, Tania was ineligible for legalization through either her parents or her husband because of the bars to readmission. She ran the family store, since she did not need to have a Social Security number to do so. Because her husband's formal work in the restaurant maintained the family economically, Tania managed everything else and was constantly stressed out in juggling home, store, and children.

The lack of papers did not confine women like Saraí and Tania to the home from fears of interacting with the outside world. Both drove, though without a license; among my interviewees, seven of eight unauthorized women living with legal-status partners drove compared to fewer than half of unauthorized women with unauthorized spouses. As table 2 shows, many always made the family's doctor appointments and interfaced with government agencies. When someone assaulted Saraí's husband at a bar, for example, she filled out the police report and health insurance forms, contacting me to ensure that she had done so correctly.

For these families, employment structured the conditions under which heightened gendered divisions of labor made sense. Male partners with legal status worked more regardless of their class background, or more intensively, to cover the family's costs of living; unauthorized women worked less outside the home because they could not do so easily even when they were well educated. Instead, they took on more of the unpaid household responsibilities.

I asked one college-educated divorced mother I interviewed to reflect on the impact of her lack of legal status on her marriage to a US citizen. Her e-mail response eloquently explains the disadvantages legal status carries for women, which intensified after September 11, 2001.

> The question is did my legal status put me at a disadvantage in my marriage? The answer is yes. Let me explain. At the beginning of the relationship, my ex-husband had control over a lot of decisions, some small, some big, such as where to live, renting an apartment, getting car insurance, making phone calls about cable, phone service, electricity. I depended on him to

go places, to order food at a restaurant, to answer questions at any place, etc. He knew how things work in this country; he spoke the language, and also some of these things required a social security number and/or a credit check.

Things changed a little once I was able to get a driver's license and I understood a little about the way of living here. . . . I was able to get to places, I got a better job, we were both paying bills, and at one point I was bringing a little more income home because I had 2 jobs. Things were going fine even though he was always the one making most of the decisions. I felt he knew more and I gave him that responsibility.

He was not legally divorced when we moved together. It took him about 3 years to finalize it because he owed money for child support and we were not able save enough money to start the process and pay the outstanding balance. I never pressured him to make this a priority; there was always the money issue, and of course there were always more important things going on. Also, I was working and driving without problems and this made my living easier. As soon as he divorced, we went to a lawyer and started the petition, but then 9/11 happened and it complicated the process.

By the time my son was born, I was home taking care of him and my 2 stepchildren (he won legal custody) and I had no source of income. My disability benefits were denied because I had an invalid Social Security number and I did not have health insurance. By this time, my ex-husband had his own business and he spent a lot of time there because financially things were not running well. He expected me to take care of things at home, and at that point I felt I had no choice because I was not contributing financially. We had major financial problems. At the same time I was arrested because I had a driver's license without having a legal status.

This was the breaking point in our marriage. I left with my son and started working for the same company I worked for several years. Two years later, my employment was terminated because I was not authorized to work in the country.

Strikingly, her account contrasts the initial dependence she experienced due to her foreignness as she adapted to the United States with the later, legally based dependency she experienced only after enforcement tactics nationwide increased. While eventually this mother was able to legalize her status through their original petition and now has applied for citizenship, illegality in this case, as in others, framed increased dependency in the relationship, dependency that ultimately undermined the marriage and led to its dissolution.

TRIPLE BURDENS

If illegality enhances unauthorized women's dependence on their spouses, we might imagine that legal-status women in relationships with unauthorized partners enjoy certain advantages. If legal status affords them power in their relationship, they may be able to negotiate for greater equality in the division of household labor. This is, after all, what household bargaining theories propose.[38] Yet interviews with women married to unauthorized men suggest the opposite. Illegality creates a structural situation in which unauthorized men depend on their legal-status spouses, so much so that these women take on even more responsibility for the household. In a twist on Arlie Hochschild's well-known second shift,[39] US-born women may do more labor at home because they have the social and cultural capital needed to help their husbands negotiate life in the United States as unauthorized residents.[40] Additionally, they may do even more tasks typically viewed as feminized labor, like cooking and cleaning, so as not to undermine their partners' masculinity by requesting help with these tasks.[41]

Mothers with legal status described assisting their unauthorized husbands in finding adequate employment. One schoolteacher, for example, recommended her college-educated unauthorized husband for part-time work in the school district so he could leave his low-paying job at a factory. Puerto Rican Betty's husband "was here working with his uncle in that Chinese restaurant for several years. . . . It wasn't until we got married that his status was legalized."

"Did you feel that was a little hard on your marriage? Having one spouse without papers?"

> It was. Sort of, I should say. Because, it can really get . . . It's hard for them to get a job when they don't have a Social Security number or, really, permission to be here. That's why he was working at the Chinese restaurant, because they didn't require that. They knew they were undocumented. They say, "Cheap labor." In that respect, yes, it was a little difficult, finding a good job for him after he got out of the restaurant. Now we are thankful. I don't remember how exactly, but we were able to get him that place at [current employer].

Betty used the pronoun *we* in describing his search for employment, indicating her joint role in the job search process, not difficult for her, as she worked as a secretary in a factory and was familiar with how to search for new job openings.

Women also may take over primary financial responsibility during periods when their partners cannot work, which can put strains on relationships. This happened to one couple who met when they both got involved in the Zapatista movement in the West Coast US college she attended. He had come on a travel visa and was able to follow her to Central America for a year. When they returned, he struggled to find work because he lacked employment authorization. She recalled her parents' reaction to their relationship. "They were like, why doesn't he just get a job, you know, they weren't understanding. I was just like, you know, Mom, he's illegal . . . She was like, okay, now I understand a little. I think they just thought he was like, lazy or something. Like a common misconception. Like, why doesn't he just get a better job? Why is he working there?"

Although all of these unauthorized husbands worked, they experienced precarious employment situations.[42] They also faced discrimination and especially low wages in the types of jobs they could access without work authorization.[43] Women often found themselves intervening on behalf of their husbands either to potential employers or to family members who did not understand their situation.

In such a mediating position, women with legal status felt responsible for more than just the economic stability of the family. For some, the added responsibilities were not an issue. Ohio-born Tiffany was separated from her husband, the unauthorized Mexican-born father of her two children; both had completed GEDs to graduate from high school. She held no resentment for the responsibility on her side of the bargain. I asked if her legal status led to her doing more work than him, like making doctor appointments. "He always said, 'My English is no good. My English is no good. You need to call. You need to call, my English is no good.'"

She went on to explain that when they were together her husband had health insurance, dental insurance, life insurance, and car insurance all through her, through her employer. "It's all through me, but he still had those things."

"So you helped him out a lot, actually?" I asked.

"Yeah. Yeah, I did. I think I did my fair share. . . . I mean, it's not his fault that he couldn't . . . So, I wasn't like, you know . . . It didn't bother me. It didn't bother me at all. It bothered him I think more, like, because he couldn't get a job except for under somebody else's name or whatever but it didn't . . . It didn't bother me at all. So, when you love someone you don't care."

Gender roles played a role here: Tiffany viewed her extra work in the home as an expression of love, of the care work she did for her family.[44]

For others, the inequality in the relationship grated, straining the relationship and becoming, at times, unbearable. Leah's forty-five-year-old husband had been in the United States since his early twenties, when he left Mexico to work on the farm where Leah's parents lived, but he had never legalized his status. For a time they separated, but when I met Leah, a white US-born woman who worked as a florist, they lived together, with their eleven-year-old son. I asked if her son knew about his father's status:

> He [son] never really said anything. He knows stuff because he used to ask me, "Why can't Daddy pick me up from school?" "Well, Daddy doesn't have a license. They won't let him if he doesn't have an ID." . . . He has questioned certain things: "Why do you have to go to get plates for his car?" I'm not going to lie to him . . . He knows. But I think there's also the fact that he's lived with me alone before. So he knows that even if something happens with his dad, he'll be okay. I'm his security. Who's the one he relies on? He relies on me. From getting him up in the morning, feeding him, taking him to the doctor, taking care of him when he's sick. Not that his dad won't. But I do it. I always have. Even for him taking his medication, his father can't read English. So he doesn't understand when he is reading the medication what he is supposed to do. It's me who does it. They play and I'm the caretaker.

Leah highlights her husband's lack of a legal status as the reason why she does more in the home, from picking up and dropping off her son from school to reading and administering medicine when necessary. In the past, taking full responsibility for all of the family duties had stressed the marriage, leading to their temporary separation. "Sometimes I felt I was completely alone and while you're married you feel completely alone. That was part of our issue to begin with. That I was doing it all. I've gotten to a point that I've realized that regardless of that we do have a good relationship. He is a good guy and works really hard. He is a good father and he is a good husband. He doesn't want to do all the little things, but I can handle it. Sometimes I get like [growls] 'Would you do something?'" When Leah decided to accept the inequalities in the marriage, she and her husband reconciled.

Cristina, on the other hand, did not accept the unequal arrangement. A Latina US citizen, she divorced her daughter's father, a Mexican who had attended a university prior to migration and who had been unauthorized while they lived together. Cristina, a schoolteacher with a master's degree, explained why the status difference had created insurmountable differences in expectations in their marriage:

> Because one has the "official" responsibility for the home, to pay the bills, to fill out the income taxes, to have your name on all of the debts and even in driving the car to the supermarket becomes an official [task] because you have a license. Sometimes your partner doesn't understand and doesn't help you with the work supporting you at home like he should. . . . in fact, I think he resents it too, and that makes everything more difficult. Like instead of being on the due dates for bills, you have to go looking for them and asking for money to pay the bills on different dates all month long . . . one feels like a collection agent. Maybe when he controls the money in this way he feels it is a way of maintaining control in a relationship in which he feels inferior.
>
> There is so much machismo in a Latino relationship and so much more if your partner is undocumented and doesn't speak the language [English] well. His undocumented status feels like daggers during discussions about the responsibilities for the home . . . that he doesn't do this or doesn't do that because he doesn't know English. . . . The condition of the relationship and knowing that there is someone who will help them limits them too. . . . I would say they limit themselves. I imagine that for some guys it's very uncomfortable.
>
> Also, I remember my own need to validate his place in the home. Sometimes you never talk about these inequalities in a relationship very openly, but I made the effort to give him his place in certain decisions.

For Cristina, the need to do the typical tasks that women take on in the household combined with the extra burdens associated with the financial responsibility for the household was too much.

When spouses had similar legal statuses, like college-educated June and Martín, these structurally based inequalities did not exist. June met Martín in Mexico, while on vacation. They married, and because she sponsored his fiancé visa he immediately had worker's authorization upon arrival in the United States. I asked the couple, sitting together in the interview, who did the laundry. June said, "Laundry? Me. Laundry is me. He cleans the kitchen all the time."

"I think it is pretty balanced," added Martín.

"Really?" I asked them both. "Is that something you talked about?"

June replied, "I don't think we've ever talked about it. Someone notices the floor needs sweeping, they'll sweep it. If he knows that I have a meeting and I'm working late, he'll do the dishes."

Similarly, another citizen mother who had not graduated from high school explained that her legalized husband with a similar background "helps with the laundry and dishes and sometimes little projects. You know, just like cleaning up." And Rosa, a Puerto Rican, worked full time in a college program for teenagers and left early for work. Since her husband left later for work, she explained that "he usually packs [lunch for daughter] in the mornings. . . . bananas, grapes, cheese sticks, if we have cookies." Once couples have an equal legal status in the partnership, women may feel more at liberty to petition for their partners' greater contributions in the home. While class differences and gender ideologies influence the negotiation of housework, mixed-status partners with varying class backgrounds described a similar experience. Living with a partner who did not share a legal status further heightened inequalities in the home.

LIVING WITH RAÚL

I relate to these women's stories. The inconveniences caused by Raúl's legal status bothered me early on. But not until I listened to, reread, wrote up, and digested women's accounts did I realize how much these power differences also affected our relationship.

Raúl and I first moved in together to a ninth-floor apartment with a fabulous view of the annual Fourth of July fireworks display over the river, paying an extra $40 per month in rent for the balcony. Raúl worked Saturdays; on those days I puttered alone. Each week after cleaning the one-room apartment, I relaxed, destressing after three hours of scrubbing the bathroom and kitchen and doing a thorough dusting, sweeping, and mopping.

After Raúl got home I hated picking up the snack wrappers he left out on the single bed stacked with pillows, our living room sofa, when he watched TV; I despised cable, but he insisted we order. He needed the mind-numbing entertainment after so many hours of manual labor per week.

I much preferred Sundays, when we set out early to go garage sale shopping, or when we went to the park and I watched Raúl play soccer from the sidelines with the wives of his teammates. In those days I liked joining Raúl's routine rather than making my own, but our patterns cultivated distance.

My friends helped run the volunteer ESL school; spending time with them involved obligations Raúl did not always want on his days off. With his friends, Raúl watched soccer, sipping beer in his friends' living rooms, and I—well, I knew I was to hang out in the kitchen, with the women. They politely entertained me despite our differences, I having grown up in New Jersey and they having been born and raised in Mexico. Raúl tried to help me feel comfortable, often inviting me to sit with him and drink a Corona. Mostly, though, I complied with the gender separation of these visits, learning to make small talk, to adapt, to watch the women cook— albondigas, tamales—and to ask about the ingredients they used. Inside, though, I began to feel extremely lonely.

At home, I tried to make some of these foods. Raúl ate everything but began to take me out with him to visit more and more friends, to eat, on the weekends. I never noticed a problem until a Friday night a few weeks before our first lease was up. I brought out our plates from the kitchen, chicken—seasoned with cilantro, simmered in onions and tomatoes—and rice.

"What is this?" he asked, looking down at the plate, disgust twisting his mouth.

"Um," I reddened, and then grew angry. I made the dish once a week. "It's chicken. I've been making this all year."

"I know," he answered, curtly. Now I recognize the temper; in Temo it comes out when his blood sugar drops. "I can't stand it anymore." Raúl pushed the plate away, stomped out of the apartment and came back a half hour later with greasy Chinese takeout.

I laugh when I tell this story, so recognizable an example of marital discord; I really was not the best cook. But it hurt: when you're trying to relate to someone through food, rejection stings.[45] The gulf widened. I began to hassle Raúl about the cleaning; I think I may have nagged a lot. We moved into a different apartment, with two rooms, right near the train so I could walk to my graduate sociology classes in New York. We continued—me with the weekly routine of housework, badgering Raúl to help, and Raúl bringing in his own food more frequently, taking me to new friends, always to eat—the cautionary emptiness gnawing inside me, unheeded.

And so, we married. I thought marrying would equalize us before the law, diminishing the ever growing differences. I got pregnant with Temo, and the next year we bought a home and filed the paperwork to adjust Raúl's status. Raúl expertly sanded the floors, repainted the interior (he had worked previously as a painter in Texas), and found contractors to retile the basement and replace the second-floor apartment's rugs. He redesigned the front yard, planting delicate Japanese maples and constructing a new set of front steps with extra material from one of his many landscaping jobs. After Temo came, Raúl helped change diapers and watched him when I went to New York City to teach. Raúl's contributions balanced my weekly housecleaning routine. Marriage and legalization worked, for a time.

Yet loneliness haunts and takes a toll. We never talked about the gulf I felt, nor the one Raúl surely experienced, since he so often left for the apartment of his best friend from Veracruz, sitting with their family for dinner instead of ours. And as the power differences imposed by his prior illegal status eased up, others took their place. Graduate work suited me: I did well and had some success. Raúl felt proud; he still does, giving me unconditional permission to draw on our story for this book. But it changed me, gave me new perspectives and goals, just as legalization changed Raúl. Raúl began traveling to see his children in Mexico. Now that he saw them more frequently, ensuring their future became a more pressing challenge, and economic stress increased. If I worked, instead of staying in school, we would be better off. But I had begun dissertation research and envisioned a PhD. Our priorities began to clash. I applied for a Fulbright—Raúl moved out before I received the good news that would take me to Mexico for a full year with toddler Temo. Raúl stayed in New Jersey.

We never spent years fighting. The split felt fairly amicable, chalked up to cultural differences. Yet the webs of dependency continue, a legacy of the past carried forward into our postdivorce relationship. We used to argue, and continue to, when he feels I do not help him enough with my greater understandings of US society, and when I feel he does not do enough to support my raising Temo and Dylan. Early on we agreed to forgo formal child support arrangements, but that issue persists, bothering me when money feels tight. And why do the boys see their father only when I drive them to New Jersey instead of him coming to visit? I sometimes whine. The last time he drove upstate we spent the whole time filling out the boys' passport applications, frustrated. Then, to travel to Mexico, I needed a notarized letter from Raúl. How frazzled we both got when he did not get me the letter in time. As I came to New Jersey at the last minute before our trip, Raúl had to go to an after-hours *notario* who charged $40 for something that should have been free.

The dynamic of dependency and unmet expectations is ongoing, never quite finalized. As I reflect on these problems spinning around in what C.W. Mills would call my private orbit I see how immigration policy codifies this dependency.[46] Raúl's immigration application required my affidavit of support; I signed papers that oblige me to cover any costs the government might incur to support Raúl until the time he becomes a US citizen. Now, with Raúl's pathway to citizenship blocked because of a problem in our divorce papers, from the government's perspective I continue to be liable. Raúl and I are both stuck.

DEPENDENCY AND PARENTING

"She likes school."

Isabel is telling me about Alexa; the seven-year-old second grader has just run off, her thick straight black hair swishing against the middle of her back. Funny, it always seems to happen like this: I am here to learn about daughter Alexa and her younger siblings, Isabel and *el güero's* children. Preoccupied with the intensity of Isabel's own situation, I learn little about daughter Alexa until I have already been at the house for more than two hours.

In the kitchen, Isabel has graduated from breakfast cleanup to preparing pozole, the typical Mexican dish with jumbo-sized corn kernels, pale white, saturated in chicken broth with bits of meat. Sometimes spicy *chile*-seasoned broth tints pozole green or red. Isabel makes it plain, for her son: "It is his favorite dish." She will freeze most of it to eat on the weekdays when she doesn't have time to cook.

"She was a problematic child for a time. I don't know if the teacher doesn't like her. But she always had these reports, that she didn't listen, that she misbehaved."

Alexa doesn't like to speak Spanish, although she understands most of my conversation with her mother in Spanish. "Do your friends at school know that you speak some Spanish?" I have just asked her in English.

"I don't wanna tell them," she replies.

"How come? Why don't you wanna tell them?"

"'Cause it's my secret."

El güero speaks Spanish; he picked it up while living with Isabel. He usually communicates with the children's teachers. Says Isabel, "I tell the teachers, 'You know, I don't speak English well. If you send something home, please send it to me in Spanish."

"Do they do it?"

"Sometimes, yes. Alexa has a teacher who speaks Spanish. I talk with her. But I don't really have time for the meetings. *El güero* does it all. There they don't know much about Mexicans. But the children get treated equally."

Except that Isabel suspects that Alexa's teacher does not like her.

Power imbalances created by legal status shape intimate relationships, such as Isabel's relationship with *el güero*. They also influence the way mothers like Isabel parent their US-born children. Unauthorized parents with US citizen children face unique challenges, perhaps inhibiting their involvement in their children's schooling.[47] For Isabel, it is not that she fears school officials; she has had plenty of interaction with the police because of the tumultuous relationship with *el güero*. Her disengagement from Alexa's schooling also cannot be attributed to her English, as she herself suggests. Along with regularly communicating effectively with the police and her English-speaking employer, Isabel addresses Alexa and her siblings in English on all my visits; she speaks English quite well. When it comes to parenting Alexa, however, Isabel defers to *el güero*, having him act as a go-between. She seems to lack the confidence to navigate success-fully on her own. It seems as if the legal-status disadvantage Isabel experi-ences vis-à-vis *el güero* augments her overall sense of dependency, filtering into the ways she raises Alexa and her two other US-born children.

BROKERING

Not only does *el güero* act as a go-between for Isabel, but so too, at times, does her daughter Alexa. This is not uncommon among immigrant fami-lies, with the children of immigrants often working as translators or "cul-tural brokers" in their families.[48] Attending US public schools, they may speak English better than their parents born and raised abroad, so parents call on them to interpret.[49] Children fill out documents for their parents and attend appointments, helping to navigate what can be confusing for those with limited English-language skills and limited experience with US social institutions. Children's work as brokers extends beyond language, with immigrant parents at times asking their children to help with family decisions, like purchases or school enrollment decisions, trusting that their children better understand the intricacies of US consumer culture and the educational system than they themselves do. Children of immigrant par-ents may also help out with their siblings, attending conferences with par-ents, helping with homework and other general child care duties.[50]

The parents and children I interviewed in both New Jersey and in Ohio spoke of numerous incidents in which children helped their parents. Of the 110 children I interviewed, 71 children had translated or interpreted for their parents. They talked about helping in medical settings, in schools, and at stores. One twelve-year-old girl, to give just one example, often helped at parent-teacher meetings because "sometimes they don't have enough translators and they need help." She also interpreted at the store, "like sometimes they need help saying the word or what they're telling them, they don't understand, so they tell me to translate."

Despite the need to help with language, the work children do in immi-grant families may not be all that different from that which occurs in sin-gle-parent households or families with large number of children in which the oldest child has many familial responsibilities. Scholars describe the impact of these types of brokering activities on different family outcomes, such as school performance and parents' and children's ability to acculturate.[51] It can, in fact, be a positive experience when there are high levels of parental support and cooperation for these activities.[52]

Not all children I interviewed talked about how they felt about these experiences, but among those that did, just a quarter distinctly said they enjoyed the experience: for example, an enthusiastic ten-year-old boy explained, "I like doing it. I feel very helpful." Another group of children, one in five, felt ambivalent about the work. A teenage girl wavered: "No, I'm okay with it as long as I know what they're trying to say. 'Cause if I don't know, then it just feels awkward." And a twelve-year-old explained, "Sometimes I like it, sometimes I don't, 'cause it's kind of like, they use really like strong words and it's hard to pronounce."

More than half went further, explaining why they distinctly disliked translating. Children especially seemed to feel uncomfortable when their parents' dependence on them stood out. An eleven-year-old said, "I feel uncomfortable because there are words I do not understand." A ten-year-old said she didn't like to translate "because sometimes I don't know how to say some things in English in Spanish so it's hard." Similarly a seven-year-old complained, "I feel a bit uncomfortable. I don't know how to explain to my mom some words in English." And a ten-year-old felt bad translating because "sometimes I don't understand some words, or how to say them, or I don't know what they mean."

Translating, or brokering, indicates a specific type of relationship dynamic between parents and children, one characterized by webs of dependency. When the dependency is minimal, children do not mind translating and may enjoy helping their parents. Yet when children feel that their parents really need them, they feel uncomfortable, and stressed about whether they are getting it right. Although children gain power in their relationships with parents through brokering, they view this undermining of parental authority as unnatural and may resent the added responsibility.[53]

According to thirteen-year-old Luís, for example, "Like yesterday, we went to Walmart and my mom asked me to ask the—what you call it—the person that was working there, um, if they could help us, and so I had to translate that."

"Do you like doing that, or do you not like translating for your mom?"

"Not really."

"How come?" I asked.

"Because um, sometime my mom should learn how to speak English instead of me every time helping her." Luís felt frustrated that he had to translate and wished his mother would learn English so that he would not have to get involved in tasks he viewed as his mother's job.

Similarly, fourteen-year-old Marjorie speculated that brokering created an undue weight on her at a young age. At the end of our interview, when I asked if she had any final comments about what it was like growing up in Mexican family in New Jersey, she explained, "Most Hispanic kids and their parents, well, both their parents are working or something. So we usually have to grow up faster than we usually, than usual kids do."

"You mean 'cause you're like watching your brother?" I asked. Marjorie took care of her younger brother every day after school while her mother worked.

"Yeah, 'cause we like have to watch like siblings and stuff."

Translating for her unauthorized mother also made her feel that she grew up too quickly. "'Cause I used to translate, like my mom didn't speak Spanish, I mean English before, like in elementary. So I would have to translate. So I would know like more than I was supposed to when I was younger."

"That makes a lot of sense. So do you think it's bad to grow up quicker? Or it's okay?"

"I mean I wish it wasn't like that. . . . Like maybe, I mean it's good and bad at the same time because um, I, I don't know, usually kids my age won't like be, won't have like as much responsibility as I do now. And then like it's good because like it makes me like learn more and it shows me like what I'm gonna like go through like later in my life."

Marjorie talked herself into the potential benefits over time of what she perceived to be an inversion of the normal responsibilities of children and parents. However, for the time being, she felt it differentiated her from her peers in the ninth grade at the school she attended who did not have such adult responsibilities. In fact, Marjorie spent much of her free time (not watching her brother) with friends, sleeping over most weekend nights. She told me that if she had any problems at school she would talk to her best friend or another friend's father's girlfriend about them rather than her mother. Her activities suggest attempts to escape the weight of the work at home. A year after we met, I heard that Marjorie had been suspended when caught smoking pot at school. As explained to me by a family friend, "I know all the kids smoke pot these days, but the way she did it, she was just asking to get caught."

Often the oldest children, and girls like Marjorie, bear the brunt of brokering responsibilities,[54] although this is not always the case. Nelva, the mother of three, two grown children and one fifteen-year-old, explained how her children fought over who would help her out, since no one wanted to, and her youngest ended up helping the most. "[My oldest] liked to be involved in all sorts of programs, on committees, as a leader. So she was almost never at home; so she could not translate. The middle one, as I said before, had a lot of trouble learning [English]. The youngest, since she was little I took her with me to the school to translate for me."

I asked her if her daughter felt uncomfortable or if she liked to translate.

> She was uncomfortable. [She complained.] First, it was the oldest, "Oh, but, why me?" Because her uncles always asked her for help. "It's that you are the oldest and you are the one who knows the most. Your sister is just starting to learn." The middle child understood, but she couldn't speak well. I said, "If God gave you a gift, you have to share it. You want me to ask for help from my neighbors when I have my daughter? That would be shameful. You have to do it. You don't have any other chore. If I am asking you for help, it is because I can't. If I could, believe me, I would do it." . . . The youngest, the same. "Oh Mommy! To the school again?" It was the same with her.

This account suggests that parents and children negotiate the brokering responsibilities and that children may view them to be undesirable. Especially during the teenage years, parents' reliance on children can increase conflicts between parents and children.[55]

The perceived imbalance of power between parents and children can also lead to other types of conflict. Parents in a wide variety of immigrant communities fear that children use their presumed understanding of US society to threaten to call Child Protective Services during arguments, much as *el güero* threatened to call the police when Isabel did not do what he wanted.[56] Although very few parents reported official involvement with this agency, one father's story about his eight-year-old son illustrates parents' fears that children's authority will go so far as to inhibit parents' ability to discipline them.

> He was behaving badly. He came and he told me that it wasn't true, that he hadn't done it, that it was other children and that he had nothing to do with it. We went to the school, and they told us that yes, it was him. He came here and he said no . . . I told him, "Tell me the truth, I won't hit you if you tell me the truth." "Dad, I'm telling the truth." "I hate lies. Tell me the truth and I promise that I won't punish you nor hit you. Speak to me truthfully." "It's not true, I have been good."
>
> So we went to school and they asked him, "Wasn't it you the one who threw water in the bathroom? You know that it's true." So I hit him with my belt. Twice. I am not like that, I don't like to hit. But it didn't leave a mark or anything. So then he went to school and told them that I abused him, that I hit him. "They hit me." I was sad for a long time. He went in and said that he was afraid of me. That boy got me into a lot of trouble. . . . They [CPS] came and they interrogated us.

After two visits, Child Protective Services closed the case, the accusations unfounded, since discipline like this is not child abuse.

The incident marks the extent to which an inversion in power relations disrupts parental authority. In this case, the third grader's position as the liaison between parents and school led him to report his parents' abuse when he felt unfairly punished. In other cases, children use their mediatory position to prevent parents from closely monitoring their school performance, including attendance and behavior.[57] Children may use this to their advantage in the short term, but in the long run those like Marjorie do not appreciate such advantages.

Alexa answers the door on my next visit, home on this weekday, a school holiday. Clothes scattered across the living room; Isabel seems to be in the process of folding laundry. From upstairs, she calls that she will be down in a minute. Alexa frets over her homework; school folders are spread over the dining room table and the matching glass coffee table in the living room. I try to calm her: "Can I look at your papers?"

She diligently brings over test, quiz, and homework. A bright red sharpie marks the assignments: D+, C-. "I am surprised they give you letter grades like this," I tell the second grader. "Temo doesn't get letter grades yet. He is in third." Alexa exhales hard, puffing up bangs, exasperated.

"Is the teacher strict?" I later ask Isabel after she comes down.

"She is very demanding."

"I think I would be upset if Temo came home with grades like this."

"No, it's good. I like it. I think it helps her," Isabel explains. Isabel believes that having a strict teacher will help keep Alexa on task.

Six months later, Isabel tells me that Alexa's school performance has deteriorated. Recently, on garbage night, Isabel found a whole bunch of workbook pages crumpled up in the trash can, so she went in to talk to the teacher. She learned that Alexa, without her mother's knowledge, had been signing Isabel's name on her homework sheet to indicate that her homework had been completed when actually she was throwing out the incomplete work in the trash can at home.

Upstairs, when it is time to leave, I find Alexa, Temo, and Dylan scrunched into three pink miniature plastic chairs of a children's table set. Alexa holds a small green blackboard and points at it with white chalk. Temo secretly rolls his eyes at me. "She wanted to play school," he later admits uncomfortably on the car ride home, feeling perhaps too old for such girly games. Alexa uses her greater familiarity of the school system to hide her difficulties in school from her mother. But in play, Alexa thinks about school, taking on the role of the teacher.

Bill Corsaro describes children as using role play in order to exert some control over features of the adult world over which they have little control.[58] I suspect Alexa wants to do much better in school. Although she feels adept at negotiating between her mother and her schoolteacher to avoid trouble over the schoolwork she finds difficult, Alexa may not know how to ask for the help she needs in order to complete her work successfully, or may feel embarrassed doing so. The inversion in authority she experiences vis-à-vis her mother does not seem to improve her school performance.[59]

CHILDREN'S HOUSEHOLD LABOR

Accounts of children's brokering experiences suggest that immigration shapes child rearing in unique ways, much as race and class have been shown to shape parenting practices.[60] But to what extent does legal status matter? Alexa may dare to throw her schoolwork into the trash simply because she has been raised in the United States and her mother has not; she may feel entitled because she has a greater familiarity with US schools in contrast to her mother's status as a foreigner. This is what the existing literature suggests by emphasizing brokering as a feature of the immigrant family experience. But does legal status have anything to do with the authority negotiations between parents and their children, and children's willingness to help out in the home?

Directly asking children, or parents, to explain how their legal status shapes children's chores would not answer this question. Instead, as with intimate partners, I turn to families' accounts of children's household contributions as they vary by parents' and children's legal statuses. Scholars rarely view children's chores as indicative of power inequalities to the same extent as with spousal relationships.[61] However, the contributions of children to certain types of household tasks—such as family decision making and translating—may indicate greater authority vis-à-vis parents, whereas contributions to other types of household tasks—such as child care, cleaning, and laundry—may indicate less power in their relationships with parents.

Table 3 shows the percentages of those reportedly making no contributions to household work among the four groups of children I interviewed:[62] US citizen children with unauthorized parents, US citizen children with parents of legal status, unauthorized children with parents of legal status, and unauthorized children with unauthorized parents. The number of unauthorized children with legal-status parents was much smaller than the other groups; as with all the descriptions of the sample, these patterns are simply suggestive.

Most children did not help with decision-making tasks. US-born children with legal-status parents and unauthorized children with legal-status parents reported helping out slightly more than the children of unauthorized parents. Perhaps parents with legal status more often encouraged their children's participation in family decisions than unauthorized parents.[63] However, the differences were minimal.

As for common household responsibilities, among those with mixed-status parents, unauthorized children did more work than US-born

Table 3 Percentage of Children Interviewed Who **Never** Completed the Following Domestic Tasks

	Mixed-Status Parents		Same-Status Parents	
	US-BORN (N = 48)	UNAUTHORIZED (N = 8)	US-BORN (N = 22)	UNAUTHORIZED (N = 23)
Decision-Making Tasks				
Making family decisions	98	75	91	87
Making child decisions	96	88	91	96
Coordinating schedule	96	88	91	96
Common Household Responsibilities				
Laundry	74	50	68	57
Shopping	73	50	91	70
Cooking	92	38	68	65
Cleaning	37	13	14	17
Yard work	98	50	86	100
Outdoor maintenance	98	50	87	100
Indoor maintenance	98	75	96	96
Tasks Linking Family to Services				
Making appointments	94	88	100	73
Interacting with gov't agencies	92	88	100	68
Translating	33	38	68	23
Child-Rearing Duties				
Child care	80	64	82	57
Help with homework	81	63	96	65
Transporting children	100	100	96	100

NOTE: Not all children interviewed answered these questions.

children. The same held for children living with same-status parents: unauthorized children (with unauthorized parents) reported more contributions to household labor than did US-born children. Of all four groups, unauthorized children with legal-status parents typically contributed the most to household labor, and US-born children with unauthorized parents contributed the least (except in outdoor maintenance and yard work). Lacking a legal status may have diminished children's ability to negotiate how much they helped out in the home, especially for those whose parents had a legal status. And US-born children helped out less in the home, but they seemed to help with common household responsibilities even less when their parents were unauthorized.

The picture varies somewhat when it comes to the tasks linking families to social services. Predictably, US-born children whose parents have legal status reported the least amount of work translating and interacting with social and medical services; since their parents could presumably do these tasks on their own, they might not be needed. While one might expect that US-born children's citizenship would help link parents to outside resources they did not report helping out with these tasks as much as unauthorized children did, regardless of their living situation.[64] And unauthorized children with unauthorized parents helped the most with these tasks. Similarly unauthorized children more frequently helped with child care tasks (except for transporting children, a task only one child I interviewed did), regardless of their living situation, than did US-born children.

These patterns suggest that brokering practices may not be equally shared by all children in Mexican immigrant households. In fact, legal status seems to shape children's contributions to their families, with unauthorized children helping out with brokering, child care, and household tasks more than US-born children. If children's greater integration into US society than their parents explained their brokering activities, we would expect the opposite. If children brokered because they better understood US society than their foreign born parents, US-born children of the unauthorized would more often translate, make doctor appointments, do child care, help with homework, and interact with government agencies. Instead US-born children with unauthorized parents seemed to help out less often. They even did less of the most mundane of household tasks, such as cooking, cleaning, and laundry. This suggests that, as between spouses, brokering may reflect the power negotiations between parents and children more than parents' and children's relative assimilation.

Strikingly, gender has been shown to influence children's housework, and the girls I interviewed more often reported helping out with most household tasks than did boys.[65] However, across the board unauthorized boys contributed more to every single household task than did US-born boys. And unauthorized girls contributed more often to household tasks than US-born girls. If children's contribution to household labor is an expression of their power in the family bargaining unit, legal status clearly seems to be—at the very least—a factor that complicates existing gender and generational negotiations within families.

Of course, participating in household work is not necessarily a bad thing. The reasons why unauthorized children contribute more work to the family are complex, perhaps in part related to their different ideas about children's roles in the family a greater sense of what scholars sometimes describe as familism.[66] I return to the different positions that unauthorized and US-born children have in their families, and the subsequent possible manifestations in daily activities, in the following chapter.

GENDER AND POWER IN FAMILIES

"Do you have chores you are supposed to do?" I ask second grader Alexa.

"Yes. I clean my room, the bathroom, Mommy's room. Everything."

"You do a lot of chores." I am impressed. "Does your brother do any chores?"

"No."

"How about your little sister?"

"No."

"How about your mom?"

"No." She laughed really hard at her mistake. "I mean yes."

"What chores does your mom do?"

"Everything."

The story of the impact of legal status on family relationships is a gender story. Women in abusive relationships suffer with abusive partners, yet those in mixed-status relationships like Isabel experience even greater inequalities with their partners who use legal-status differences as another source of privilege by which they control their wives. And while women tend to do more housework than men, illegality further enhances these divisions between partners. Unauthorized women depend economically on their legal-status spouses who work, so they take on more of the unpaid family labor. Unauthorized men depend on their legal-status spouses to help out with everything; women with status feel uncomfortable further challenging their unauthorized husbands' masculinity by asking them to help out at home. As a result they not only do a second shift at home but carry what seems to be a triple burden:[67] they work outside the home, they work inside the home, and they work to bolster their partners' masculinity, which is so often undermined because of unauthorized men's marginality in US society. Not only is "the power of legalization closely linked to masculinity,"[68] but legal-status differences heighten gender inequality in the everyday lives of women.

As for the power relationships between adults and children, this too is a gender story, as girls help out at home more than boys. But again, legal status appears to considerably complicate. Scholarship points to the work children in immigrant families do to assist their families' integration in the United States, suggesting that children's greater proximity to US society explains these contributions. However, reports from the families I interviewed suggest that the children who are most like their parents—that is, unauthorized boys and girls—help out more in the home than US citizen children, especially when those children have unauthorized parents. This suggests that family power negotiations may better explain children's contributions to household labor than their level of integration.

This is not a story of generational exploitation, but rather one in which legal status complicates the webs of dependency between parents and children. Parents depend on their children to help with the family, but they describe their fears that children take increased authority too far. Children may call CPS, undermining parents' disciplinary roles. They may throw their schoolwork in the trash can, preventing parents from properly monitoring their school progress. Although parents rely on their children, and praise their children for helping out, they view their help as a double-edged sword. Parents feel stuck and look to their children for help. And children may enjoy helping out their parents, but they do not seem to like their added responsibilities in the home, especially when their parents' dependencies are obvious to others; they tend to see these tasks as a burden unfitting to the typical roles they imagine American children to have in families. In fact, it appears that when children have enough symbolic power in their families—that is, when they are US citizen children with unauthorized parents—they may negotiate their way out of family household duties.

Codified legal-status distinctions within families further accentuate gender differences between spouses and potentially confound authority relationships, between parents and children. Although the United States extols its immigration system as one that prioritizes the family, and family relationships, the current system does little to support families and often undermines them. The most obvious way policy destabilizes families is through enforcement efforts that threaten familial stability and remove fathers from their family members living in the United States. Restrictive legalization also undercuts family functioning in less overt ways. When members with different legal statuses face administrative restrictions that differentiate them from each other, illegality also subtly alters gender and generational power dynamics.

Women's power in their families weakens, and women are frustrated when legal-status issues increase their subordination to men, causing conflicts in many—although not all—relationships. Parents and children, too, feel undermined when children's power in the household increases. Of course, children's increased authority is not always a bad thing: children may successfully transfer skills learned from brokering into other settings.[69] Children also may feel empowered when parents take their opinions into account, improving parent-child bonds. Children's contributions to families work best, however, when they do not infringe upon children's ability to feel normal in a society that expects little work from children and highlights their need for parental guidance.[70] For many of the families I interviewed, this was not the case. Children typically felt uncomfortably burdened by parents' reliance on them. And while parents encouraged their children to help, they worried that such reliance could go too far, preventing them from being able to properly guide their children. Stuck in webs of dependency not of their own choosing, parents and children lose the autonomy to work out gender and generational distinctions in family relationships on their own terms.

4 It's Not Fair

THE PECKING ORDER IN IMMIGRANT FAMILIES

In each American family there exists a pecking order between siblings—a status hierarchy, if you will. This hierarchy emerges over the course of childhood and both reflects and determines the siblings' positions in the overall status ordering in society. It is not just the will of the parents or the "natural" abilities of the children themselves that determines who is on top in the family pecking order; the pecking order is conditioned by the swirling winds of society, which envelop the family.

Dalton Conley, *The Pecking Order*

I'm exhausted by the time we make it to the park. I've persuaded Temo and Dylan to come along by buying them vanilla ice cream cones, ordering them to lick the cones quickly so the drips don't end up on the gray fabric seats of the car. Once I park in the now abandoned school lot, I relax. It is six o'clock. The heavy late afternoon air makes the ice cream drips come more quickly as we climb out. But now the seats won't be ruined by the melting. And all the rushing has been for nothing. I do not see the coach or any nine- and ten-year-olds running around in the long, uncut grass in front of the four steel-posted goals, all missing nets, staggered in different parts of the city park, none belonging to a proper soccer field. Not sure where the practice will be held, I can see that the team captain Camilo—a star who stands out both on and off the field—is not here. I am not late.

Opposite: Photograph by Bob Anderson

When Camilo's father Carlos invited my nine-year-old son Temo along to practice with his son's soccer team, I was elated. It was the perfect setup. Even if only for a month, while taking Temo to the practices and games I could spend more time with the family. But when Temo heard the invitation in Spanish, which he clearly understood with his basic Spanish skills, he groaned, "I am *not* going!" as soon as Carlos and Camilo were out of earshot.

"Yes, you are." I replied, "It is important to me." The standoff continued until a few days later we set up a contract, written out in black Crayola marker.

"It's not fair," Temo had argued. "Why is it always me? Why doesn't Dylan have to do stuff like this?" I'm impressed by the allusion to inequalities between him and his brother, inequalities I came to learn also plagued Camilo and his siblings.

Still, Temo signed his name, in cursive, with a faded green marker and handed the contract over to me. I signed too. And so we have come to soccer so I can observe Camilo doing the activity he loves most, and excels at, procuring much of his parents' resources and time.

Camilo reminds me of the Energizer bunny, his schedule like those of middle-class children whose multiple activities academics posit as having both positive and negative consequences.[1] "He does dance practice on Mondays, three soccer practices a week, and then the games on the weekend," Camilo's father, Carlos—who ferries him to all these various activities—told me.

"He doesn't get tired?" I once asked his mother, Milagros.

"*Como quisiera.* How I wish he would, but no. *El sigue,* he always wants more."

By most accounts, Camilo is a success story. At age nine, Camilo plays for two of the city teams. With the U10 group, his peers, he plays center—a striker. For the older team, the U12s, he plays goalie. But Camilo excels in more than just soccer. He dances with the Mexican folkloric troop at his elementary school. He is among the most popular third graders in his class—well liked by both students and teachers. When I asked to hang out in his classroom for a few days, the teacher didn't object but simply asked, "Why him? He is one of our best students." "Every trimester he gets diplomas and medals," said his father Carlos. His mother Milagros added, "He has tons of medals, he even has one on his key chain."

An archetype of the mixed-status family, Camilo's household epitomizes a pattern in the contemporary United States, and the ensuing complexities that legal status creates. Camilo, the youngest in the family, is a US-born citizen. His two older siblings and his parents are unauthorized migrants. Although families often are loath to outwardly discuss such vast inequalities between siblings and children in the same peer groups, inequality is a hallmark of the current immigration system, which intensifies existing pecking orders among children.

Camilo enjoys a number of advantages, aiding his success as an elementary school–age child in his neighborhood. These advantages are, however, tempered by his status as the child of unauthorized immigrants because in many ways the odds stack up against Camilo. Camilo is the youngest of three, born and raised in a city where one in four survives below the poverty line.[2] The state's median household income is $69,711; in this city it is just $44,543.[3] Camilo's parents' combined income is less. Camilo's father earns a little over the minimum for a manufacturer of realistic-looking white plastic dining plates and pseudo-steel utensils. Although his mother Milagros taught elementary school back in Mexico, like twenty-two of the eighty-one mothers I interviewed, her occupational prestige declined after migration:[4] she now works as a factory temp. "She makes paper for me," Camilo boasts, showing me his math notebook. "I like it because it has pockets on it. That's what I like mostly about it, 'cause it has pockets on it and when I finish something I just put it in here."

The family rents a three-bedroom apartment for $1,100, which they afford with the economic contribution of Camilo's seventeen-year-old brother, Silvio. Silvio was born in Mexico and came to the United States when he was twelve, just a little older than Camilo is now. He works two shifts at a mechanic shop and is rarely at home. I am not even really sure what he looks like, having glimpsed him striding in or out of the apartment only once or twice.

Camilo shares his bedroom with his fourteen-year-old sister, Rebecca, who, also born in Mexico, attends a vocational-technical school and aspires to be a beautician. She is slim; her complexion is a clear milky brown, *café con leche*. With thin lips widening into a gentle smile and carefully lined hazel cat-eyes, Rebecca is a cover girl image for *Seventeen* magazine. I think she might succeed in her goals, if she graduates. At the vocational school she attends, only three out of four incoming students finish with a degree.[5] Still this is higher than at the public high school where her brother Silvio studied. There the graduation rate is only 68 percent and only 19 percent of those graduates expect to attend a four-year college.[6] This is particularly dismal in a state that boasted a graduation rate of 87.2 percent in 2009–10.[7]

Camilo's prospects seem better. He too attends a struggling public school in the district. But he has time. So far, he stands out, having exceeded all expectations.

LEGAL-STATUS DISTINCTIONS

Immigrants and native born alike share a lasting commitment to the American dream;[8] popular mythology dictates that high-achieving children like Camilo will succeed later in life despite modest upbringings. Yet social inequalities are stubborn. Research shows that racial gaps in education and wealth still endure and income inequalities continue to rise.[9] Camilo is Hispanic and of Mexican origin, comes from a low-income family, lives in a relatively poor community, and attends a low-achieving school. Because inequalities pass down from generation to generation no matter how hard Camilo works, or how well he does in school, if he overcomes the barriers of his background, he will be an anomaly, the result of what Robert C. Smith would describe as an exceptional combination of intrafamilial dynamics and extrafamilial support.[10] Because racial and class disadvantages cling to families, more often than not these disadvantages come to affect children's chances over the long run.[11] Intergenerational social mobility in the United States declined dramatically at the end of the twentieth century.[12]

Theoretically, legal-status distinctions should work differently than race and class: obtaining legal status should be an administrative process similar to applying for a library card. The differences between those who have a library card and those who do not certainly shape one's daily routines, access to books, DVD collections, computers, and—in the case of some libraries—day passes to regional museums. Access to a library card alters one's resources. However, because obtaining a library card is an option for nearly all those who meet the rather simple criteria for proving residence at a particular address, we hardly think of this as the source of deep social status distinctions. Of course, the requirements for a library card prove more difficult for some, such as the homeless population who may not have a permanent address, than for others. Typically, however, most can eventually meet the criteria. Those who do not can access many library resources on site.

Legal status in a restrictive immigration policy environment, in contrast, becomes much more than an administrative hurdle. Because so many individuals have been excluded from the criteria necessary to legally live in the United States, illegality has begun to accrue a social significance similar to that of racial or class background. When no line exists for those who want to legalize, social mobility later in life becomes ever more difficult for unauthorized youth, like Rebecca and Silvio, and even for US citizen children like Camilo living in mixed-status families. Under an inflexible immigration system, legal uncertainty becomes the source of family-based social status inequality, with specific costs for children.

Illegality has numerous consequences for children's development.[13] For one, unauthorized children face educational barriers. Under *Plyer v. Doe* all children, regardless of legal status, are entitled to public school education.[14] However, when states have implemented local laws that target the unauthorized—like Alabama, which ordered schools to ask for citizenship status (a measure that was ultimately overturned)—children in immigrant families grow nervous at the threat of deportation, resulting in significant drops in school attendance.[15] More strikingly, unauthorized youth's education is constrained once they enter high school and begin to make plans for after graduation, since often they are ineligible for student loans, in-state tuition benefits, and other programs that will finance their college education.[16]

Children I met described educational barriers as significantly affecting their daily lives at even earlier ages. One seventh grader, for example, described the limitations his legal status created for his educational goals, already a prime concern: "Actually, I am a bit sad about this. Because of the two years I got left back [due to his transition to the US school system], when I am eighteen I will only be in the eleventh grade. I think then they are going to send me to the adult school. I want to finish high school like any other kid. I also want, when I am of age, to drive. But I cannot. I cannot get a license. There are things I want to study, in the university. I would love to go to the university here."

I asked him if he thought about going back to Mexico instead to study.

"Yes, but I cannot tell you an answer about that yet. If I go to Mexico, I can study there. But the career in Mexico will only be valid in Mexico. I want to be a chef, and maybe I can do it there, but it is going to cost a little more than here. And if I study here it will be valid in other countries, they would recognize the degree. It would be better. I would speak Spanish and English. For this reason I would love to stay here and study. But because I don't have papers, I don't know."

"Does this stress you out?" I asked him.

"A lot of stress, a lot of sadness."

"During a normal day, how much do you think about it?"

"Every day. Every single day."

Educational barriers may create low levels of stress about future prospects that children may experience on a daily basis. Over time, knowledge of these limitations may affect children's motivation to succeed in school.

Unauthorized children also may lack access to adequate health care: since they are often uninsured, their parents may forgo preventative care appointments and resort to emergency room care for routine illnesses.[17] Of the 212 children living in the eighty-one families I interviewed, legal status was the primary indicator of insurance coverage. While nearly two-thirds of US citizen children were insured, *none* of the forty-eight unauthorized children in the families I met had health insurance coverage. Although unauthorized children lack insurance, they may have greater health needs, with new studies suggesting that unauthorized youth suffer from greater anxiety and depression because of their status.[18]

Unauthorized children may also experience food insecurity.[19] Among children in families I interviewed, one in ten of the US-born children received food stamps and a little over half received WIC. None of the legal migrant children or the unauthorized children had received benefits under either program. This is not to say that they didn't have similar economic needs, since many of those I interviewed lived in the same households as US-born children. And the unauthorized children in the families I interviewed did rely heavily on school-based food programs; eight out of ten unauthorized children ate lunch through a free program at school, while only just over half of the US-born children did. And while nearly one in three unauthorized children ate breakfast at school, only 15 percent of US-born children did.

Illegality, however, does not affect only unauthorized immigrant children. The citizen children of unauthorized immigrants may face stunted prospects of social mobility. Hiro Yoshikawa, for example, finds that parents without legal status may have fewer resources for their US-born children than parents with legal status. Illegality limits parents' access to social services, curtails their informal social support, and magnifies the economic stressors associated with parenting.[20] These in turn shape children's learning, socioemotional well-being, and physical health. Economic factors stand out; national estimates suggest that one-third of the children of the unauthorized live in poverty, as compared to 18 percent of children with US citizen parents.[21]

Unauthorized parents face a myriad of economic constraints related to their employment prospects and lack of benefits. These factors undoubtedly shape the types of environments US-born citizen children grow up in. Consider home ownership, often used by sociologists as one measure of social inequality.[22] Among the families I interviewed, forty-three of the forty-five unauthorized children lived in rented apartments or homes, whereas one in four US-born children lived in homes their parents owned. Significantly, these patterns were stronger for children living in mixed-status households. The majority of US-born children with unauthorized parents lived in rented dwellings (eighty-seven of ninety-eight), while the majority of US-born children who shared a legal status with their parents lived in homes their parents owned (eighteen of twenty-nine). Strikingly, among those I interviewed there was a similar pattern in health insurance coverage. Eight out of ten US-born children with legal-status parents had health insurance, while only six in ten US-born children with unauthorized parents were insured.

Legal status is not simply a matter of having papers, or *papeles*, as the families I interviewed often referred to legal status. Rather, it creates a social hierarchy—what Dalton Conley describes as a pecking order[23]—among children. Family members experience disadvantages due to the threat of deportation and the dependencies caused by illegality. Yet legal-status differences also shape the long-term prospects of children growing up in the United States, causing insidious inequalities even between siblings, like Camilo and his older siblings Silvio and Rebecca and the twenty-three other families like them whom I interviewed. Research on sibling inequalities typically focuses on factors such as birth order, gender, personality, parental preferences for resource distribution, and changes in family resources over time.[24] For siblings who vary in legal status, all of these factors may matter, but they are overshadowed by much more obvious inequalities.

Camilo, a US-born citizen with a gregarious personality, is the youngest male child in the family. Yet personality and birth order are not the only factors at play because legal status marks Camilo's experiences when compared to those of his older siblings and other unauthorized children. And it does so in more complex ways than simply the presence or absence of a Social Security number. Camilo's citizenship status shapes, at the very least, the rhythms of his daily life, including language usage and participation in housework, his relationship to the migratory process, his resources and subsequent schooling pathways, and his emerging identity as a Mexican American growing up in the United States. These experiences differentiate the lives of unauthorized and citizen children.

LANGUAGE IN CHILDREN'S DAILY LIVES

I first met sometimes shy nine-year-old Camilo at an impromptu Sunday afternoon gathering. He was tagging along with his father, Carlos, who sipped a Coca-Cola while chatting with friends who downed Corona after Corona. Camilo stared listlessly for over an hour at the Nintendo DS he had brought with him. He barely acknowledged anyone else in the room, leaning into his game, hiding behind shaggy bangs. His dark brown locks hung in the style of Messi,[25] who plays for Barcelona and is Camilo's inspiration. "I mean, I always wanted to play soccer, but it was Messi that really inspired me. When I saw him play, the way he moves, that's what I want to be," he once told me. But Camilo plays soccer with the light-footed energy—and poacher's mentality—of Chicharito, a star on Camilo's favorite team, the Mexican Nationals.

Camilo enters a room with a vibe of detached aloofness that contributes to his allure, until you get to know him and find out that he is a nonstop talker. I imagine him unaware of the effect he has on others, although his mother tells me that he knows that girls find him attractive. Camilo denies having a girlfriend, but he lists off the girls at his school who have crushes on him. "At church the girls are always coming up to me and asking me, 'Where's your son, where's Camilo?'" recounts his mother Milagros, laughing.

I think that Camilo intimidates Temo, which is why he does not want to go to soccer practice with Camilo. At the field, after he finishes his ice cream, Temo rolls his eyes again, looking at me as if to say, "I told you so." What he does say is, "So . . . where *is* this practice?"

"I'm not sure," I answer on an exhale. "Why don't we take a little walk?" We make a big circle around the park, starting at the side near the elementary school, a sprawling one-story building. It is another ten or fifteen minutes before the boys start to arrive, one by one, congregating by a goal that they help the coach move into position. Camilo and Carlos arrive now too. I walk over with them to meet the coach, who is around my height, somewhat stocky, sporting gleaming white Nike trainers and a pair of navy Adidas pants with two white lines stitched down the sides. Camilo takes Temo with him out to the field and joins in the center of the action, stealing the ball away from one of the others and taking it down to score.

I sit with Carlos, who pushes mirrored sunglasses up onto black hair, spiked short, hard with gel. He smiles broadly, introducing me to others, at ease, making small talk. But Carlos doesn't stay, saying he promised to give a friend a ride, confirming that I have his number before leaving. He asks me to drop Camilo off if he isn't back in time. For the next hour I fend off the mosquitoes as I sit in uncut grass. I watch.

The scrimmage is chaotic, a free-for-all. The coach splits the boys up but does not assign positions. The boys order themselves, some drawn into the pack following the ball, while others—like Temo—play back, in positions, anticipating the movement on the field. The coach, in the middle of the boys, belts out encouragement as he runs along with the play.

"*Ataque, ataque*" (Attack, attack), he yells, "*Adelante, así es*" (Go forward, that's it). Off the field, the boys all speak English to each other. On the field, they use Spanish. Physical space and generation pattern children's language usage on and off the field.[26] So does legal status.

In general, children of all legal statuses primarily spoke Spanish with their parents. Approximately three out of four children reported speaking all or mostly Spanish with their mothers, and over half spoke Spanish with their fathers. With other children, they spoke English: approximately three out of four spoke all or mostly English with their peers, and half spoke only English with their siblings. At one nine-year-old's birthday party, for example, the adults sat in a circle on chairs in the main room while the children played in the back bedroom. When one child ventured into the main room to ask for a piece of cake and another to complain to his father about a sibling, the children spoke Spanish. Walking back into the bedroom to collect my boys to leave, I found the children jumping on the beds, rattling off to each other in English, some more fluently than others, some with strong accents, while playing a wild game of basketball and with SpongeBob blaring, in English, on a small nineteen-inch box TV on the dresser. An eleven-year-old summarized the common practice: "I speak Spanish with my mother and my father. But with the other kids, in English."

Camilo is fluent in both Spanish and English. He is not in bilingual classes, so he mostly speaks English at school, although I have watched him switch comfortably into Spanish occasionally in the lunchroom and at recess, as he is doing now on the soccer field. At home, Camilo sometimes speaks English with his dad; his mother has taught him to read and write in Spanish. They prefer that he be bilingual, and Camilo says he likes Spanish and English equally. Indeed, *regardless of legal status*, children in interviews reported similar levels of English proficiency, with approximately six out of ten US-born and unauthorized children reporting that they were either near-fluent or fluent in English. They also reported nearly identical language preferences, with a little over half preferring English and more than a quarter preferring both.

Language usage, as opposed to English proficiency or preference, was different for US-born and unauthorized children. Nearly half of the unauthorized said they spoke all Spanish at home, while only one in ten of the

US-born children did. And while very few unauthorized children spoke mostly English at home, almost a third of the US-born children did. Language use across settings also varied by legal status, with unauthorized children much more often reporting that they spoke all or mostly Spanish with their siblings or friends than did US-born children. US-born children reported speaking all English at school more frequently than did unauthorized children. Because children reported similar levels of English proficiency, it is possible that Spanish proficiency explains these differences: while eight out of ten unauthorized children reported being near-fluent or fluent in Spanish, only four out of ten US-born children did.

Researchers often use language as a primary measure of assimilation.[27] However, the greater use of Spanish by unauthorized children does not indicate greater isolation. Both US-born and unauthorized children reported a similar prevalence of cross-racial friendships with whites, Asians, other Latinos, and Middle Easterners. In fact, unauthorized children reported friendships with blacks twice as frequently as US-born children did. And unauthorized children much more often reported that friends came over to their houses to play and that they did sleepovers, a consistent pattern across age categories.[28] Clearly, legal status does not inhibit children from forming friendships with other children in their communities. Unauthorized children do not experience greater isolation from their peers because of their greater use of Spanish and their Spanish-language proficiency. If anything, unauthorized children are more adept at speaking Spanish and thus more frequently use Spanish with their parents and siblings.

HOME-BASED ACTIVITIES

Legal status also patterns children's activities within the home, a theme from chapter 3 that I return to here. Individual families have different approaches to child rearing and expectations of their children.[29] While class background shapes parenting significantly, research suggests that class does not affect children's contributions to housework in the United States, nor does family structure and maternal employment.[30] Rather, within-family factors, including child's age and gender, consistently

Table 4   Percentage of Children Who *Never* Helped with Domestic Tasks

	Unauthorized Children (n = 45)	US-Born Children	
		NO MIXED-STATUS SIBLINGS (N = 106)	MIXED-STATUS SIBLINGS (N = 38)
Chores			
Laundry	52	83	90
Shopping	61	86	92
Cooking	61	89	97
Cleaning	9	55	79
Child care	52	85	95

matter, with older children and girls helping out more than boys and younger children.[31]

Scholarship does suggest that children's housework contributions may vary by race and immigrant status. Children in Hispanic families have been found to help out more in the home than others; scholars hypothesize that a cultural propensity toward "familism" may explain these greater contributions.[32] Similarly, case studies show that children in immigrant families work hard to help their parents as they adapt to life in a new country.[33] Among the children in Mexican immigrant households I interviewed, however, I found variations in patterns of housework contributions by children's legal status. This suggests that housework may be more about children's relative position within their family than a cultural propensity toward familial cooperation among Hispanics or among immigrants as a group.

Among children aged six through seventeen in the families I interviewed, children who were unauthorized helped out in the home with domestic tasks, including cleaning, cooking, and laundry, more frequently than US-born children. They also more often helped with child care for siblings (table 4).

On average the unauthorized children I interviewed were older than the US-born children yet I found these patterns to be consistent across many different age groups, even though the numbers of children in each specific age group were small. Perhaps even more tellingly, US-born children in households with siblings of mixed legal statuses reported never helping out with laundry, shopping, cooking, cleaning, and child care more frequently than US-born children who didn't live with mixed-status siblings. In other words, US-born children who have unauthorized siblings may contribute the least to family housework.

This is the case in Camilo's family. When I ask about chores, Camilo offers, "Clean my bed, other stuff. Or sometimes help my brother or sister clean the bathroom . . . Like sometimes, sometimes I need to like, if I get punished or something I need to clean my room every single day for like a month or two." But Camilo's sister, Rebecca, frequently does stuff in the house. According to her mother, Milagros, "Even here, in the house, she helps me with household. She on her own says, 'Mommy, what are you doing? Can I help you?' If I am cooking, she helps." Of course, there gender differences are perhaps at play, as girls tend to do more housework than boys. In Camilo's family, however, father Carlos models male involvement in housework, cooking and cleaning on days when he is not working.[34]

One might also attribute Camilo's fewer contributions to housework to his being the youngest, the baby of the family; age significantly shapes children's contribution to chores.[35] The conflation of birth order and legal status—as unauthorized youth are often older siblings—helps explain why US-born children contribute less to household chores. Yet the experiences of another family suggest that legal status may yield certain disadvantages for children, effectively increasing their responsibilities in the home.

Anita's family, previously described, was a legal anomaly because both parents and the eldest daughter María had naturalized while the younger four siblings remained unauthorized. In this family, María did not contribute as much to work in the home as her younger sisters. This was because María had won a scholarship to a college preparatory high school. Her parents encouraged her involvement in the school's extracurricular activities, and every day after school she spent two to three hours on her homework and didn't have time to do anything else. Instead, Carmen, the second oldest, supervised her younger siblings while her parents were at work; she directed the others in completing daily chores, including vacuuming the living room and cleaning the kitchen after school. This pattern continued even over the summer when María was out of school. One summer she was invited by a friend to attend a weeklong sleepaway camp, and the following summer she worked at a part-time job as a restaurant hostess.

Why would parents view unauthorized children as resources in the home much more than US-born children? US citizen children may, as this case suggests, have greater opportunities outside the home, whether employment based or at school, that parents hope to support. Anita and her husband wanted María to take full advantage of her scholarship, and other opportunities that unfolded, and thus did not require her to help out as much at home. Similarly, Camilo is an extremely talented soccer player. So Carlos and Milagros support his athletic development by taking him to practices and games nearly all week long. Camilo surely returns home tired from these events, with little time to do anything more than complete his homework. In short, parents may find themselves unknowingly investing more in their US citizen children's activities outside the home because their US citizen children have opportunities that their unauthorized children cannot access. Unauthorized children, at home and available, pick up the slack.

Unauthorized children may help with housework for other reasons aside from fewer opportunities outside the home. They may have a very different type of relationship with their parents than US-born children. Unauthorized children, after all, migrated just as their parents did; they understand the difficulties of adjustment to life in the United States more poignantly as they share this history with their parents. Drawing on this shared history, children may view their relationships with parents as more cooperative. Rebecca may have brought with her from Mexico different expectations about her place in the home and thus may voluntarily offer to help her mother Milagros with housework because, to her, it seems natural to do so. One unauthorized eleven-year old told me, for example, when I asked her what chores she did at home, "Sometimes I help my mother. I ask her, 'How can I help you?' and she says, 'You can pick up the clothes.'" Unauthorized children may feel they should help with chores.

Although Rebecca shares the migration history of her parents, she did not migrate with them. In fact, more than eight in ten unauthorized children in the families I interviewed experienced a period of physical separation from one or both of their parents, while only one in five US-born children did. In Camilo's family, I come to learn on the soccer field, experiences of separation have had long-term repercussions that have continued to affect Camilo's siblings long after reunification. The aftermath of family separations may also help explain the different trajectories of unauthorized and US-born children growing up in the United States.

THE AFTERMATH OF FAMILY SEPARATION

It is not at this first practice, but at the next one a few days later, at the same park, swatting at some of the same mosquitoes, that I learn more about the ways Camilo's experiences diverge so significantly from those of his brother and sister. I sit with Carlos making the type of small talk parents often do at such events, about how busy the kids keep us. "But don't you want another?" Carlos asks, teasing, "a little girl this time?"

I laugh too; this isn't the first time I've been asked this question. "Nah," I break into my standard response, "I like kids and all, a lot, but two is about all I can manage on my own." I do not add as I sometimes do, with women, that I would need a good man first.

Perhaps it is implied, because Carlos now asks about how involved Temo and Dylan's dad, Raúl, is in their lives. Carlos has met Raúl before. I feel uncomfortably pressed. "He didn't used to visit at all," I answer truthfully. "But now he sees them a lot more," I add, monitoring my voice, trying to keep superficial.

And now the unexpected: Carlos begins to tell me how hard it was when his two older children came up from Mexico. They are not Carlos's biological children, he explains. This I suspected, not because Carlos mentioned it before, but because Rebecca called him her stepfather, repeatedly, in our interview.

Carlos met Milagros when Silvio was just three and Rebecca under a year old. He had been working on an engineering construction project in the small town on the coast of Guerrero where Milagros worked as a schoolteacher. They moved in together until, in 2000, he came—alone—to the United States. Within a year he saved enough money so that Milagros could join him. For four years, Rebecca and Silvio lived with an aunt and uncle and their cousins in Mexico.

In the United States, Carlos and Milagros had Camilo, and then, when Camilo was three, they sent for the older children. "At first they didn't want to come," Milagros had told me, "but then they decided to because the older one began to complain that I wasn't there." They also wanted to meet their little brother, Camilo. "When they were in Mexico, he was really little, and he couldn't talk well. But still, they talked to each other on the phone. They wanted to have some contact with their little brother. And when they came, Camilo waited for them anxiously."

They imagined the reunion would be easier than it was. "We didn't recognize each other." This is Rebecca talking about her arrival. "I remember just standing there and looking at them because I remembered that when my mom left them she was all skinny and then she got a little fat here. It took about a month to get used to living with them again."

While we sit in the itchy long grass in the park, Carlos tells me how difficult it was for the boys to adjust to each other. Camilo admired Silvio and wanted to be like his older brother. But Silvio felt jealous of Camilo for being the baby in the family. "For two or three months he [Silvio] cried almost every night, uncontrollably." Silvio resented that his mother had left him back in Mexico and had gone on to have another child. "We didn't know what to do," Carlos says. "He even had suicidal thoughts. He said he was going to get a knife and cut himself and hurt himself and his siblings."

The emotion in Carlos's voice disarms me. I gulp, thinking about what I don't want to talk about, about the choices I have made and the consequences these choices have had for my children, and Raúl's. The idea of fundamental inequality between siblings plagues me; Temo's claims that "it's not fair" always hold double meaning. I wonder if Carlos also worries about the intrinsic inequality between his two boys: one born in Mexico, the other here, one a biological son he has always lived with, the other a stepchild from whom he lived apart for five years.

RAÚL'S CHILDREN

Much as Carlos's children have diverging opportunities given their different pathways to the United States, over time the differences between Raúl and my children have seemed to only become more noticeable. Unlike in

Carlos's family, Raúl's two children from his previous marriage remain in Mexico. When I first met Raúl, I accepted them as my own, or rather, thought I did. But since then I have been awkward in my ex-stepmother role and have not done much to parent them. When Raúl's oldest son Facebook-friended me at age eighteen, the unexpected emotional turmoil brought me to tears. We reconnected online and then visited in Mexico for the first time in eight years. I felt the family connection so strongly, snapping photos of Temo and him leaning forward over their knees in the same fashion next to each other on the sofa, laughing when they each separately asked me quietly, "Do I really look like my brother?"

Raúl and I had planned to bring the boys to live with us in the United States when we married. At the time they lived with their maternal grandmother; in Mexico we visited, buying them new sets of clothes and school supplies. Raúl decided to wait to apply for them until he became a US citizen, allowing time for custody issues to get sorted out. Also, this way no wait times would be attached to their application.[36] When Raúl's citizenship jammed, so did their opportunity to reunite. Adamantly opposed to their unauthorized migration, like most parents Raúl wants his children to have a different—better—life than he had when he migrated north unauthorized as a teenager. Raúl's oldest finished high school after moving in with Raúl's parents but now works a low-wage retail job. The other, living with his maternal grandmother still, also works. Neither has yet attended college. Their prospects growing up in Mexico look so different from those of their siblings in the United States.

You see, Raúl, now remarried, has three more children—aside from Dylan and Temo—growing up in a community similar to that of Camilo and his siblings. Living with both of their parents seems an advantage, one that Raúl's children in Mexico never had. They have traveled to visit family in Mexico, as Raúl has covered the 2,600-mile route by van quite a few times, yet Raúl's children in Mexico cannot migrate legally or even obtain a tourist visa to visit their father. They cannot see with their own eyes life in *el norte*. In contrast, like Temo and Dylan, Raúl's youngest children are US citizens.

Even so, experiences diverge given that they live with Raúl, a former unauthorized migrant, and Temo and Dylan live with me, a US-born citizen. My boys, sons of an academic, squirm as they listen to me read these sections of my book out loud to them. They constantly have to field my questions on what happened in school on a particular day, how they feel about—well—almost everything, and which kids "love each other" and have started dating—I'm curious since I teach a class on the sociology of childhood every year. My stable salary provides opportunities; we travel frequently, often in conjunction with conference or research trips. When Raúl's children travel to Mexico, it is to the house Raúl built for his parents with remittances; they never stay in hotels as we do.

Our children's daily activities also differ. My boys have played hockey, even though it stretches our budget, and travel team soccer. Raúl's son has played rec soccer, but only in the spring, and occasionally he and his sisters participate in folkloric dance events, the cost free. They attend a struggling urban school, similar to the ones children I interviewed attended. In contrast, my boys first attended excellent public schools in a middle-income, white college town in Ohio, and then attended even better schools in the economically and internationally diverse middle- to high-income town where we lived in New Jersey for six months. At lower-performing, diverse urban schools in upstate New York, they benefit from my flexible schedule; I am home most days right after school. And, after Temo spent sixth grade struggling to keep a low profile and avoid fights at the expense of his schoolwork, we have decided to move to a private school for seventh and eighth grade. In New Jersey, Raúl's children share a bedroom in a two room apartment located across the street from a bar on a dangerous city block, while Temo and Dylan each have their own bedrooms in the house I own in one of the nicer neighborhoods in Albany.

My boys enjoy visits to their father, practically glowing in the love they feel from participating in Raúl's family. When the weather is nice, they play soccer outside together enthusiastically, go to the park, and ride bikes up and down the sidewalk. Raúl's children eagerly and affectionately hug Penny, our little Boston terrier, when I drop the boys off, asking in accented English for her to stay with them and their own little poodle, Chiquis—at least they did before Chiquis jumped out of Raúl's Chevy Astro and ran off. They help my boys when they struggle to understand Raúl's quick speech in a Veracruz accent.

Rarely do Temo and Dylan comment on the differences between us and their stepsiblings, differences I know they must notice. After all, they so often comment on the things their friends have that we don't: the back-yard trampoline, the home movie theater, the seasonal ice rinks that enthusiastic fathers construct of treated wood and fill by the garden hose in their large backyards when the temperature drops below freezing. Perhaps they downplay their understandings of the class differences between Raúl and me for my benefit, or perhaps for their own. It is surely easier for them to enjoy their connections with their siblings by not thinking too much about it. That one father has three sets of children facing such unequal pathways feels a little uncomfortable. So many factors at play, some that we control and others that we do not. But one, illegality, has come to frame our children's experiences in ways we never anticipated when Raúl and I first met.

FAMILY MIGRATION PATTERNS

Temo's and Dylan's daily lives, so different from those of their siblings, suggest that children's position in the family pecking order may arise from a combination of the timing of migration and parents' formation of conjugal relationships. In fact, that siblings with different legal statuses sometimes had different biological fathers—as Silvio and Rebecca do—was not uncommon among the families with mixed-status siblings I met.

The factors surrounding women's migration north help explain why children may have different fathers. Migrant mothers from Mexico are often unmarried single mothers or divorced women who seek migration north as a means out of economic difficulties.[37] This was the case for one mother, Elvira. "I married good, with the father of my daughter," she explained, "in the church and everything." But the marriage fell apart while Elvira was seven months pregnant. Her husband came home one evening to their room drunk, and when she refused his advances, uncomfortable in her pregnant body, he dragged her by her hair and pushed her. In the morning, he left. So Elvira moved back in with her own parents, as a single mother; they supported her through the birth of her daughter and after. Two years later Elvira met her current partner, who unconditionally accepted her daughter as his own. "She has always known him as her father." But then he migrated to New Jersey, and the couple separated.

Elvira grew desperate at her economic situation and decided to migrate as well to make ends meet. She lived alone in New Jersey for a time but reconciled with her ex when they met at a party. Now they had two US-born children, whom they were raising along with Elvira's first daughter.

Women spoke highly of their new partners who accepted their children from a previous marriage, much as Carlos readily accepted Silvio and Rebecca. Their praise hinted at the pride felt for partners acting differently from the perceived typical *machista* male who does not accept children from previous relationships.[38] I learned from a third party that Ana had a fifteen-year-old daughter in addition to the three children under age six that I met. In our formal interview—in which I spoke with both Ana and her current partner—the existence of this older daughter never came up in the conversation, even when I explicitly asked each about their children. Perched on the edge of the sofa, Ana occasionally glanced over at her husband, I now think for cues about how much to tell. Later with me informally, Ana spoke openly about her daughter. Ana had split with her daughter's father in Mexico. She had migrated to the United States, leaving her daughter with her mother. Her ex-husband also had come to work in New Jersey, but Ana did not have contact with him until she sent for her daughter and when, after arriving, her daughter had problems living with Ana and her new husband. So the daughter moved in with her father, visiting with Ana every other weekend. Although Ana was not ashamed of her daughter, that she did not mention her daughter in our interview illustrates the worst-case scenario. When new partners do not welcome children from previous relationships, inequalities between unauthorized and US-born siblings potentially become even more pronounced.

Transnational separations had specific consequences for children and were fairly common among the families I interviewed. Nineteen of the eighty-one mothers I interviewed had been separated from their children at some point during the migratory process. Seventeen of these migrant mothers had been separated from their own parents as children because of US migration. Nearly half of the fathers—thirty-eight—had been separated from children during the families' migratory process.

Carlos's confessions about Silvio's difficulties after family reunification surprised me, though the story of family separation was familiar. I interviewed so many parents who had left their children in Mexico, and so many children in Mexico whose parents lived in the United States.[39] Parents described feeling guilty at having left their children but believed the sacrifice was worth it. Yessenia, a mother to one child in Mexico and two in New Jersey with her, said, "I feel bad about my son in Mexico. Sometimes sadness overcomes me, and I feel like crying. I have my two children here, but it isn't the same." Yessenia did not communicate this sadness to her son over the phone. Instead, she rationalized the separation of mother and son as something that had been good for the family and important to their survival. She explained,

> I tell him, "Do you remember when I was there and you wanted something; I couldn't buy it for you? My mom gave me something, but it wasn't enough. I had to work to buy you things." . . . He [son] has never told these things to me [over the phone]. But at school he writes poems. My aunt said she found them. My mom said she found the papers from May 10th [Mother's Day], from the Day of the Child, [and he writes] that he feels sad, and alone. That sometimes he wants to tell his mom that he feels alone, that he loves her very much. But when I talk to him, he doesn't tell me this.

Yessenia's son colluded in the narrative of familial sacrifice, although he, like his mother, seemed upset by her prolonged absence.

For both parents and children, years living apart weigh heavily. Family reunification promises to soften parent-child tensions. For parents, family reunification validates the period of separation as ultimately worthwhile; they view the period of time living apart, and the distance it created, as surmountable with time together.[40] But resentment often clings to children during periods of separation and beyond, no matter how well they get along with their parents and caregivers in Mexico, and no matter how clearly they understand the circumstances surrounding their parents' migration.[41]

Even adults, who had lived apart from a parent years earlier as children described ongoing feelings of detachment in these relationships. One woman at age thirty-two, for example, described her relationship with her mother as close and with her father as distant. "It was very sad," she told me describing the time he had been away. "Because I didn't have my father and because the kids younger than me were always crying." For five years her father had nearly no communication with his family in Mexico. "I remember that day. . . . We were outside playing in the yard just like the kids now are outside playing. And we saw this man coming towards us, and he had on some ugly clothes and his hair down to the middle of his back, and he was walking all crooked. We thought he was a robber and we ran inside to hide."

The man, of course, turned out to be their father. She said her youngest brother had slapped him and hit him when her mother tried to hug him. "He wasn't like a normal father. We always saw him as really distant." Another woman tracked down her own mother who had left her as a child to raise her younger siblings. When she found out that her mother been living on the streets of Chicago she worried about her mental health and brought her to live with her husband and son. The reunion was not as she expected. "It was like she was never used to living with us and we argued all the time about . . . that she didn't like anything . . . .and that—all the time she felt like I hated her." Ongoing guilt and apprehension of resentment by the mother led to many fights and strained their relationship until her mother decided to move out.

For parents the time away may be stressful, but it amounts to a small fraction of their adult lives. For children, like for Silvio and Rebecca, periods apart from their parents represent, at times, more than half of their short lifetimes. And, although many lived with relatives whom they loved dearly, children told me again and again that living with their relatives was not the same as living with parents. "I missed my mother [Milagros] a lot. I didn't feel like I could talk to my aunt the same way that I talk to my mother," Rebecca explained. Similarly, a nineteen-year-old I interviewed in New Jersey said of the two years she had lived without her parents, between the ages of eleven and thirteen, "It was really hard at the beginning." This was because, as other children also told me, "I didn't have the same kind of *confianza* [trust] with my grandmother as I did with my mother." Later in the interview she specified, "To a parent you can say, [with childish voice] 'No, I don't want to eat this.' And with your grandmother it's 'No, you have to eat this.'"

Imagine, then, what it was like for Silvio, who had not lived with his parents since the time he started school in Mexico, to move, at the age of twelve, to the United States, entering a classroom where he didn't speak the language and a household where he didn't know his parents or their routines. No wonder Silvio wanted to be Camilo. Camilo, born in the United States, had lived with both his parents, always, the baby of the house. Camilo had it made.

ON SUBSEQUENT RESOURCES AND FUTURE PROSPECTS

Silvio and Rebecca came up from Mexico during the summer. Worried about their transition, Milagros snuck Silvio and not Rebecca—because he was older—into adult ESL classes before school started. "At school he adapted well," she told me. "At home, he became a bit rebellious . . . because 'we had abandoned him.'" Milagros and Carlos worried about him. "At school he was an exemplary child. I even went to his school to talk to his teacher because at home it was a total disaster. But they didn't believe me because he was so well behaved." Milagros explained, "Sometimes he didn't do well. When he was mad at me he would say, 'I am going to get all Fs.' And he did. Then he would say, 'Don't worry, Mommy. I am going to get good grades.' And he would bring home As and Bs and honor roll certificates. He is very smart." Milagros and Carlos eventually got him into therapy. But it is unclear whether it was the therapy or early fatherhood that turned things around.

> It was when he started in the tenth grade. He just wanted to go out with his friends. At first I let him go out. . . . Then he just wanted to do what he wanted to do, without asking, at any time he felt like it. He skipped school so he could go hang out. Then he started going out with this girl. When she finished middle school, it came out that she had gotten pregnant. We went to talk to her parents and everything. They said if she wanted to come live with us. So she decided to come here. Living here, she started high school. We sent them both. But neither wanted to keep studying. They wouldn't go. So I said, no. "If you don't want to study and you want to work instead, well, work."

Carlos and Milagros continue to help with child care, when needed, but now expect Silvio to contribute to the household on his own.

The transition for Rebecca was less problematic. "I don't know why," says Milagros. "Maybe because she is younger. Her sentiments are very different. She is very different." Mother and daughter are especially close;

Rebecca spends more time at home than her siblings. She doesn't participate in any extracurricular activities, like Camilo. Instead, Rebecca often
helps with Camilo; since both her parents are already at work when the
children wake up in the mornings, she is the one to make sure that Camilo
gets off to school. Since reunification she seems to be "making up for lost
time."[42] So far, adolescence has been easier for Rebecca than for Silvio,
whether because of her age at migration, gender, or personality—which
both Milagros and Carlos describe as being much less emotional.

Camilo is different. His hectic schedule dictates the routines of the family.[43] On school days he walks himself to school, where he has breakfast;
when school lets out, he often stays at the free after-school program and
does his homework there. But if he doesn't feel like staying he walks himself home and does his homework. The rest of the evening, he spends time
with his dad, Carlos. On Mondays, "I go to dance. If not, I tell my dad to
take me to, um, my cousins' house." Other days, he has soccer practice. The
weekends are taken up by soccer as well. "When I don't have school I go to
my soccer games." Milagros and Rebecca take Camilo to his soccer games
on the weekends because Carlos works. Carlos ferries Camilo to and from
all the after-school activities during the week.

Of course, Carlos and Milagros love all three of their children. But, as
most parents do, they invest their energies into each in different ways.
Because unauthorized and US-born children's experiences within the
family migration history are different, their needs differ. As the oldest,
Silvio spent formative years away from his parents who sought economic
stability via international migration. Reunification, however, did not erase
the resentment Silvio felt about the separation. Ongoing resentments carried over into his schooling and affected his emotional well-being more
broadly and, seemingly, his motivation to excel in school specifically. Not
only did Silvio's unauthorized status affect his prospects in the United
States, but so did the decisions he made as a result of the process by which
he arrived to live with his parents in the United States after what was, for
him, a prolonged period of separation. Silvio at a young age opted out of
any academic track by dropping out of high school. After an early entry
into fatherhood, Silvio joined his parents as a full-time worker and con-
tributor to the joint household with his parents and partner and daughter.
According to Milagros, "Now that he is working he says, 'If I had the

opportunity to get my papers, it would be easier to find a better job.' In one place he was working, they wanted to keep him, but they asked for his papers."

Silvio has not ultimately been able to translate his parents' sacrifice via migration into tangible benefits in terms of educational achievement and, in fact, has a lower educational level than both of his parents. He is a proud father of a lovely boy and supports his partner and son with full-time employment. Nonetheless, he has experienced what sociologists describe as downward mobility as a result of the family's migration.[44]

For Rebecca, the middle female child, the transition to the United States proceeded more smoothly than it did for Silvio. Surely aware of her brother's adjustment difficulties, Rebecca has demanded less of her parents' time and energy and helped out more in the home. Although she too lacks legal status and was separated from her parents for as long as Silvio, Rebecca is not a wave maker. She plans to finish high school but is not thinking about college. For this reason she chose to go to the vocational-technical high school; she wants to leave high school with a career, since she knows she will not be able to attend college in the United States because of her lack of papers. Rebecca explains, "It isn't fair that there are kids who don't have opportunities because of the papers." She is disappointed that the DREAM Act, which would allow students, like her, who do well in US schools, has not yet been passed. It is likely that she will benefit from the Deferred Action for Childhood Arrivals, as long as she stays in school and graduates.[45] "When I graduate I want to try to start my own business, have my own beauty salon. I don't know if I can, but I want to here. If I can't, I may have to go back to Mexico to do it." Though Silvio has already opted out of formal school after family reunification and therefore will not be eligible for deferred action, it remains to be seen how Rebecca's legal status and her educational experiences will pan out in terms of her employment prospects over the next five or six years.

Camilo, the youngest, was born into a different family than Silvio and Rebecca because his parents, although still unauthorized low-wage workers, stabilized the family's economic situation during his lifetime.[46] Camilo wants to be a soccer player or a singer when he grows up, goals that—typical of young children—may not be all that realistic. Yet his parents have invested money and time into Camilo's love for the sport. In fact, in the fall after I met him, Camilo was selected on scholarship to play for a Premier League, one that typically costs $2,000 per season. Of course, he probably will not play professionally, but the opportunity may make him eligible for a sports scholarship, if not to college perhaps to a private high school, if he continues to excel. Camilo continues to do well in school. His parents are considering moving to a different school district by the time he reaches middle school so that he doesn't experience the same problems as his older brother did in school. As is the case with Rebecca, Camilo's long-term prospects remain to be seen. But he has direct access to his parents' resources—now supplemented by his older brother's income—and may ultimately be able to benefit from their migratory sacrifice.

CHILDREN'S IDENTITY AND STATUS DIFFERENCES

Unauthorized and US-born children's citizenship status also has consequences for the ways they come to terms with growing up as members of Mexican immigrant families. Camilo, as a third grader, tells me that he is Mexican American, "'Cause I'm, my family is Mexican. That makes me half Mexican, and I was born here so that makes me American too. So I'm half Mexican and half American." I asked all the children I interviewed to pick the best ethnic or racial descriptor. They identified with a diverse set of labels, including *black, white, Hispanic, Latino, Spanish, Spanish American,* and more. Most often, children of all legal statuses chose *Mexican* or *Mexican American.* However, more unauthorized children than US-born children chose the label of *Mexican.* A fourteen-year-old girl explained, "Because I was born in Mexico and I guess you could say I am more Mexican. Even though I was technically raised here in America, I'd still consider myself Mexican." More US-born children, like Camilo, than unauthorized children chose the label of *Mexican American.*

Children matter-of-factly described the differences between themselves and their family members and defined their identities as being tied to their nativity, which they described in very concrete terms. Nearly all were able to correctly tell me where they had been born and also where their parents and siblings had been born. And place of birth, in their minds, extended to their understandings of ethnic identity even at young ages.[47]

Carlitos, an eight-year-old, said that he was Spanish American but that his mother, father, and older sister were "Mexicans" and that his brother was, like him, "American, Spanish." When I asked why, he explained, "'Cause we were born here, and me and my brother were born here, and my sister was born in Mexico." And when I asked an unauthorized nine-year-old, "How come you say your parents and your brother are Latino but your little brother's American?" He explained, "'Cause my brother, my little brother is from Ohio and he looks like, more lighter. And we look like more darker." For children, race and/or ethnicity was tied to their varying citizenship statuses.

Scholars suggest that factors such as peer relationships, school context, perceived discrimination, parental support, and language proficiency shape the identity formation of ethnic minority youth.[48] Age also may be especially important, with sociologists finding that children develop a sense of symbolic ethnicity as they grow older and that pan-ethnic identification becomes particularly strong for college-aged students.[49] Children's accounts suggest that legal status also may shape children's identity formation, and the way they understand belonging, and that this process may occur at earlier ages than for those not confronted with such differences.[50]

Despite identifying their different citizenship statuses, siblings resisted assigning any social significance to these differences. When I asked Carlitos point blank if he thought his older sister was different from him because she was born in Mexico and he wasn't, he answered, "No, 'cause we're related to each other." Similarly, eleven-year-old Lupe explained that she and her siblings went to different doctors, "well, because they have those little cards, they go to a specific doctor."

"You don't have one?" I asked.

"No, because they were born here."

When I suggested that maybe it wasn't fair, Lupe responded quickly, "That doesn't matter to me."

Siblings were reluctant to call any attention to the meanings of these status differences: that their place of birth—something that children clearly understood—brought advantages. As Lupe's observation suggested, she knew of these differences, although she claimed they did not matter. Just as parents like to talk about treating their children equally, children resist the idea that structural inequalities give them different opportunities, possibly because children are so often determined to ensure that relations in families be as fair as they can be.[51]

Yet it isn't fair, and children know it. Health care access, for one, strikingly differentiates children of varying legal statuses. Patricia, fifteen, explained when I asked where she went if she got sick, "There's a clinic. We have to apply for . . . I don't know. It's something. I think it's like a discount. Because otherwise it's expensive. We haven't had the time to go."

"Do you ever worry about getting sick?" I asked.

Patricia nodded yes.

In Camilo's family, he is the only one to have health insurance through the state Medicaid program. His sister Rebecca cautiously admits, "It is a little unfair because my brother gets health insurance and I don't." Camilo too knows of the difference. He explains, "My sister and brother were born in Mexico. My whole family actually. I'm the only one that was born here." I ask Carlos and Milagros, "So does he know there is a difference between him and his siblings because of the papers?"

"He is beginning to notice," Milagros answers.

"What does he say?"

"He asks why we cannot go [to Mexico]. We say we don't have papers. 'Why does this happen?' We'll tell him the truth." This is Carlos.

"[He asks,] Why don't you get the papers?" adds Milagros. "Why haven't you gone to do it? Is it expensive?"

"How do you explain?" I ask.

"He has to understand," Milagros says. "He is born here; he is a citizen of this country. His brother and sister, no, because they were born in Mexico. It is very difficult for them to get their papers. They can work and study, but they don't have the same rights as he has."

As children grow up in the United States, they learn that legal status affords differential access to services, health and otherwise. An unauthorized fifteen-year-old explained, "I don't know. It seems like a lot of doors close on you."

"What kind of doors?" I asked her.

"You can't go to a good college. I can't have a good health insurance. You can't drive when you're old enough."

"Have you felt those doors close on you?"

"Yes. For summer programs, sometimes you need a Social Security card."

Similarly, a teenage sister, unauthorized, with an eight-year-old US citizen brother explained, "It's hard. You feel different from others. Others have more opportunities. You feel different."

Aside from access to services, children know that illegality curtails educational opportunities. A fourteen-year-old Mexican-born sister to two US-born younger brothers, for example, explained,

> It's kind of, um, how would I say it, like it's kind of unfair for us because, for example, I want to become a doctor. . . . But I probably can't do college here because first of all, it's so expensive and you need to like have papers, I guess. My, well, my mentality has been, well, I'm not going to do college here, I'm going to do it in Mexico. But to the kids that want to do it here, that's not fair for them. Especially if they're like really good in school, I feel like it's not fair because they have worked for so long to be like at the point where they're done with high school but they want to go to college but they can't. I feel that's unfair.

Clearly her brothers will not have to return to Mexico if they decide to study medicine. Similarly, Anita's daughter Carmen—described earlier as the unauthorized, second-oldest daughter in a family where the oldest daughter was a US citizen—avoided directly talking about how legal status affected her own life. She denied feeling jealous of her naturalized older sister. But during my visits with the family for approximately six months, I often asked about school. Carmen alluded to the scholarship her sister had received as an opportunity she would not be able to take advantage of despite her better grades.

UNDERSTANDING MEXICO

Children also know that legal status limits travel opportunities. Of all the children in the families I interviewed, nearly one in three US-born children had been back to visit Mexico, while only three of forty-seven unauthorized children had (nine of fourteen legalized children had been back to visit). Children, and parents, most openly discussed differences between siblings related to travel. One teen born in Mexico felt she was the same as her US-born siblings except that "I just feel different at the fact that they actually get to go to Mexico and see my family because I haven't seen them in so long. But other than that, no." In Anita's family, the eldest daughter, María, had been back to Mexico periodically with her parents, usually once or twice a year. Anita told me that after she and María had returned to Mexico recently for two weeks for an aunt's graduation, "The others complain[ed], how come you don't take us?"

Camilo has yet to visit Mexico, "He wants to go," Milagros explains, "but he doesn't want to go alone. He wants to go with his brother and sister. But . . ." The conversation about travel has spurred Milagros and Carlos to explain to Camilo about the legal differences between him and his siblings.

Mexico, for US-born children, may be a vacation spot, a place to visit family. For unauthorized children, Mexico represents the place they are from, a place they feel intimately connected to. Although the unauthorized children I spoke with did not travel back to Mexico, they described more frequent contact with families in Mexico, with one in four saying they chatted with family members in Mexico or sent e-mail, compared to just one in ten US-born children. Unauthorized children in the families I interviewed also participated in two types of extracurricular activities more frequently than did US-born children: youth church groups (nearly half of unauthorized youth and just 23 of 144 US-born children) and dance classes (ten of forty-six unauthorized children and just 9 of 144 US-born children). With only one or two exceptions, the dance classes these children participated in, both in Ohio and in New Jersey, were with Mexican folkloric dance troupes. Unauthorized children engaged much more frequently in activities related to their Catholic and Mexican heritage. These activities signaled a difference in identity formation between the children who had been born in the United States, like Camilo, and those who had not. However Mexico, for unauthorized children, was also a place they could not visit, which was perhaps why the ability to travel arose most significantly in children's minds when they discussed the differences between themselves and their US-born siblings and friends.

Unauthorized children also talked openly about potential permanent returns to Mexico—the result of a deportation or enforcement act. Regardless of their own legal status, children spoke about their fears of deportation. Yet children distinguished between what would happen to themselves and to their siblings, aware that illegality potentially could determine where they would live in the future, shaping their life course. Recall the comments of Moisés and his cousin Andrés from chapter 2. When I asked if it was scary to have immigrants in his family, Moisés, an unauthorized migrant said it was "because, what happens if some cops come to our house and they want to see our papers? We don't have it. And my little brother and my four cousins have it. And we have to go. That's what's scary about it." Andrés, his US citizen cousin, explained, "No, well, yes. if everyone leaves, it's only going to be me and my sister, my little cousin that you were just talking to and my little sister and my little cousin." Similarly, another eleven-year-old US citizen told me it was scary, "'cause if they get caught, her, if my mom or dad get caught, my sister and me and Luís would have to get a passport to get back. 'Cause we have passports and they don't."

Legal status differentiates siblings and they know it. Unauthorized children grow up longing to connect with Mexico, which they do through participation in folkloric dance classes and church youth groups, as well as via Internet communication with family members back home. They consider themselves Mexican as they sense their political exclusion from the United States. Yet they cannot travel to Mexico. They grow up aware that they are different from US citizen children; they don't have health insurance and cannot participate in the same types of programs as US citizen children. They must forge different educational goals that take into consideration their limitations. Siblings perhaps do not like to think that status makes their identity any different from that of their brothers and sisters, with whom they share so much. But it does.

IT'S NOT FAIR

Dalton Conley writes about the inequality between siblings that we like to ignore, as it is somewhat embarrassing to think that we—as parents—give greater advantages to one of our children when we usually feel that we love all equally. Ultimately, though, the pecking order within the family is not about the love that we give our children. Rather, "The pecking order is conditioned by the swirling winds of society, which envelop the family."[52]

Silvio, Rebecca, and Camilo face extremely different prospects. Inequality due to illegality has already marked the young lives of these siblings and others like them. US-born and unauthorized children have different daily routines. Although they both speak English, unauthorized children use Spanish more than US-born children, as they report speaking better Spanish. They also participate in household tasks to differing degrees; unauthorized children help parents the most with housework. Perhaps this is due to US-born children's greater opportunities outside the home and parents' efforts to invest in these opportunities. Or perhaps it is unauthorized children's different experiences during migration that lead them to take on more active roles in the household. Unauthorized children, who so often have been separated from their parents during migration, may feel more invested in what Rob Smith calls "the immigrant bargain":[53] they may help at home because they feel much more a part of the project of familial sacrifice during migration than do US-born children.

Family separation shapes children's trajectories in other ways as well. Because separation can be so difficult, with ongoing feelings of guilt and resentment, there may be a powerful and harmful emotional impact on children even after reunification.[54] Children like Silvio may be smart but may fall behind in school as they come to terms with the complex feelings around family separation and reunification.[55] Many feel strong ties to Mexico, their birthplace, but they cannot travel to visit their former homes. Still, they may seek connection, sending e-mails and chatting with family and friends, dancing with folkloric dance troupes, attending church youth group meetings.

Over time, without opportunities in the United States and unable to physically connect in Mexico, they may begin to feel lost. Schools foster the belief in equal opportunity for both unauthorized students and those with legal status.[56] Yet their opportunities are not equal. Ultimately excluded, some, like many undocumented youth activists, may develop an oppositional consciousness.[57] Others, like Silvio, will join their parents as low-wage workers struggling to make ends meet in the US economy. This seems the most likely outcome, as recent research suggests that unauthorized Mexican and Central American youth are less likely to enroll in college and more likely to drop out of high school than those with legal status.[58]

US-born children, like Camilo, have been born into different types of families than their unauthorized siblings, families that are settled, even if still experiencing precarious employment and lacking economic resources.

Camilo considers his ties to be both to the United States and to Mexico. But Mexico, for him, is home to his favorite soccer team, and a place he may visit in the future, not his home. Instead, as time goes on he may seek future opportunities in the United States, opportunities that will further differentiate him from his siblings as long as immigration policy continues to block family sponsorship for those who entered the United States by walking across the border, without inspection.

To some extent Camilo experiences advantages from being the youngest. Yet the advantage of his legal status is likely to become more pronounced, not less, over time. Despite Carlos and Milagros's best intentions, Silvio is now an unauthorized low-wage worker, like themselves. Rebecca, although still in school, will follow a similar path unless some sort of immigration decision makes deferred action permanent and grants her the right to stay in the United States legally. But Camilo, and other US-born children like him, have a different trajectory. Of the three he is the only one with the chance of experiencing some level of social mobility due to his parents' migration. While explained to some extent by birth order, at a time when immigration policy is stagnant, Camilo's future prospects are shaped most strongly by one overwhelming factor: legal status. Like race, class, and gender, illegality is likely to shape children's mobility, and their place in US society's pecking order, over time.

Numerous factors influence the unequal prospects of these siblings, as they unequally affect those of my children and the other children of Raúl, the two living in Mexico and his US-born children growing up in New Jersey. That our children, and others, have diverging pathways does not mean that one pathway is necessarily better than another. But opportunities certainly differ. And while economic stability, education, birth order, and even personality affect these pathways, so too—it seems quite clear—does illegality. Whether immigration restrictions result in not migrating to avoid becoming illegal, as in the case of Raúl's children in Mexico, being "illegal" in the United States, or having illegal—or even previously illegal—parents, it shapes children's experiences differently even as they live in the same families. And, as Temo reminded me when we first sought Camilo out on the soccer field, this hardly seems fair.

5 Stigma

The term stigma, then, will be used to refer to an attribute
that is deeply discrediting, but it should be seen that a language of relationships, not attributes, is really needed.

Erving Goffman, *Stigma*

"I don't have friends," he tells me, seriously, in carefully pronounced
English. The accompanying smile, dimple on each cheek, makes me
almost not believe him.

Preciliano wears a stained school uniform: navy blue trousers and a
white collared T-shirt. A rough-and-tumble third grader with a slight
build, I imagine him the type to play a pickup soccer game on a dusty
street in Mexico, not in the urban streets of central New Jersey. He has not
yet learned that his uniform pants should look like neatly pressed baggy
jeans or that his polo shirt should gleam as a sign of prosperity in this
community of second-generation immigrant children. Perhaps he is a little different.

We sit squinting at each other in the sun at the end of our interview.
The hot metal-covered-in-red-rubber park bench burns my back every
time I lean against it, causing me to shift uncomfortably. Preciliano's
mother, Carmela, has moved into the shade of a tree, taking the stroller
with her. A handful of children, two my own and two Preciliano's younger

Opposite: Photograph by Bob Anderson

brothers, run around shrieking on the nearby jungle gym. My boys enter-
tain themselves by pounding each other with a recently pumped soccer
ball. Every once in a while the ball ends up outside of the wood chip area.
I already called them over when it rolled too close to the guys hanging out
near the brick structure that was probably once bathrooms but is now
permanently locked. When we got to the park a little after 3:00 p.m. they
were there. Low jeans, flat-brimmed baseball caps covering eyes; one or
two at a time they disappeared, walking down across the short field to the
few sparse trees by the train tracks. Then each one came back to the others, to hang, enjoying the sunny spring afternoon and his high. I'm not the
only parent monitoring her children's contact with the junkies, regular
fixtures at the park. No one looks over in their direction. Our eyes trained
on our children, we make sure they don't venture too close.

I laugh a little too hard. "You don't have friends at school?" He is too
cute for me not to respond playfully, at first. Preciliano smiles, black hair
spiked with gel. Light often plays across his brown eyes, drawing me into
his stories when I ask him to tell me about what life is like for a third
grader living in New Jersey.

"Sometimes they play with me ... eh ... they don't play with me
sometimes."

"Really. Why do you think they don't play with you?"

"I don't know," he says looking down at swinging feet. His black Velcro
sketchers don't quite reach the ground. His trousers have hiked up, revealing skinny brown legs and bleach-clean white socks.

"Does that make you feel sad?"

"Yes." He meets my eyes and then looks away.

"Well, who do you play with when you have recess?"

"With no one."

CHILDREN'S PEER GROUPS

Legal status marks children's relationships within their families and significantly shapes their daily lives,[1] whether distinguishing the prospects of
siblings, heightening existing gendered distinctions between partners that
create extra burdens on women, or amplifying the dependency of parents

on children and the tensions this causes. Yet children spend significant amounts of their time in the company of other children. And in the structured environment of formal schooling, children typically forge group hierarchies at early ages cultivating gender-, race-, and class based distinctions in school-based interactions.[2] Children also form significant ties with other children in organized extracurricular activities, where they may develop gender, racial, and class identities, especially through participation in formal sports.[3] In what ways do children negotiate legal-status distinctions with their friends, both inside and outside the classroom?

Knowledge of immigrant youth's friendships derives primarily from a focus on their adaptation experiences,[4] with peer groups either aiding or abetting children's integration, overall assimilation of language, cultural practices, and future aspirations. On the one hand, peers may negatively influence immigrant youth—creating the conditions for downward assimilation—especially when children move into neighborhoods with widespread youth gangs, drug use, and small-scale violence.[5] Both historically and today, reformers have viewed cultural dissonance in the second generation as a pressing social problem, one that affects both families and communities when youth do not integrate.[6] On the other hand, in certain communities ethnic peer groups may buffer children from the negative influences of wider youth cultures in difficult neighborhoods and schools.[7] Coethnic peer relationships may become a source of positive identity formation for immigrant children and the children of immigrants who struggle to adapt to a society different from that of their parents,[8] and racial authenticity among the second generation may give youth social status among peers.[9]

Nearly exclusive attention to assimilation experiences obscures the fact that the children of immigrants do not simply socialize—or get socialized—in peer interactions; rather, children appropriate, reinvent, reproduce, and contest features of adult society in their interactions.[10] "From this perspective, children enter into a social nexus and, by interacting and negotiating with others, establish understandings that become fundamental social knowledge on which they continually build."[11] With their peers, children—and the children of immigrants—create social knowledge as much as they absorb it. In elementary school, children especially recreate and contest status distinctions along the lines of gender, differentiating boy and girl culture in classroom settings.[12] As they age, racial and ethnic distinctions become particularly salient in children's interactions, which may vary across diverse school environments.[13] By high school, children create gender, racial, and class distinctions simultaneously, evident in complex clique formations, in the hierarchies of the jocks and the popular girls, and in the racial and economic background of a particular school's social outcasts.[14]

Third grader Preciliano doesn't look like the typical loner child in elementary school.[15] Usually something marks such children physically as different, like being overweight or having a mild form of a disability. Or they may smell funny, or their clothes may not be as clean or fashionable as those of other students. Sometimes they are poor.[16] Notably loner behavior reinforces itself, with outcast children often rejecting other children's attempts to bring them into social activities, further perpetuating a cycle of isolation.[17] For example, I watched one loner at a school in New Jersey walk up and down a faded yellow painted line on the blacktop, barely looking up when someone invited him to play tag. A little shorter than the others, he wore thick square glasses and received special education instruction in a pullout program a few times a week. This East Asian boy looked and acted differently than children in the diverse school he attended, composed of nearly equal proportions of South Asian, Latino, white, and African American students. To my trained eye, Preciliano seems remarkably normal. I don't quite believe that he has no friends; it takes time to understand what sets him apart.

I come to find out that Preciliano indeed struggles to connect with his classmates. His story illustrates the ways legal status affects children in peer group interactions conditionally, varying by the specific features of the community where they live. For children like Preciliano growing up in a primarily second-generation Mexican and Latino community in central New Jersey, being a Mexican immigrant works differently than it does for other third graders like him growing up in northeastern Ohio. In 2009, 3.5 million immigrants were estimated to be living in "new destination" states, like New Jersey and Ohio, more than a third of whom were Mexicans.[18] Illegality—or the negotiations around needing or lacking a legal status—shapes children's lives according to the specific dynamics of the community context in these new destination sites.

This makes sense. In Ohio, more families reported detentions and deportations of male members, and also varying whims of police officers and others law enforcement professionals with whom they interacted. Although all families feared enforcement, families in Ohio experienced greater vulnerability. So illegality might more significantly shape children's peer groups in Ohio than in New Jersey, where, after all, the children I interviewed lived in a community with many unauthorized migrants among them.

Surprisingly, I found the opposite to be true. Children in Ohio rarely employed legal-status distinctions in relationships with peers, whereas children in New Jersey actively utilized, or pointedly avoided, concepts of legality in peer group interactions. Children socially constructed illegality negatively: they remained silent on legal status, describing it as a secret, and may have come to stigmatize those, like Preciliano, to whom they attributed characteristics of illegality.

ALONE IN NEW JERSEY

At recess, a few weeks later, Preciliano leans up against the gray, twenty-foot-high chain-link fence right by the door for almost the entire recess period. Two large groups of boys organize their daily soccer games on the far part of the blacktop, while another group plays basketball. Girls and boys chase each other in the middle in the gender play that Barrie Thorne has written about.[19] A group of girls follow around a green-eyed, light-skinned girl who has brought a baby doll set from home against school rules. Her tight curls bounce as she skips around hugging the doll to her chest. She is popular for a few minutes before the other girls get annoyed. Some others are light-skinned, like her. Most have darker brown skin tones, like Preciliano. At this school nearly 97 percent of children are Latino, and 89 percent of children speak Spanish at home.[20] Here there is no jungle gym, but kids play, busy. Everyone chatters, seemingly having fun, except for Preciliano.

The next day Preciliano sits against the same stretch of fence and pulls out a stash from his pocket: two green plastic soldiers and a red and white plastic tractor trailer that turns into a police station. I can't stand it any longer; I break my own rules of disengagement.[21]

I sit with Preciliano. I ask if I can play.

We chase each other around, plastic toy police soldier—me—chasing plastic toy robber—Preciliano. I make shooting noises. Preciliano hides his figure under piles of little stones that have loosened from the pavement. We enact the police chasing game that others play at recess with our plastic figures. A short, chubby boy with tan pants and a pale yellow shirt comes over, interested. He looks on for a few minutes and then walks away. He circles back, after having run off to join the chasing game, this time with a taller, skinny boy with mismatched navy blue shirt and pants, more disheveled than those of Preciliano next to me. This time they ask Preciliano what he is playing. "Police," he answers annoyed by their interruption.

Suddenly aware of how funny I must look, I feel foolish squatting down against the fence with Preciliano in my tan capris and white shirt, my feeble attempt to match the colors of the school's lax uniform policy. No clothes I can wear can make me, a tall, white sociologist with long brown hair, and glasses, fit in. I don't even know how to play toy soldier chase games, usually refusing make-believe games like this with my own children. I desperately want these two boys to take over. I look up at them and smile, as invitingly as possible, without saying a word. I will them in my mind to ask, "Can we play?" so I can stand up, stretch my legs, and lean against the fence like the passive observer I want to be.

But they move on.

Everyone knows what it feels like to be different, as I do at the school and as Preciliano appears to be reminded every day at recess. But still, his exclusion perplexes me. In Ohio one in four children I met reported feeling excluded by their peers, which made sense given that so many were the only brown faces in their classrooms and the only ones to speak Spanish. But in New Jersey just four children reported feeling excluded, one of them Preciliano. What makes him, of all the kids at his school, a loner, a "stigmatized person" in the language of Erving Goffman?

A MEXICAN COMMUNITY IN NEW JERSEY

Preciliano's mother Carmela knows he doesn't have friends. Looking ten years younger than me, she wears tight dyed blue jeans and a sleeveless bright red shirt that hugs her midsection. Energetic, she has walked more than twenty minutes across the city to meet me at the park for the interview. She has lived in the United States for four years and she birthed her youngest child in a nearby hospital, but I can easily imagine her walking as briskly among mango and palm trees on wet dirt roads along the coast of Oaxaca.

Fifteen years ago, most of the new immigrants to this small city in central New Jersey came from small towns in the primarily rural state of Oaxaca, on the coast or just inland, like Carmela, who—orphaned at a young age—grew up with her aging grandfather in a small village in the Sierra Sur of Oaxaca.[22] She came to the United States after she met her husband, who grew up in a neighboring village, also as an orphan, which, she explains, "is why we understand each other." Neither attended school past the sixth grade; employment prospects in Mexico were few. After they married, an acquaintance offered to help Carmela's husband come to New Jersey; he jumped on the offer, leaving her with Preciliano as an infant. He returned to visit after three years, at which point they had a second son. This time he decided to bring his family north with him.

Their destination, a little over an hour from New York City, attracted many Mexican migrants during the 1990s because a growing manufacturing sector as well as a vibrant service sector (especially in landscaping and construction) was replacing the declining industries of the 1970s and 1980s.[23] Most, like Carmela's husband working nights for a cleaning company, worked for low wages in a community where the cost of living was quite high. The families I interviewed most often shared homes or apartments with friends or relatives, doubling up two or three families per housing unit.[24] Of those interviewed in New Jersey, only four owned their own homes. Approximately two-thirds of the mothers worked. Parents often arranged alternate shifts so that one of them could always be available for their children. When Carmela arrived in New Jersey she worked for the same cleaning company as her husband for about a year. Once pregnant with their third child, she began to stay at home—in the one room that the family sublet for $400 in a three-bedroom apartment. She hopes to continue to do so until her youngest can attend preschool.

By 2011, when I first met third grader Preciliano, the Mexican community in this small city in central New Jersey had grown considerably. Some still came from small towns and rural communities, like Carmela. Others had grown up in large cities: Acapulco, Puebla, Mexico City. The Oaxacan origins of the migrant community, however, lingered, evident in the Oaxaqueño stores and restaurants that the city boasted, the names of men's soccer league teams, and the cultural events commemorating Oaxacan traditions such as the dances of the Guelaguetza.

The social service infrastructure in this city seemed to have developed in ways to meet the needs of Spanish speakers, in part because of strong Puerto Rican and Dominican advocates who had lived in the area prior to the growth of the Mexican population. Many agencies, state and also nongovernmental, hired bilingual staff.[25] Numerous churches offered services in Spanish, three Catholic along with a number of other denominations. In 2000, when I first lived in the city, I translated at the hospital ER frequently because this was the only place migrants without insurance could go. Mexicans routinely experienced differential treatment. One incident sticks out: I accompanied an uninsured in-law to the ER when he experienced sudden and severe trouble hearing. The doctor dismissively attended him, annoyed that he had come in for what turned out to be a heavy buildup of ear wax due to the safety equipment he used at work. In 2011, I accompanied an uninsured mother who had hurt her back after having fallen on the ice to the same ER. I thought I would help to translate but ended up providing just the ride and conversation. Everyone who attended her, from the receptionist to the nurse to the doctor, spoke enough Spanish for registration, diagnosis, treatment, and discharge.[26]

By the time Carmela had given birth to Preciliano's eighteen-month-old brother in that same local hospital, numerous pregnant Mexican women, and those with young children, knew the hospital services well. At the district elementary school that Preciliano attended, the school superintendent estimated that a full 80 percent of students had Mexican immigrant parents. The city had rapidly changed from being a community of new immigrants to one of an emerging young Mexican-identified second generation.

Difficulties accompanied this transition. Children described Mexican- or Central American–identified gangs as especially problematic.[27] A fifteen-year-old in the ninth grade explained,

The school I went to, there was like I guess two major gangs that were there. I had a friend for a while that, he was really like, he was always like joking around with that, but he ended joining one in the end. The friend I told you that died, he got stabbed by a . . . 'Cause he was in a gang and you know so he would go out, get high, um, and stuff like that with them and one night he was like that. It was around four in the morning, I heard and went out, it was a rival gang, the other people started talking, and to, you know, to defend his whatever, he started fighting back, and after a while he got stabbed.

I asked another ninth grader who commented on the many boys in gangs at her school about what she did to stay safe. She explained, "I try not to talk to them much. That is I don't talk to everybody."

At Preciliano's elementary school, gangs stopped being a major problem a few years ago. In the early 2000s, back when the school went through the eighth grade, older students recruited fourth and fifth graders. This was before the district established a distinct middle school. Now Preciliano's school has a student body of 820 students in grades pre-K through 5.

A PROTOTYPICAL KID

"He gets in trouble at school," Carmela explains to me at the park, in Spanish, while we sit in the sun on the benches whose squares feel now imprinted on my bottom. "The other kids tease him, but the teacher blames him for causing trouble." Preciliano, who plays alone at recess, is definitely not shy or quiet. He messes with the other children when we file down from his third-floor classroom to art on the first floor. On the way to ESL he teases the two girls with him on the walk down to the basement, and again when they are running back upstairs at the end of the hour.

Carmela's voice hikes up an octave, shrill with anger when talking about Preciliano's teacher. The teacher, Ms. Rodríguez, is young and Latina, with loose black curls down to her shoulders and occasionally sympathetic eyes. She means well but rarely smiles and mutes emotions behind her Kohl's-style wardrobe. Preciliano is not her favorite.

"How did you decide on your boys' names?" I ask Carmela, changing the subject.

Shaking her head in disgust, she blames her husband for wanting to name Preciliano after his own father. She spits the words with a level of emotion missing during most of our interview, except when talking about Ms. Rodríguez. "I don't know why he couldn't have picked a normal one." Carmela adds, proudly, that she picked the more mainstream names of her two younger sons.

Naming does not, however, explain Preciliano's loner status. At PS 13, he is not the only child with a unique name; I heard many during the full nine days I spent at the school. There 98 percent of the children receive free and reduced lunches and nearly the same percentage are Latino. Twelve percent of students have an IEP, an individualized education program, meaning they have some sort of special education need.[28] They either attend one of four self-contained special education classrooms or, when teachers deem them ready, move to an "inclusion" designated room. Preciliano does not have special education needs that make him stand out. He is in a bilingual classroom, a fact that hardly makes him different at PS 13, where 37 percent of the students are LEP or limited English proficiency.[29] In addition, the district designates the school as a port of entry for new immigrants: it is one of only two schools with a special newcomer classroom to help children who arrive drastically below grade level, regardless of language skills, to catch up before moving into a regular classroom. Students at this school have access to three types of services, depending on their specific needs as determined by an entrance exam administered by the school district at the time of registration: the newcomer classroom, a bilingual classroom, and an ESL pullout program. Theoretically they can transition through each until ESL is no longer needed.

Despite the difficult socioeconomic profile of PS 13 students, the school has spirit. While students' academic performance ranks among the lowest 7 percent of schools statewide, it rates among the highest for college and career readiness, at this age measured by participation and attendance rates.[30] The kids may not boast high academic test scores, but they like the school and have fun there. A handful of friends' Facebook pages boast graduation from PS 13. Teachers also seem to like the school, which has the reputation of attracting—and retaining—those who want to work with underserved students. School spirit bursts from the seams. Unlike the squeaky instruments at Temo's winter concert that stake a claim for future accomplishment, PS 13's fourth- and fifth-grade band plays a lively salsa combo, the talent real, in the moment.

At PS 13, idiosyncrasies seem more often accepted than in other schools I visited in both New Jersey and Ohio. I observed in another third-grade class there, one of the inclusion rooms, which held more than a dozen awkward boys of all sizes with unmatched uniforms in varying levels of disarray. During a multiplication baseball game, a lanky, pigeon-toed boy struck out with the easiest of questions: 3×7. As he walked to the back of the line, his eyes grew watery. My stomach clenched, fearing instant ridicule for him. But instead the most obnoxious and popular kid in the class slapped him on the back. "Don't worry about it, man," he said, his bright white teeth flashing a smile from beneath his deep brown, Indian-Guyanese skin. Two others—one overweight Dominican with slits for eyes and the other a Mexican of a similar build with a reputation for provoking the other boys—joined in with reassurances. At the back of the line, the pigeon-toed boy smiled, unscathed.

Preciliano fits the median profile of most of PS 13 students, and those in the school district. Although born in Mexico, he attended the newcomer classroom for only a few months, and teachers expect he will transition out of his bilingual classroom by fourth grade. He is Latino, his parents are Mexican, and he speaks Spanish at home but is learning English quickly. He lives in a low-income family, facing economic difficulties similar to those of other children at the school.

But relatively normal-looking Preciliano has no friends in his class. He sits in the front, paying close attention to Ms. Rodríguez when he isn't daydreaming, drawing in his notebook, answering the other children's taunts or occasionally taunting them himself. One day Preciliano shows me his drawing, an elaborate penciled window frame with two panes that he has cut out to open, revealing a bright gray landscape of mountains, birds, and sunshine. In art he works diligently to color his flag project while others goof off. He holds the green and red crayons carefully, deeply etching the colors of Mexico.

I wonder if artistic sensibilities set Preciliano apart. While I sit isolated in my second-floor closetlike office, writing, peering out the window at the blue sky bright over the dead winter grass of my backyard, and reflect on

Preciliano and all the other kids I have met at PS 13, I think that just maybe Preciliano and I feel so different, and distant, because we are artists, writers, observers. At lunch, Preciliano sits with the girls, smiling and laughing easily with them, sharing chips and passing ketchup back and forth, his grin infectious. The boys sitting at my end of the table, though, avoid him like the plague.

PEER GROUPS IN NEW JERSEY

The children I interviewed in New Jersey, like Preciliano, interacted frequently with other children like themselves, more so than those I met in Ohio: all but three children (who did not actually live in the city where Preciliano lived) had Spanish-speaking friends, and *all* had Latino friends. In Ohio, seventeen children had no Spanish-speaking friends and fourteen had no Latino friends. Twice as many children in New Jersey preferred Spanish to English (although most children in both places liked English better), and twice as many chose the labels of *Mexican* and *Mexican American* as their best identifier. Three times as many children in New Jersey as in Ohio thought their parents made the same amount of money as their friends' parents.

Children in New Jersey described their peers as being mostly just like them, something that might have positively influenced their self-esteem.[31] They frequently interacted with these peers. In New Jersey most children interviewed had friends over to their houses to play, and slightly fewer than half had sleepovers. One out of four children in New Jersey participated in school-based tutoring programs compared to only one child in Ohio. Many boys I met played soccer, and girls participated in the Mexican folkloric dance group that practiced once a week in the PS 13 auditorium. Boys and girls took swimming lessons and participated in catechism classes.

Interactions with children like themselves also occurred frequently in the neighborhoods where children lived. In Ohio 98 percent of children lived in census tracts with a Spanish-speaking population of less than 10 percent, and 97 percent lived in census tracts that were less than 10 percent Latino or Hispanic. This compared to 25 percent and 21 percent of children interviewed in New Jersey. Children in New Jersey lived in places with not only a higher concentration of Spanish speakers and Latinos but also in places with greater cultural diversity due to high levels of immigration. In Ohio, 77 percent of children lived in census tracts with less than 10 percent foreign-born residents, whereas in New Jersey only 6 percent of children did.

Given the neighborhood Preciliano lives in, and the school he attends, none of the typical social status indicators that Patricia and Peter Adler suggest as indicative of an outsider status mark Preciliano as especially different.[32] He does not have an identifiable physical or mental disability. He doesn't smell or look particularly funny; his mother dresses him in pressed, clean clothes that he dirties by the end of the day. He shares a language and an ethnic heritage with his peers. Economically he seems no better or worse off than the others at PS13.

ON BEING AN IMMIGRANT IN NEW JERSEY

The Puerto Rican social worker at PS 13 chuckles when we talk of Preciliano; she knows him, as he has been referred to her more than once. His jokes annoy the girls in his class because he constantly boasts about the things that "real men," like him, do. And it isn't hanging out at the park getting high, dressed in oversized jeans and a pristine sports jersey. It is, the social worker explains, telling the girls to go first when walking into the classroom. It is bragging about his superior strength and his ability to cut down stuff with a machete. Even his gait, she says, reminds her of a typical *machista* Mexicano.

The special skills teacher says Preciliano is misunderstood.

Yes, I think, he is misunderstood because Preciliano is unknowingly defiant. He is Mexican and is not, and does not yet try to be, Mexican American, like the other kids at school. Even after having lived in New Jersey for two years, everything about Preciliano radiates what was cool and acceptable for boys in Mexico, not New Jersey. I have visited dozens of schools in Oaxaca;[33] there Preciliano would fit right in. In New Jersey, he is what the other children in his school are distancing themselves from: an immigrant, someone who is unauthorized.

In the context of life at PS 13, his unauthorized status cannot be all that unusual. Most children are of Mexican descent with unauthorized parents. Some, like Preciliano, have migrated to New Jersey from Mexico with their parents. These Mexican-born children, however, do not talk about Mexico at school, preferring to be assumed to be second generation like their friends.

Recently an influx of legal Dominican migrants to the school contrasts sharply to the trickle of Mexican immigrants scattered among US-born Mexican children. The newcomer classroom I visit is more than half Dominican, and children chat openly about their hometowns in cutting, rural accents. Once, during a lesson on geysers, the Dominican kids were out of their chairs, jumping up and down with arms raised, talking before being called on, clamoring to tell stories about the hot springs and water-falls back home. Some spoke with such strong intonations that I, and the teacher, had trouble understanding their Spanish.

I never heard Mexican kids at PS 13 refer to their hometowns in Mexico out loud. Few have firsthand experience in Mexico. As their parents are unauthorized, they do not regularly visit relatives back home with their parents. In fact, only sixteen children in New Jersey had been back to Mexico to visit, whereas forty in Ohio had. This is not to say that the Mexican American kids at PS 13 were not proud of their Mexican heritage. They were just not necessarily proud to be immigrants, or the children of immigrants. In New Jersey, forty-two children I interviewed said they were proud to be Mexican, but only sixteen said that they were proud of their immigrant heritage.

Children in both New Jersey and Ohio told me that they did not want other children to know that they or their parents were immigrants. Remarkably, children in New Jersey were much more likely to say this than children in Ohio, despite living in and around so many children like themselves (table 5). "They are like mean because I was born in a different place from my mom," said an eight-year-old girl on why she did not like people to know her mother was an immigrant. A ten-year-old boy who attended PS 13 more explicitly explained that he didn't tell people his par-ents were born in Mexico "because then it spreads around the whole school, they start rumors."

Children in New Jersey more often hid aspects of their race/ethnic background than did children in Ohio. They especially hesitated to dis-

Table 5 Children's Reports of Peer Awareness of Key Identity Indicators

	New Jersey (n = 53)	Ohio (n = 57)
Percentage of children whose peers know what country they or their parents are from	57	71
Percentage of children who *want* peers to know what country they or their parents are from	54	65
Percentage of children whose peers know that they or their family speak Spanish	75	84
Percentage of children who *want* peers to know that they or their family speak Spanish	69	85
Percentage of children whose peers know they or their parents are immigrants	16	60
Percentage of children who *want* peers to know they or their parents are immigrants	16	53

NOTE: Not all the children answered each of the questions. I am reporting here the total number of children interviewed in each site.

cuss issues related to their immigrant heritage compared to children in Ohio.

Children may hide their parent's foreign-born status because of their fears of deportation. But this is not all, because for them the word *immigrant* has become an uncomfortable word that means "unauthorized" and means people can come take your parents away at any time. It is a stigma, best to be avoided: a social distinction they at times use in interactions with peers. And Preciliano looks and talks like an immigrant. In the cultural context of peer relationships at PS 13, Preciliano's outward immigrant status seems a subtle source of stigma.

In the basement cafeteria, the kids have doused the chicken nuggets in ketchup and distributed them among each other. Two Dominican girls sitting next to me start talking about their school lunches back home. I ask who else in the class has been to school in the DR. Sandy, on my left, points up and down the row of girls and boys on each bench and names six who were born in the DR.

"How about kids who've been to school in Mexico?"

She looks back blankly. Finally she shrugs and refers to Suraya, another Dominican next to her, who can't tell me either. Karla, the most social of the Mexican girls, sits across the table from us listening. I ask her.

"I was born at St. Josephs [the local hospital]" she tells me in perfect, sing-song Spanish. "I don't know about the others," she adds, assessing each row of her classmates sitting on the benches of the cafeteria table. Finally, a light-skinned girl next to her—who has been listening in quietly and whom I have assumed to be Puerto Rican—says she went to school in Puebla, where she was born. "People never think I'm Mexican because of the way I look," she adds.

"Are there others in your class?" I ask. She too shrugs her shoulders, unsure.

Strange that girls who know so many details about each other's lives, including which children were born in the Dominican Republic, cannot say which children were Mexican born. The social worker later confirms that in Preciliano's class of twenty-five, six kids were born in Mexico and six in the Dominican Republic. At PS 13, the Mexican children—but not the Dominicans, who mostly came to the United States with visas—are noticeably silent about their place of birth in their peer group interactions. The children at PS 13 do not talk too much about being born in Mexico.

I ask a seven-year-old, who is actually a US-born citizen but who tells me that he is an immigrant (his parents and older sister are immigrants), "Would you want your friends or other kids at your class to know you're an immigrant? [Or] is that something you prefer they don't know too?"

"I'd prefer they don't know."

"How come?"

"Because like we don't really use that word and I feel like some people are not going to understand me, then they're gonna think I know other words and they might not talk to me." Gabriela, a fourteen-year-old eighth grader in New Jersey, articulates what seemed to be the general sentiment: "They don't know I was born in Mexico but they know we're from Mexico."

"Okay. Would you want them to not know that you were born in Mexico? Is that something you try not to talk about?"

"Um, it's really a subject that we don't talk about like in general as like, like at school we really just don't talk about that in general."

TEASING IN NEW JERSEY

In New Jersey, children surprised me with all their stories of ethnic or racially based teasing.[34] Nearly half the children I interviewed reported teasing compared to 37 percent in Ohio. For example, a twelve-year-old girl recounted, "Yes, but they were one of my friends last year. There was a girl, she doesn't really like Mexicans, but [she said that] like to one of my friends, but I told her that it doesn't really matter what she thought." And a ninth grader explained that she had been teased in middle school. "Maybe like somebody has called me a spic or something."

"And like who calls you spics? 'Cause I imagine your middle school has like a lot of people, different cultures," I asked her.

"Like white girls or something."

Another ninth grader commented that people didn't tease her but they did make fun of Mexicans, saying "that they have big heads. That they are short." And an eighth grader explained, "We were reading about, what's it called, a story about Mexicans and well, um, it had to do with Mexicans, and they called a Mexican a tacohead and then my friend tried calling me that, but I called him something else and then [it stopped]."

Some children talked of shrugging off the insults, but not all did. I asked a US-born seven-year-old whom I was interviewing in Spanish whether he, or anyone he knew, had been teased for being Mexican. "Yeah . . . they say something bad when you make a mistake."

"How do you feel when you hear those things?" I asked.

"A little bad. Because I don't like that they make fun." Then he switched to English, "'cause my family is Mexican." A thirteen-year-old, son of a Mexican father and a US-born white mother, told me about being teased by a good friend at school. "He said Mexicans are poor and that they always make their money mowing lawns. And that is so not true. I threw him into the table because it made me mad." And Jasmine, a ten-year-old US-born citizen, explained that when she heard other kids being teased, "I feel bad. I don't feel bad 'cause I'm Mexican. I feel bad for them for being teased. It feels bad to be teased about who you are."

Significantly, the teasing that children reported—or feared—was often related to legal status,[35] explaining why children might be so reluctant to disclose their heritage to peers. Jasmine had denied being teased in the past, but she went on to explain that she didn't want others to know her parents were immigrants, "because I don't feel comfortable telling other people that my parents are immigrants. They will probably want to tease me or tell other people." And another recounted a common joke at his school: "They say that Mexicans can't read books." I can be especially slow.

"Why?" I asked, "I don't get it."

"They say because Mexicans don't have papers."

Similarly, a ninth-grade girl explained about being teased: "Um, I don't know, you'll be talking and then you say something that's like ethnic where you are [from], like you like spicy food or something, or they'll be like, oh, you know, that's so Mexican or something. Or they'll make a little joke about since I like to run, and I run cross country, then they'll make a joke on that 'cause my family is Mexican." Her peers joked that the preference for running was related to being Mexican and having to run across the border.

At PS 13, administrators and teachers did not condone this behavior. A student at PS 13 explained: "In the school, there was a kid, he's in fifth grade . . . and he said, 'I don't want to be Mexican 'cause I don't want to be dumb like Mexican people.' And he started doing that stuff and he got suspended, and the principal didn't want him right there 'cause there's a Dominican, Mexican, Honduran people, and they don't actually talk about their cultures. They just be normal Americans in there [at school]."

Despite adults' objections, children drew on stereotypes about Mexicans, especially about their legal status, in their play with each other, whether this was maliciously intended or not. Children in New Jersey avoided highlighting their immigrant heritage, and for some their Mexican background, in order to avoid these types of comments.

I will, of course, never know exactly why, at PS 13, other children marked Preciliano as being different, but here is what I think. The way Preciliano walks, even the way he talks in his faltering English, is "Mexico." In his few years attending school in New Jersey, he has not made an effort to alter his style or to fit in with the other Mexican and Latino kids in his school. He ignores the styles of masculinity and femininity that kids in New Jersey project, teasing others for not being manly according to his Mexican-based standards.[36] Preciliano misses the social cues of his Mexican American peers, cues that other Mexican immigrant children may pick up on better. He communicates a style of the Mexico of other children's parents, one that could be dangerous, one that is associated with the unauthorized. And so Preciliano unwittingly embodies other children's discomfort and their fears about legal status.

STANDING OUT: SCHOOLING IN OHIO

"I don't think this was such a good idea." Kevin's second-grade teacher shakes her head to emphasize her discomfort, not meeting my eyes when I walk into the classroom at 9:20 on a Monday morning at the end of May. This midfifties woman, shorter and heavier than I, with bleached blonde thinning hair in a long bob, acts the persona of a seasoned inner-city teacher who won't take anyone's bullshit. Her dour expression intimidates me.

"I can just sit in the back," I offer.

"Oh you don't have to do that." She softens some but still does not smile. I move toward two chairs at a desk in the back of the room. "Those are for students who come in late." She turns around and goes back to her seat in the cut-out middle of a semicircular table. Students, when called, sit with her one at a time to review their end-of-the-year letter grades for each subject. I find a smaller plastic blue chair at an unused computer desk in the back of the room and sit, hugging my knees. I don't dare take out my notebook and instead silently watch her tell a seven-year-old that he is getting lots of Ds and Fs on his work.

Kevin, whom I've come to observe, sits alone at a desk up against the far wall lockers working quietly on a ditto. Twelve students, mostly girls, sit grouped at three tables composed of four desks facing each other. The other six, mostly boys like Kevin, sit individually at their desks spaced throughout the room facing different directions. Eleven of the children are African American, four are white, one is Asian, and one I can't identify. Kevin is the only Latino. At the school, 52 percent are African American, 31 percent white, and 11 percent multiracial. Official statistics don't include any Asian or Latinos in 2009–10, the year I'm visiting, even though Kevin is a student. Four percent are LEP and 15 percent students with disabilities. All students qualify as economically disadvantaged.[37] "I've taught a Mexican before," the teacher tells me later at recess, "but I don't think there is another one in this school right now."

Kevin reminds me of Preciliano. With the same thin, lanky height and build, he wears the white top and blue bottom of the lax school uniform in a similar disheveled fashion. He also resembles Preciliano in that he is dark skinned, has black hair, often gelled, and even has the same mischievous sparkle in his eyes. Like Preciliano, Kevin was born in Mexico and has a younger brother, also born in Mexico. He came to Ohio with his mother a few years earlier as an unauthorized migrant. Unlike Preciliano, Kevin talks about friends at school and joins other boys playing basketball on the blacktop at recess. He does not feel like a loner, and being an immigrant in Ohio does not seem to isolate him. Ironically, no one else at his school shares his migratory experiences; minority youth in such school contexts often report discrimination from peers.[38]

In New Jersey I visited three schools, typical to the children I interviewed in my sample: one urban public school, one suburban public school, and one urban charter school. In Ohio, Mexican families did not concentrate in any one section of the city. To capture the typical school environments of the children I interviewed, I went to six different schools, five public and one parochial. I thought the two middle-income suburban schools spectacular. In one the teacher had the second graders do yoga in between lessons in order to "move their bodies around and stay focused mentally" and allowed them to stand up at their tables while working. At the other the teacher ran a school gardening program with her students, dissecting a radish they had picked and grown on her smart board to show them its parts. Nationwide, however, most children in Mexican immigrant families are overrepresented in problem schools, like the urban public schools I visited with Kevin and Preciliano, which rated low compared to other schools in the state.[39] Their students came from low-income households. Many had special needs, whether developmental (students with IEP plans) or linguistic (LEP students) or behavioral.[40] Kevin's experiences contrast to those of Preciliano, illustrating major differences in the environments of children growing up in New Jersey and Ohio and ultimately the meaning illegality has for children across these varying community contexts.

Kevin, like Preciliano, gets in trouble frequently at school, I learn over the next week after the teacher decides to tolerate me. This is why he sits alone at his desk. I watch, on this first day, the teacher reprimand him for cheating when he later stands up at the table to work on vocabulary. Then another student complains that he has taken a page of notepaper, ripped it up, and stomped on it. Present at each incident, I notice nothing. Mostly I see Kevin shoving other boys to get to the front of the line. "I don't know why he does that," the teacher complains. She theorizes, "It's like he is competitive. He always has to be first."

The ESL teacher, a tall thin brunette about my age, confirms that Kevin, together with his younger brother in kindergarten, gets in trouble for fighting. "Sometimes I think he just doesn't know what he does wrong. One time I saw him standing up against the wall and I asked what he did wrong. He just shrugged and smiled."

"He and his brother remind me of little men," she laughs. It is later that afternoon when we sit for a few minutes after she finishes working with him in a forty-minute pullout session in her small, interior office without windows. Unlike in New Jersey, where students are individually tested, in this school district in Ohio all students qualify automatically for ESL if they speak a language other than English at home. She has three Mexican students in this school: Kevin and his brother and one other. Mostly, the other ESL students are Asian. An Office for Refugee Resettlement operates nearby placing families—at that time often Burmese or Bhutanese-Nepalese—across neighborhoods. For teachers, the refugee children, who access tutoring support programs outside of school, are the faces of local immigrants. The district ESL coordinator, for example, tells me, "Our students are, approximately, 50 percent refugees. . . . The Spanish-speakers are really a [few] all over the city." Because Mexican children are so few, adults in the school do not describe concerns over the particular needs of Mexican immigrant children. They view Kevin as a troublemaker but do not see that his behavior could be related to his status as an immigrant child adjusting to a new environment.[41] Just as in the official statistics, from the school's perspective, the fact that he is a Mexican immigrant is invisible.

THE PARENT-SCHOOL CONNECTION

"His mother comes in and talks to the teacher and then it gets better for a few weeks, but then they are back to their regular stuff again." The ESL teacher doesn't blame Kevin's mother, Elizabeth, nor does his teacher, who talks instead about the negative influences of the neighborhood.[42] Elizabeth always attends when called into conferences, despite her limited English language skills. She also advocates on behalf of her children, requesting her own conferences. One day she asked me to go with her because her son was not included on the list of students honored for reading at home, an activity she supervised. She knew he had completed the required hours, diligently signing off on the form every week. In the meeting Elizabeth expressed herself with confidence, in broken English. The boys continued to get in trouble despite her efforts.

Kevin may behave better in his classroom because of my presence, since he has seen me many times visiting his mother at their house. Although he doesn't greet me when I come into the room, at lunch he passes his uneaten chicken nuggets down the table to me and tells another student that I have two children, one whose name is Dylan like his friend's brother. My boys spend many evenings with Kevin and his younger brother that spring. Typically after school the boys play outside for hours, usually by themselves, but sometimes an Asian boy down the block joins in. On visits, Temo takes turns with the other boys riding their nonfunctioning motorcycle bikes down the hill of the brick-laid street where they live. Elizabeth has learned after having lived there for three years that their street was a *zona caliente*, a bad area of the city known for its resident prostitutes.

When we first met, Elizabeth lived with her husband, who was periodically unemployed. During the year I visit, they have a falling out and he moves out, although he comes to see Kevin and his brother nearly every afternoon and often eats dinner with us during my visits.[43] Elizabeth, affectionate and loving in her parenting style, is the main breadwinner and family disciplinarian. Her husband, also warm with the children, frequently plays with them, although often he also watches TV with them or sleeps on the sofa while they run around outside. Kevin likes to play Uno with his mother; with his dad "Crocodile . . . My dad is down there, like this. And he grabs a leg."

Despite the attention from their parents, Kevin's and his brother's mischievous behavior extends outside of school. They attended a free weekend program until asked not to return for not heeding the adults in charge. On one afternoon visit, Elizabeth spends the afternoon teaching me how to make *chuletas en salsa verde*. When the boys finally come in from out-side to eat, Temo, Kevin, and his brother reek of gasoline. Elizabeth sends her boys upstairs to change while I grill Temo: he eventually confesses that the three snuck into a neighbor's garage and that, playing around, each peed into the red plastic gas container next to a lawnmower.

STRUGGLING SCHOOLS

In his classroom I watch Kevin fidget with items in his desk, rapidly fin-ishing classroom assignments ahead of the other children. Does he get in trouble because he is smart and bored? The school curriculum and the ditto after ditto handed out by the teacher, who relies on hefty textbooks for reading and vocabulary assignments, may be at the root of his boredom.[44]

"She's not so good," the ESL teacher confirms, her voice quieting to a near whisper when she senses that I've had a hard morning with Kevin's teacher. "I went into the classroom once and just had to put my head down on the table." The sister of a friend, she feels like an ally, even though we have not met before. "But you know what?" she tells me much later, after I have stopped visiting the school, "She is the best option we have got, bet-ter than the other two teachers. We always try to get our ESL students placed with her instead of the other ones."

Kevin's teacher cares. I see this when a new kid registers for school on the second day of my visit in June, something the teachers are not happy about since it is the end of the school year. He is placed with Kevin's teacher, who sympathizes when she realizes he has trouble reading. She assigns Kevin to help him with a drawing assignment, and tells him, "Honey, I like that one the best" when he shows the drawings to her, caus-ing him to break out into a bright grin. The other teachers already have decided the new kid is trouble; they think this is why he has transferred so late in the year. During the afternoon period when the teachers swap stu-dents for the unit on the butterfly cycle, I witness another teacher scream at him, her face two inches from his, so loud it startles me standing four feet away, accusing him of trying to use a pencil as a weapon against another student. She later tells me in the hallway, "I am going to break him." Again, the incident occurs right in front of me, but I don't see it happen. The kindness of Kevin's teacher stands out.

Jonathan Kozol writes about poor-performing schools, noting factors such as lack of teaching training, which may be at play here.[45] He also highlights poor school facilities and discusses how buildings in disrepair, and a lack of proper subject materials, communicate a perception of low negative worth to students.[46] That is not the case at Kevin's school. State of the art, the building, an entirely new construction, opened just two years ago. The walls and floors brightly shine from the waxed, marigold yellow tiles. Every classroom has clear windows, providing visual access to rooms from those walking down the hallways. Cutouts of Max from *Where the Wild Things Are*—and other popular children's books characters— hang from the library ceilings. Only the lunch room bothers me; as true in other district public schools in the city, students sit at one-way benches designed to keep social interaction to a minimum. Monitors require near silence at meals, making children put their heads down when they finish eating. During my lunch with Kevin, the African American vice-principal holds a microphone in the front of the room, giving out prizes to those who answer Jeopardy questions in math correctly. Although preferable to another school that showed *Magic School Bus* episodes to students to keep them quiet at lunch, from a sociologist's perspective this disciplinary tactic inhibits the positive social interactions frequent in the bustling PS 13 lunchroom in New Jersey, where the children share stories while eating.

I highlight the structural differences between Kevin's and Preciliano's school environments not in order to identify what promotes or inhibits school performance. This topic I leave to experts in education. Some children I met in Ohio—and in New Jersey—attended top-performing schools, and others—like Kevin and Preciliano—did not. Rather, the contrasting educational contexts matter because they frame the environments where children socially interact with their peers. The struggling school in New Jersey that Preciliano attended supported children of immigrants, and Spanish-speaking children specifically. Both the charter school and the higher-performing suburban school in New Jersey that I also visited similarly sought to support immigrant families. They sent fliers home in Spanish and English and organized activities for Spanish-speaking parents at their schools, including exercises classes, folkloric dance practices.

and bilingual PTA meetings. Preciliano did not necessarily feel integrated despite this supportive environment. The social distance he felt from his peers, I suspect, related to his missing cues about how to act in this community of second-generation Mexican children, a specific context where children had begun to associate immigration increasingly with illegality.

This was not the case in Ohio, where Mexican children, as a group, remained invisible. The struggling school that Kevin attended in Ohio offered fewer structural supports for immigrant children and no support targeting Mexican children, because he was one of only a few Mexican students who attended the school. The parochial urban school and the low- and middle-income suburban schools I visited also lacked institutional support, with the exception of the occasional ESL teacher, or classroom teacher, who was particularly adept at dealing with diverse student populations. One teacher, for example, invited second grader Daniela's mother in to show the class how to make tortillas by hand for Cinco de Mayo. The students loved the presentation, and Daniela seemed so pleased, reaffirmed by her mother's visit to her classroom. Yet at recess she mostly played alone. Even though she lived in a condo right across the street from the school, none of her classmates ever came to play at her house.

Kevin referred to all the boys in his class as his friends; similarly, though, none came over to play. I attended the joint birthday party for Kevin and his brother when they turned seven and nine. "I don't know," wondered Elizabeth out loud as she put out soda and chips on the plastic tables arranged on the gravel in the front yard of the two-story house she rented. "I don't know. I sent invitations to school . . . " The attendees were all Elizabeth's friends from work and from church. Peers can be an important resource for Mexican American children.[47] But children in Ohio often lacked supportive peer networks readily available to the children I met in New Jersey.

OHIO NEIGHBORS

Mexican families in Ohio lived dispersed throughout the main metropolitan area and surrounding suburban regions, explaining why children, like

Kevin, were so often the only Mexicans in their grade or their schools. One mother who lived in a trailer park and spoke no English said, "I have no friends." Another woman at the other end of the park spoke Spanish, but they rarely visited each other. Any contact with other Mexican families occurred intentionally, when planned. Kevin's mother Elizabeth had a sister, and cousins, living in the same city, but not within walking distance. They had to drive to see each other.

To shop required driving as well. The small businesses catering to the Mexican community did not concentrate in any one neighborhood but rather were scattered across strip malls in different parts of the city. As in New Jersey, the Mexican community had grown in the late 1990s but at a much slower pace. A Puerto Rican mother recalled when Mexicans first started to arrive: "When my cousin came from Chicago, . . . he came and started bringing tortillas and chorizos and small things that he could keep in a freezer in my dad's garage. After that everybody spread the word that if you need anything just go to . . . [Dad's garage]."

In northeastern Ohio many migrated directly from traditional immigrant sending regions in Mexico—such as Guanajuato, Jalisco, and Aguascalientes—at the recommendation of compatriots, to work in the food service industry. Others found jobs at local factories, in construction, in cleaning, or at national chains, like Elizabeth, who had worked in kitchen prep for a chain restaurant ever since her arrival. As in New Jersey, Mexican migrants in Ohio were low-wage workers, but because it was an economically depressed region they enjoyed relatively low housing costs. Elizabeth paid just $400 a month for her small house, which included a living room and dining room, a small kitchen, and two bedrooms and a bath on the second floor—a much larger space than the one room Preciliano's family squeezed into for the same price in New Jersey. Most in Ohio rented their own homes or apartments on minimum-wage incomes. A third of families I interviewed had purchased their own homes.

Because few children in Ohio attended school with other Mexican families (with a few exceptions) or lived near other Mexican children, they reported greater diversity in their friendships. Twice as many in Ohio as in New Jersey had black friends, and two-thirds reported white friends, compared to just under half in New Jersey. Yet these friendships developed primarily in settings outside the home. While most children in New

Jersey had friends over to their houses, only half of the children in Ohio reported that friends visited their homes and even fewer, just a quarter, had sleepovers. Children in Ohio, in general, experienced more isolation from their peers, often interacting with them only at school.[48]

BULLYING

The teasing events that children in Ohio described often seemed more malicious than those in New Jersey, meeting the definition scholars often use for bullying "in which (1) the behavior is intended to harm or disturb, (2) the behavior occurs repeatedly over time, and (3) there is an imbalance of power, with a more powerful person or group attacking a less powerful one."[49] Moreover, race and ethnicity loomed large in children's and parents' accounts of these incidents. An eight-year-old girl told me she was teased: "These African people . . . Well, it was a person, my friend. He always teased me. Well, not always, but one time he was like . . . fighting with me. And he was saying that they are better. But some of my friends were helping me not to be sad for it." A second grader said, "Sometimes they say to me that I'm stupid [because my mom is from Mexico]. . . . Stephen sometimes says to me, 'I don't care about Mexico, and I don't care about where your stupid mom is [from].'" A thirteen-year-old recalled that back when she was in the fifth grade a boy once came over to her while she sat with her friends and, imitating a rural accent, said, "Girl, why don't you go back to Mexico?" And the mother of a nine-year-old explained that her son often got jumped at school. He described an incident when he was teased while riding the bus: "This boy like, like on the seat next to me, he said that Mexicans were ignorant." His mother thought "that is why he [her son] is always saying that he is not Mexican."

Parents in Ohio also often described race as marking their daily interactions. According to one mother, who had lived in Ohio since she was eighteen, "The black people look at you and there is no problem. But the white people . . . sometimes there are people (*hesitates*) . . . . They don't like us. There are times when you go out shopping, like for example, to the mall or something, and the people there are watching you. They think we are going to rob something." And I asked thirty-four-year-old Celia, who had worked in a fast-food restaurant for the last three years that she had lived in Ohio, about her experiences with discrimination. She told me she heard stuff all the time at work, mostly from her boss. "What kinds of things do they say?" I asked her.

"Fuck you *mexicano, estúpido mexicano.*" I am taken aback at the language from this petite rather overly polite mother. She explained further.

"It's just you can tell from the looks, like the way they just look at you, or how they look at you with their eyes like this (*furrowing her brows together*), or sometimes you go fill out a job application and they yell, 'No, no there is no work, go away.' It is more from the American side . . . well, from the . . . not from black people."[50]

Some children spoke of discrimination from other minority children, while some parents felt rejected by white Americans, but not all. Significantly, stories of teasing and discrimination were racializing incidents for families in Ohio.[51] According to Amanda Lewis in writing on how children negotiate racial boundaries in different school settings, "Although racialization processes exist in all settings, they do not operate uniformly across time and space. Thus, local contexts, although operating within a larger racial formation, have some impact on the shape of racial boundaries and on how they operate in everyday life."[52] Differences in the ways children and families experience teasing—and infer discrimination through teasing events—are telling.

In fact, a number of the children in New Jersey shrugged off the teasing as other kids "messing around" and, even though it could hurt their feelings, said it wasn't important. One mother of a seventh-grade boy in New Jersey explained,

> The boys that are his age, the new thing now . . . It seems this is what is going on: if there is a Jewish boy, "Oh, you're a Jew; you're black." They're starting to do this at school. I get so aggravated with Brandon. I tell him, "You're Mexican; you're a minority. You might think it's funny to joke around with each other." His friend Mike is Jewish. They've had spots arguing with each other. Michael makes reference to Brian being Mexican, joking with each other. Then Brian makes a reference to him being Jewish. "Come on, you guys! That's really inappropriate. How would you like it if . . ."

If in New Jersey the teasing around ethnic identity constituted part of peer group play, accounts from children in Ohio suggested more harsh interactions, bullying from children who were not friends, and more severe consequences from these interactions.

Twelve-year-old Amalia in Ohio explained what happened in her middle school when she hung out with other Spanish-speaking friends, "'cause in school, if we say something English, they hear us and are like, 'Oh my gosh,' you know, so we kind of like say it to ourselves in Spanish. . . . And sometimes, they get mad at like . . . they're like, 'Uh, this is not Mexico.' I was like, 'I don't care. I feel comfortable speaking in Spanish. Why? You got a problem with it?' And they're like, 'Yeah, I got a problem with it . . .'" The interaction, as she described it, escalated quickly into a racially tinged altercation: "Like, there's like, these, this girl, she was like, she was like, 'Oh, you know why, Oh, you know why people can't, Mexican people can't play Uno?' And I was like, 'Why?' And she was like, 'Because they get all the green cards.' And then I was like, 'Why are you telling me that?' 'Because I don't like Spanish people, and I don't like, like you.' . . . And I was like, 'So?' And she was just like, 'So? What you mean, so?'"

Mexican children in Ohio, at times, might have been considered illegal by their peers, with legal status implied in some teasing incidents. However, from children's perspectives, it was their being Mexican, not their legal status, that marked altercations. Unlike in New Jersey, where children often reported incidents among friends, for children in Ohio teasing contributed to a school environment in which they often felt excluded.

RAISING MY CHILDREN

"Would you want your friends or the kids in your class to know what country your parents are from?" I asked Temo at age seven when he was in the first grade in Ohio, while practicing the interview questions I would be using with children.

"No."

"Why not?"

"'Cause it's really embarrassing."

"Which part of it is embarrassing?" His answer surprised me. We spoke Spanish at home and spent a lot of time with Latino families in New Jersey and in Ohio. I hoped he might develop a sense of self-esteem even though we lived in a primarily white college town.

"I'm not telling." I pushed, asking what about it embarrassed him, "The whole thing. It's embarrassing." Growing uncomfortable, he would not elaborate.

For fun I interviewed both my boys at the beginning of the project in Ohio, when Temo was seven and Dylan just three, and then again after I completed my last interviews, Temo at age ten and Dylan at age seven, a first grader just as Temo had been when I started the whole endeavor. I meant the interviews to be personal family mementos, but when I read them over through the gaze of a sociologist contemplating the effects of migration and community on children's development, Temo's comments hit on this theme of difference that other children also articulated. And who better understood the differences between growing up in New Jersey and in Ohio than Temo, who had made the move from schools between northeastern Ohio and central New Jersey, not once but twice, and then again to upstate New York.

"Would you want your friends or kids from school to know that your dad is from Mexico or would you prefer that they don't know?" I asked Temo the same question I had four years earlier, this time over the summer right before he started fifth grade sitting on the front porch of our Albany home.

"I prefer that they don't know."

"Why?"

"Because all the kids call me Chinese, and they tease me about being Chinese because I look like it, and if they found out I'm Mexican I wouldn't really like that because then they'd start teasing me about what different kinds of gross foods they think I like." Temo's complaints about being mistaken for Chinese actually had started in second grade in Ohio. Although he didn't talk about it much, Temo usually described himself as Mexican American and felt upset when people thought he was Chinese.

"Why do you think they might tease you?"

"I don't know, because maybe it's just a friendly welcome or something, but it kind of really hurts my feelings."

"But you never feel like you want to correct them when they call you Chinese, you don't feel like you wanna say, 'No wait, I'm Mexican'?" I asked.

"I'm too shy. And then they'd start teasing me that I'm just white . . . not like tan."

In his primarily majority-white school in Ohio, at a young age, Temo felt embarrassed by being different, and this perhaps explained his discomfort at being singled out when misidentified as Chinese. A bit older in elementary school in Albany, where 51 percent of the students were Caucasian, 31 percent African American, 11 percent Asian, and 6 percent Latino, Temo's discomfort arose more from not looking the part than from his father's immigrant background. In fact, Dylan in first grade at the same school said he didn't care if other kids knew about his father and that he would tell if asked directly. Still, his friends did not know that Raul had been born in Mexico. "No, I don't tell because it's not like . . . it's weird to say, 'Oh everybody, my dad is from Mexico.'"

I wanted to know if Temo had felt the same way about being called Chinese at the other schools he had attended in New Jersey and in Ohio. "Now, you've been to other schools, right? This isn't the only school that you've ever been to. Did you have the same problems in other schools?" I thought he might talk about Ohio.

"Yeah . . . except for one. When I went to New Jersey for a couple months." Temo attended a school in New Jersey for the second half of third grade. The school lay across the river from the one Preciliano attended, in an extremely diverse pocket of a range of middle-income families, many immigrants and many professionals. The parents of one classmate down the block were lawyers, the father white and the mother African American, and another friend's Italian mother stayed home while his Salvadoran father worked in construction.

"They didn't tease you there?" This surprised me, as I had not remembered Temo feeling especially welcomed at that school, and the transition for six months had not been easy.

"No. They understood that I was Mexican. And that was pretty nice."

Temo had not felt out of place with peers in New Jersey, while at school in both Ohio and Albany differences had felt uncomfortable.

HOSTILE SCHOOL ENVIRONMENTS

For younger children like Temo attention to racial or ethnic distinctions may hurt feelings but not prevent children's friendship development. At

Kevin's school in Ohio, I frequently saw white and black kids playing together at recess, girls sitting on each other's laps on the swings and Kevin playing basketball with both white and black kids. Yet by the time children enter middle school, racial/ethnic markers become more salient and the teasing more severe. Several older children in Ohio faced especially hostile school environments.[53]

In one case, a girl, Faviola, was harassed so much that her mother returned with her to Mexico. They had first moved to Detroit but then came to Ohio when Faviola was ten, all with visas, as legal migrants. "[My daughter] had a really hard time in school. . . . She would come home crying every day from school because the other children said things to her. I told her, 'Don't worry, daughter; ignore them. Go to the principal.' 'No, [my daughter would answer], it's that the director doesn't listen to me either.'" Eventually, someone pushed Faviola down the stairs at school, breaking her arm. Her mother was so enraged that nothing was done about the incident that she took Faviola back to Mexico to finish high school there. I met them after they had returned to the United States. Faviola's mother felt that people in Ohio were racist and looked down upon Mexicans, more so than in Detroit. Recently they had gone to a fair at the high school: "We went to walk around, but the girls and boys there were making fun of us. The youth were laughing and saying things that I didn't understand." Particularly important in this story was that the family perceived administrators and teachers to be turning a blind eye to the incidents.[54] Teachers might not notice, or be loath to address, the racial nature of the incidents because Mexican immigrant children in schools were so invisible as a social group,

Carolina had four children, two US-born children and two older children, ages seventeen and eighteen, who had migrated with her from Mexico when they were ten and eleven. Both had dropped out of high school and, when I met the family, worked full time. She recalled, "In school they felt bad because the other kids laughed at them . . . the black kids. They would call them all sorts of names because they came from Mexico."

"Do you think that's why they didn't like school?" I asked.

"Well, they didn't like it because they always complained to us that, look, this guy said something to me or this other one said this . . . 'and I don't answer him,' my son, the older one, would say, 'because I am going to have to fight in school and I can't handle them saying these things.' And then my other son, they younger one, had a teacher that was always against him, on top of him . . . always calling on him and always correcting him, and he noticed. He said, 'Mom, I think the teacher of such and such subject is racist because he doesn't like me, he said he doesn't like me.' And now they don't go to school."

"You think that is why they dropped out?"

"I think it's because of that. Besides that they didn't complain. But they did say . . . there was a teacher who always yelled at them in front of everyone else."

Older children in New Jersey described gang involvement or a teenage pregnancy, as in the case of Camilo's brother, as potentially derailing their educational pathways. At the time of my interviews, there were no Mexican- or Latino-affiliated gangs at the schools in Ohio that children attended. Instead, older children might drop out of school because they were bullied, were ignored, or felt excluded and because schoolteachers and staff did not address these problems.

BEING AN IMMIGRANT IN OHIO

In Ohio, legal status minimally affected children on a daily basis. Although young children understood the threat of deportability, they described—and I observed—few moments in which legality came up during children's everyday interactions, even in bullying incidents with peers. As children in Ohio navigated social environments composed primarily of non-Hispanic whites and blacks, Mexican children's social status related to their own or their parents' legality loomed less significant compared to tensions they experienced related to their race or ethnicity.

Still children in Ohio talked about being proud to be Mexican and about their immigrant heritage more often than did children in New Jersey. Perhaps because of their obvious differences children did not see any reason to hide their background as much as children in New Jersey. Significantly, however, when I asked what words best described them, children in Ohio picked more heterogeneous identifiers. In New Jersey

Table 6   Children's Choice of the Best Word to Describe Them

	New Jersey (n = 52)	Ohio (n = 50)
Percentage of children who chose *Mexican*	42	20
Percentage of children who chose *Mexican American*	31	16
Percentage of children who chose *Hispanic*	2	4
Percentage of children who chose *Latino*	2	7
Percentage of children who chose *white*	2	9
Percentage of children who chose *American*	4	8
Percentage of children who chose *Spanish*	4	20
Percentage of children who chose *Spanish American*	6	7
Percentage of children who chose *black*[a]	0	2

[a] Not all children interviewed answered this question. Though only one child chose *black* as the *best* identifier, seventeen of the children I interviewed in both states said they were black None of the children I interviewed looked to me to be Afro-Mexican or seemed to identify as such, so I am not sure why they said this. But ten of the seventeen were ages five, six, and seven, and I often thought that perhaps they considered their hair color to qualify them as black.

nearly three out of four chose *Mexican* or *Mexican American* compared to just one in three in Ohio (table 6). In Ohio, twice as many identified as white or American as in New Jersey. Especially telling, a large group in Ohio chose *Spanish* as the best identifier; they seemed to recognize that their heritage made them somewhat different, but they identified in ways that marked the difference between them and their peers as related to their language ability. In Ohio, children felt no need to hide the heritage, but they did seem to want to minimize these differences.

I visit Kevin and Elizabeth, still living in the blue, slightly crooked, two-bedroom house on a street known for housing prostitutes a year after I observed Kevin in his second-grade classroom. Before the boys had been living with just their mother. Kevin's father has now moved back in again.

Kevin has just finished third grade. He had three teachers this year. "The first moved to a different school. And then I moved to a different third-grade class," he tells me.

"How did you do [on your report card]?" I ask.

"D."

"All Ds?"

"No. D, B, A, C+."

In second grade, Kevin didn't tell other children that he was Mexican. This year, he did. "Sometimes I don't like it that they know," he explains.

"Do you know people who are immigrants?" I ask him at the end of our interview.

"Me," he answers, laughing nervously.

"What do you think it is like to be an immigrant?"

"Different."

"What kind of different?"

"Sort of bad."

"What's bad about it?"

"I don't really want to be different," Kevin answers.

ON BEING DIFFERENT

Most children, like Kevin, do not like to feel different from their peers. How do children determine who is different? In other words, what makes children draw distinctions between themselves and others, what sociologists sometimes describe as symbolic boundaries?[55] On the surface, children like Preciliano might feel more integrated living in the environment in central New Jersey, with a vibrant Mexican American community, as compared to children like Kevin, living in a place where the Mexican community was relatively invisible. Yet for Kevin and Preciliano, both unauthorized migrants, symbolic boundaries in peer interactions were drawn in different ways.

For Kevin and for others living in northeastern Ohio where the Mexican community was small and the infrastructure to support members of the community was underdeveloped, illegality rarely manifested itself in children's daily interactions with peers. To be sure, legal status affected children in Ohio; they feared the intervention of the state in their home life and worried about what could happen in the event of a deportation or detention. And in the cases in which parents were detained or deported, children's daily lives in their households changed dramatically.

In their peer group interactions, however, children described teasing and exclusion based on their racial or ethnic background as Spanish speakers or Mexicans.[56] Interactions with children about their immigrant heritage often took on a racial tone, with children pointing out the race of the children who teased them for being Mexican. Children took these incidents seriously, not as jokes, and felt—at times—that school administrators and teachers supported the behavior by ignoring it, much as they overlooked the very small population of Mexican immigrant children in the area schools. Of course, for many nonimmigrant residents in Ohio, *Mexican* was synonymous with *illegal,* and thus legality does matter in shaping the negative connotation that being different had for Kevin. However, children like him took care in defining themselves as Mexicans, often describing themselves as white or even black and often Spanish, minimizing the ethnic difference with their peers who were, so often, white and black native-born Americans.

In central New Jersey, a new community of Mexicans with a large and concentrated settlement pattern, children acted differently. There they carefully monitored knowledge of their and their parents' nativity for fear that legal status would become the means for exclusion. In a local context with a highly visible Latino and Mexican community, the threat of deportability affected children's neighbors and other community members. Aware of this, children used nativity as a social status marker among peers that potentially differentiated children from each other. More so than in Ohio, children's interactions with peers were fraught with seemingly innocuous references to legal status. Though bothered by these references, children might at times not give them much importance. After all, they well knew that other children were in similar situations to their own as Spanish-speaking newcomers in New Jersey. Teachers and administrators in their schools openly addressed this type of teasing, castigating the behavior.

Yet in these interactions they reinvented illegality as a negative social trait, as a source of difference not to be confused with being Mexican. When children tease each other about legal status and remain silent, much more often than not, about their own or their parents' immigrant background for fear of being associated with this source of difference, the stigma associated with being illegal is recreated in peer group interactions.

Goffman writes of those individuals whose stigma is not visibly evident, explaining, "The issue is not that of managing tension generated during social contacts, but rather that of managing information about his failing. To display or not to display; to tell or not to tell; to let on or not to let on; to lie or not to lie; and in each case, to whom, and how, when and where."[57] Children in both Ohio and New Jersey thought about, and engaged in, disclosure management about their immigrant heritage, and in some cases in Ohio their Mexican heritage, suggesting just how much legal status has become, in some situations, a managed identity. It has begun to accrue the power of a social status distinction. This social status distinction affects children both at home with their family members and in their schools and other activities with their peers.

The social boundaries—or the "objectified forms of social differences manifest in unequal access to and unequal distribution of resources (material and nonmaterial) and social opportunities"—that exist in a particular location matter greatly to children's drawing of symbolic boundaries.[58] In certain community contexts, like the specific site in New Jersey where the Mexican community was quite concentrated, immigration status might matter more in the ways children enacted symbolic boundaries, reflecting their understandings of differential access to resources due to legal status. In other settings, like the site in northeastern Ohio where the Mexican community was small and relatively invisible to the white majority population, nonwhite minority status might produce significant social boundary distinctions. There children conflated immigration with the more salient racial or ethnic distinctions in the symbolic boundaries they enacted in interactions with other children.

My heart sinks the day after I gave in and played cops and robbers with Preciliano's army green plastic figurines. It is hot on the playground at PS 13; I lean against the mesh of the chain-link fence, scanning the different games on the playground. The third-grade inclusion classroom organizes its daily soccer game in the back corner. Another group of boys plays a less organized game to the far right. The girls still stalk behind the light-skinned, green-eyed beauty; she has not brought the doll today, but they continue to squabble. I hear a boy playing the daily cops and robbers game. My gaze trails him for a moment as he chases two girls. He shouts out, in English with a strong Spanish accent, that he is "Immigration" and will take them to jail.[59]

"Kids want to gain control of their lives, and they want to share that sense of control with each other."[60] William Corsaro suggests that kids enact unique peer group cultures characterized by children's desire "to create and share emotionally in the power and control adults have over them."[61] Under circumstances in which US immigration policy is inflexible, and immigration reform is at a national impasse, children understand the ways immigration policy controls their lives and those of their parents. It is perhaps not surprising, then, that symbolic boundaries based on children's understandings of legal-status differences emerge as a salient feature of children's peer group culture, with illegality becoming a source of stigma in children's relationships.

6 Conclusion

REFRAMING ILLEGALITY

By the end of the first decade of the twenty-first century, the US foreign-born population numbered approximately forty million.[1] Of these, more than one in four were unauthorized, a significantly higher proportion than in the 1990s.[2] Enforcement policies have targeted this population, seeking to deport four hundred thousand individuals every year regardless of the length of time they have lived in the country and the types of family ties they have with US citizens. Legalization programs have diminished, so that most of the 11.7 million unauthorized migrants cannot regularize their status, no matter how long they have lived in the country and what types of family ties they have with US citizens. What does it mean to be illegal, to be legal, and to be an immigrant, or the child of immigrants, under these conditions?

Immigrant community members, activists, and advocates articulate urgent concerns over the new meanings that legal status has for their families and communities. DREAMers, or undocumented youth who arrived in the country as children, were raised here, and were educated in US schools, have come out of the shadows "undocumented and unafraid," challenging lawmakers across the country to fix what everyone refers to as

Opposite: Photograph by Bob Anderson

the broken immigration system.[3] Public policy institutes, like the Applied Research Council, have published on the devastating costs of deportation on children and families, especially when children end up in foster care after a parent's detention or deportation.[4] Think tanks like the Center for American Progress promote immigration reform, while advocacy groups like First Focus frame immigration reform as essential for children's health and well-being, and activist organizations like the Domestic Workers Alliance define immigration policy as a women's issue.[5]

Attentive to this emerging social problem, a burgeoning body of academic literature focuses specifically on legal-status complexities.[6] De Genova defines illegality as a political identity,[7] while others qualify legal status as just one aspect of citizenship, along with rights, participation, and belonging.[8] Gonzales suggests that the impact of legal status varies in quality over the life course.[9] And Menjívar reminds that the concept of illegality does not fully account for "many in-between and ambiguous legal categories that the law creates nor the fluidity with which individuals sometimes move from one category to another, often to a realm of legal uncertainty."[10]

In this vein, I have considered in *Everyday Illegal* how children and families fare in a specific demographic and policy climate in which legal uncertainty is heightened, the unauthorized population grows, and simultaneously the efforts to remove this population intensify. Children's experiences, and those of their families, suggest remarkably pervasive relationships between public policy and familial life. Immigration policy directly defines what—and who—is illegal. Yet under restrictive policies illegality becomes a socially constructed category wielding great influence on young children as they begin to make sense of the increasing influence of legal status on everyday life. Of course, as the accounts of the families I interviewed show, the impacts depend on each individual family member's position in the family, his or her identification with the categories of legal or illegal, and the legal status of the other members of the family.

IMPACTS FOR FAMILIES

First, today's enforcement tactics create a gendered culture of fear, elevating illegality, and legal uncertainty, into a public health issue.[11] This social problem affects all families with any unauthorized members, no matter whether the family in fact faces a deportation or has had a direct interaction with Immigration and Customs Enforcement agents. When deportation tactics target wage-earning fathers, fear, stress, and anxiety result. Women like Inés, whose husband has never been detained nor deported, experience mental health impacts from the threat of deportation. Given the severe economic and emotional hardships that Inés's friend Sandra experienced in the wake of her husband's incarceration, the mere possibility of an unanticipated family separation causes Inés great stress. Children at remarkably young ages also fear the separations that deportation entails. They often do not discuss their fears with their parents, but they worry greatly about what may happen to their parents or siblings—even when they have only seen these stories on the news—if the "police-ICE" take parents away.

These are not irrational fears. When ICE does deport a parent—usually fathers—"suddenly single mothers" face great economic challenges and accompanying lifestyle changes, like the former stay-at-home mother in New Jersey who moved eight times in three years after her husband's deportation, and whose eleven-year-old daughter began to babysit her younger brother every day while she worked. When ICE deports a father, he cannot provide for his children in the United States from low-wage jobs in Mexico, especially if he experiences stigma as a former migrant. Those who cannot find a way to return to the United States are likely to lose touch with their children, like the father I interviewed in Mexico who could not find stable work and whose US citizen ex-wife had remarried. When she finally called to give him a surprise Father's Day present, his youngest son wouldn't talk to him, breaking his heart. Deportation tactics create single-parent households and cripple fathers' ability to play active roles in their children's lives. They place undue burdens on women and children who face stresses associated with severe, and sudden, economic hardship.

Second, illegality alters gender and generational relationships within families. When spouses do not share statuses, imbalances heighten existing gender inequities in relationships. For women like Isabel, the status difference compounds their vulnerability in abusive relationships with men in their lives, who may threaten to report them in order to exert power over them or keep them from leaving. Although most evident in cases of abuse, vulnerability due to status differences also marks nonabusive relationships. Women without status depend more on their legal-status partners, especially if they face problems in their own employment; the man's employment takes precedence, often dictating the family routines. In contrast, women with legal status who live with partners lacking legal status have the economic edge. However, these women contribute even more to all types of family labor, perhaps—as one mother suggested—to buoy their husbands' masculinity when illegality otherwise may undermine it. When illegality compounds gender disadvantages in families, women may feel stuck and especially burdened.

Legal-status distinctions within families also create tensions in parent-child relationships. US citizen children's full legal rights may give them an advantage over unauthorized parents, who do not feel at liberty to exert their authority in certain situations. Additionally, unauthorized parents may depend more on their children, as translators or child "brokers," than they might otherwise. Yet children do not necessarily like the added responsibility and may resent parents' increased dependence on them. Tellingly, US citizen children in the mixed-status families I interviewed did less housework than children in same-status families, suggesting that children may be able to use the symbolic power of legal-status distinctions given them to negotiate out of doing work at home. Children without legal status, and especially unauthorized girls, contribute the most to household labor, further suggesting how legal status compounds gender inequalities in families.

Third, illegality makes for unequal outcomes for children's social mobility over time—evident in the different trajectories of US-born children and unauthorized children. These differential pathways cause insidious inequalities between children and especially siblings of different legal statuses, like Camilo and his older siblings Silvio and Rebecca. Legal status shapes children's own migratory processes, with long-term consequences especially in cases of family separation, such as that experienced by Silvio. It also alters children's daily routines, since those with status have access to greater resources when US citizen children like Camilo succeed. This, in turn, results in unequal prospects both within and outside school. Legal status also may affect children's identity formation, with unauthorized children feeling that they are politically excluded from the United States and that they belong to Mexico, but simultaneously feeling excluded from Mexico, since they cannot travel there and thus are more at home in the United States. In contrast, US citizen children may know more about Mexico, but they relate merely symbolically to this identity. Legal uncertainty for children living in Mexico, those living unauthorized in the United States, and US-born children creates a discernible pecking order, with US-born children experiencing the greatest advantages. These inequalities in daily experiences likely have long-term consequences—exacerbating the intergenerational transmission of inequality and creating highly unequal outcomes among children that will only further increase over time.

Fourth, illegality shapes children's identity development in peer group settings, affecting all children regardless of their own legal status or that of their family members. The impacts vary across different local community contexts. While the children I interviewed in both New Jersey and Ohio described negative connotations with immigration and foreign-born status, for children in Ohio legal status correlated highly with their racial or ethnic identities. Racializing incidents characterized the stigma they experienced as Mexicans and the bullying episodes that marked their peer group interactions. Children in Ohio chose identifiers that downplayed differences from their peers.

In contrast, children in New Jersey claimed their Mexican American identity yet simultaneously actively utilized, or pointedly avoided, concepts of legality in peer relationships. Children socially constructed illegality negatively, remained silent on legal status in interactions with their peers, and may—in cases like Preciliano's—have come to stigmatize others to whom they attributed the characteristics of illegality. For children in New Jersey, legal status was a secret, and legal status distinctions arose in their creation of symbolic boundaries with peers. Being Mexican American or Mexican was not problematic, but being illegal was, something even US-born citizen children of immigrants, and legal migrant children, picked up on and enacted in their interactions.

Today illegality shapes power relationships between spouses and between parents and children, creates unequal opportunities for youth, and emerges as a stigma, marking symbolic boundaries in peer group settings. It generates public health concerns. Evidence from the families I met and interviewed during a period of heightened enforcement and few opportunities for legalization suggests a reframing of how we understand legal status in contemporary society.

REFRAMING ILLEGALITY

I often have considered legal status to be an administrative category that marks inclusion or exclusion from the United States. Even as such, the categorization is messy. If you need legal status to obtain a driver's license, being unauthorized means being unable to drive without great risk. In 2013, eleven states granted driver's licenses to the unauthorized; the administrative hurdles legal status caused were thus greater for the unauthorized living in the other thirty-nine states, like in Ohio and New Jersey, where the unauthorized cannot obtain drivers' licenses. If you need an official photo ID to ride Amtrak or to board a plane, and if you must show proof of legal residence to obtain this ID, than legal status matters differently than if you can board a train by merely paying for a ticket.[12] Thus the meaning of legal status as an administrative category shifts depending on its importance for navigating daily life. Being an unauthorized migrant from Italy in the 1920s would not have prevented you from finding a job in New York City, when one did not need a Social Security number to work, and there were few unauthorized immigrants in city at the time.[13] Today, however, not only must you present a series of documents to work, but the documents must be valid, as many employers now participate in the E-Verify system.[14] Furthermore, presenting falsified paperwork can lead to an arrest for immigration fraud and a permanent bar from future legalization.[15] Legal status administratively complicates daily life in different ways depending on when and where one lives.

But these administrative issues do not capture the stories I have told in these pages. Families certainly described difficulties associated with not being able to drive, struggles to find well-paid, nonexploitative work, and travel and health care restrictions. Legal status nearly entirely explains the differences in health insurance coverage among those I interviewed, for example. And children spoke of legal status as the most important factor in decisions related to future college attendance. Yet an intimate look at the meanings of illegality within family relationships suggests the need for an alternate frame for understanding the impact of legal status on children and families' lives.

When children avoid revealing immigration status in peer group settings, and subtly express the stigma they relate to legal status, it sounds remarkably like the ways children negotiate ethnic and racial boundaries in peer group interactions.[16] Symbolic boundaries lie at the heart of social inequality;[17] children's practice of drawing symbolic boundaries based on immigrant and legal status distinctions suggests that legal status is more than an administrative category for children. Like race and ethnicity, illegality becomes a primary axis for social difference.

In a similar vein, legal status creates concrete differences in features of children's daily lives—in the types of work they do at home and in their activities outside the home— ultimately affecting their prospects over time and creating a social status pecking order. The process is similar to the way child-rearing practices among middle-class, working-class, and low-income families create unequal outcomes for children over time, as described by Annette Lareau.[18] Just as class distinctions have been shown to be highly correlated with social mobility, being legal or illegal is likely to have long-term consequences over the life course.[19] An administrative fix to legal status later in life will thus not necessarily resolve the negative impacts of having had an unauthorized status as a child—as the impacts of any period of time out of status are likely to cascade, influencing children's future social mobility over time.

Within families, legal status alters power relationships between spouses and between parents and children and affects gender and generational negotiations.[20] Regardless of who in the family lacks legal status, illegality creates greater burdens in the home for women. It also inverts power relations between parents and children, since the typical mixed-status family comprises unauthorized parents and US-born children.[21] Ironically, children experience the inversion as a burden. Intersections between legal status, age, and gender complicate familial relationships, just as race and class may intersect with gender in negotiating family relationships.[22] As Mary Romero has suggested, under restrictive immigration enforcement practices, analysis of family life must include the consideration of citizenship status along with race, class, ethnicity, and gender.[23] Legal status may invert traditional power distinctions between parents and children while heightening power distinctions between men and women.

Gender, race or ethnicity, and class have impacts outside family relationships. Indeed, health disparity research typically considers both biological and social disparities related to gender, race or ethnicity, and class, as well as disability, geographic location, and sexual orientation.[24] Accounts from the families I interviewed suggest significant emerging health disparities related to legal status distinctions.[25] Punitive immigration policies underlie the emergence of this public health issue, just as segregation policies in the early twentieth century may explain some unequal health outcomes along the lines of race.[26]

Stories from those I interviewed call for a reframing of our understanding of illegality. Under restrictive immigration policy the social impacts of illegality intensify and legal status becomes, not just an administrative category, but a departure point for social differentiation. Public policy creates the conditions under which legality becomes a prominent feature of the social hierarchy. When legalization programs exist, those who want to remain in the United States—spouses of US citizens or parents of US citizen children—have a mechanism by which to do so. Illegality, under a more open system of immigration, has fewer social consequences within families and remains much more of an administrative classification. When legalization programs do not exist and when enforcement practices target the unauthorized, illegality accrues greater power to differentiate members of the population, something that children of all ages acutely understand.

CHANGING PERSPECTIVES

I struggle to qualify the extent to which my own perspective has evolved and the ways it may have altered my understanding of legal-status distinctions. I grew up in a South Jersey town where developers finished buying surrounding farmlands while I was still in elementary school. Trucks stopped picking up carrot deliveries shortly after I was old enough to ride my bike down to the concrete lot next to the train tracks that was covered with flattened, blackened carrots you only knew were carrots from the squishy sweet smell released when you wobbled riding over them. Farmworkers lived nearby, but I had not known that, not at the time. They harvested corn, tomatoes, zucchini, blueberries, and carrots (of course), among other crops, a bit further south, but lived isolated on the farms where they worked seasonally. Slowly, in the late 1980s and early 1990s, a Mexican-born workforce began to outnumber Puerto Rican and Caribbean migrants who had previously labored on the fields and orchards of the Northeast.[27]

Although ignorant of these neighbors in the 1980s, I knew something of the plight of Central American refugees.[28] I grew up Quaker, attending meeting and the Friends school where my parents worked, surrounded by some involved in the early Sanctuary movement. Nearly too young to recall the time in 1985 when a Salvadoran woman in sanctuary at a nearby Methodist church came to speak at the Friday morning school assembly, I remember the hushed tones in which adults spoke of her after a tenth grader called the police and a teacher hid with "Paz" in a library closet for a tense hour or so.[29] After they had fled war-torn countries, legality loomed large for those living in the shadows, this I knew.[30] Later between tenth and eleventh grade I tutored Central American children in Tucson, Arizona, for a group with ties to Quakers and also to John Fife.[31] That summer, we befriended young men in sanctuary at the Southside Presbyterian Church. I recall nights I lay awake in my bunk listening to helicopters circling above and wondering if they sought the friends we played soccer with. Legal status mattered greatly to these young men, who could not leave the church grounds without risking the game of cat-and-mouse perpetrated by local agents who knew where they were staying, and the status that the address implied.[32]

In New Jersey in the late 1990s, legal status did not carry with it the same restrictions. I like to tell people that Miguel was my first Mexican friend in New Jersey; I think it's true. We met in a haze of smoke at one of my stoner boyfriend's fabulously tiresome parties in 1997. Miguel and I locked eyes in the dark room where everyone else sat on the wall-to-wall carpet, backs up against the sides of the room, conversing, ever so occasionally, in a slow daze. Bored, we moved into the bright light of the kitchen, whose cream-colored linoleum flooring had begun to curl, unglued, at the corners. Leaning against prefabricated faux-wood cabinets, we talked for what seemed hours, complaining about the capitalists, idealizing revolutions.

Originally from rural Oaxaca but having won admission to study at a prestigious Mexico City university, Miguel came to work in New Jersey when he could no longer afford to study. He went from college classrooms to harvesting watermelon, cantaloupe, peaches, tomatoes, eggplant, peppers, and cabbage an hour south of the town where I grew up. The work was hard; when he learned of the more exploitative conditions on neighboring farms, Miguel tried to help organize fellow farmworkers. That too proved difficult. Frustrated, he met someone who took him a few hours north, where he found work in a restaurant. "Actually, I didn't even have to look [for a job]" he explained. "A friend took me to another friend's house and introduced me as the new guy. They asked if I wanted to work and I said yes." The owners knew he did not have papers. With the advantage of his education, Miguel seamlessly transitioned into the central New Jersey economy the same year I graduated college. We plotted, at times, around his lack of a valid Social Security number, Miguel teaching me his creative strategies to stay straight despite lacking "papers." Eventually Miguel finished his studies at a community college and began an engineering career in manufacturing.

Raúl too fashioned a decent life around the legal-status dilemma; this was why he originally worked as Luís. He drove, despite his unauthorized status, and earned a good salary from his landscaping job. Ten to twelve dollars an hour usually fifty or sixty hours a week seemed plenty to me as a twenty-one-year-old college graduate in 2000—less than I made at my first full-time job as director of social services at the Puerto Rican Action Board, but more than my earnings a few years later as a graduate student. Illegal status did not force Raúl to hide from the police, as it did to my Central American refugee friends in Tucson. And Miguel left his farming job fairly easily, even though he did not have permission to work in the United States. Although both are perhaps remarkable men, with advantages that not all migrant workers had, neither lived hiding in the shadows of New Jersey in the late 1990s.

By the early 2000s, New Jersey—along with Long Island and many other parts of the country—had undergone a demographic transition, becoming a new destination for Mexican migrants.[33] In 2005 I spent the weekend in my hometown visiting my mother. I had forgotten my promise to call a family I had spent time with during fieldwork in Mexico, but at both the local 7–11 and Wawa phone cards to Mexico had sold out. Mexican and Central American workers now staffed the local pizzeria blocks from our home, this population of immigrants no longer confined to farm labor. New Jersey communities had changed.

Probably a bit naive about the difficulties that legal status presented, I worked with Miguel, and other friends, distributing fliers and educating about legal rights regardless of immigration status. We organized ESL classes and workshops on things like workers' compensation and on how to apply for an ITIN number, which enabled one to file taxes without a Social Security number. The activist reasoning: the longer one had a record of outstanding "citizenship" in this country, the easier it would be to legalize when the option arose.

I just looked in my old files and dug up the flier we used titled "Information for Non-Citizens." The top of the flier lists what to do when in contact with police, and the bottom when in contact with INS. "If stopped by the police while in a car," the flier states, "upon request you must show license, registration, and proof of insurance. You do not have to consent to a car search, but you may. If you are not the driver of the vehicle, you are not required to show any identification." By 2010, local police had arrested some men and women I met in Ohio when they were passengers in vehicles and reported them to ICE. The culture surrounding legal rights in the United States since 9/11, since the Patriot Act, since the replacement of the INS by the USCIS and ICE, and since the rise of Secure Communities programs has changed.[34] Although technically the advice may still hold, concretely for many of those I met during my fieldwork who were detained by local police it did not.

Miguel stopped community organizing years ago, busy with family and work obligations. Recently he explained a new level of his frustrations. "Next year is my last year," Miguel told me over the phone, "I am leaving, I am fed up." Married to a US citizen but with no possibilities for legalization, Miguel explained that this was one of the reasons he stopped being so involved. "Why do it anymore?" Life for any immigrant is hard, no matter the historical period. But to hit a full stop because of legal status, even after having learned English, finished a career, married a US citizen, and contributed to the community by organizing and teaching ESL classes, is demoralizing. Miguel had no interest in offering false hope, or dreams deferred, to others.

I also stopped grassroots work. Age changes standpoint, perspective, priorities, and energy. I married and became a mother; I divorced and got my PhD. I went to Mexico on a Fulbright and then to Ohio for my first job. I watched my oldest son grapple with his identity, now defining himself squarely as Mexican American, and my younger son struggle to understand the nuances of immigration.[35] I sought understanding of the Mexican community in Ohio as compared to the one I had known in New Jersey. And I came to find out that the circumstances of families I knew in New Jersey and in Ohio had changed in response to a steady shift in immigration policy over the same time period. Friends faced risks they had not previously worried about; some had been detained. One young man who had helped organize our outreach workshops disappeared on his way back to New Jersey after returning to Puebla to visit his sick mother and then attend her funeral. He spent months in a midwestern prison before anyone could locate him. Today my legal permanent resident ex-husband faces the possibility of deportation if he applies for citizenship, and his children in Mexico have come of age without reunifying with their father.

Though less idealistic than I was fifteen years ago, I refuse to consider myself jaded. I have changed, but so have immigration policies, and family relationships right along with them. As policies have grown more exclusive, and more difficult to negotiate, outcomes have begun to have a much more long-standing impact on me and Raúl and our children and on the 110 children I interviewed in New Jersey and in Ohio, and 91 of their parents. Under these policy conditions, legal status is not a temporary characteristic or a clerical problem to work around. It has become a part of the contemporary social status hierarchy.

THE MEANINGS OF LEGAL STATUS

Historically, in the United States, specific immigrant groups have been targeted during different periods by immigration policy and legislation.

Deportation campaigns in the 1920s and 1930s devastated many communities, illegally removing Mexican families—nearly 60 percent of whom were US citizens.[36] Similarly, the Chinese Exclusion Act (1882) halted new Chinese immigration and prevented Chinese in the United States from becoming citizens. This legislation, in place until 1943, limited immigration on the basis of race and had huge social impacts on families—leading to the rise of what Nakano Glenn refers to as the split-household family strategy—and ultimately entire communities.[37] Those immigration policies, similarly restrictive to those in place today, had devastating social impacts on families. However, they identified race, rather than legal status, as the primary characteristic on which exclusion was based. Even the Central Americans aided through the Sanctuary movement in the 1980s experienced exclusionary immigration policies based to some extent on nationality, on their race and ethnic background, with refugees leaving communist Cuba in the same years welcomed into the United States while those fleeing civil wars in Guatemala, El Salvador, and Nicaragua were rejected.

No doubt, today's restrictive immigration policies disproportionately affect Latino and black immigrant communities.[38] However, they differ in a few crucial ways from past patterns, contributing to the salience of illegality as an independent category of social status differentiation. First, as Nancy Foner has pointed out, the sheer volume of families affected by exclusionary immigration policies during earlier historical periods was relatively small compared to the numbers of unauthorized today.[39] As more and more families feel the crunch of restrictive immigration policies, their social impacts magnify.

Second, these social impacts affect families living more than a thousand miles from the US-Mexican border. Past policies have often targeted specific regions of the country. The border region, for example, experienced the scrutiny of the increased militarization of the US-Mexican border in the 1980s,[40] with communities in those areas feeling impacts related to immigration status and illegality. I found in my interviews that families living in Ohio and New Jersey—two distinct states located far from the US-Mexican border—felt similar impacts, suggesting that the repercussions of illegality have extended outside a particular region of the country. The contemporary restrictive policy environment has social impacts nationwide.

Third, living out of status today restricts families' everyday lives signifi-cantly. The families I met feared family separation and at times experi-enced more acute symptoms like Inés's anxiety attack. However, they did not seem to live in fear every single day of the week, hiding in their homes or apartments, although perhaps they simply habituated to their fears. Often they went about their lives as normally as possible. Nearly half par-ticipated actively in various activities from dance class, to soccer practice, to school-based exercise programs; those I met were contributing mem-bers of the communities where they lived. Yet because of the increase in documentation in all aspects of contemporary life, the lack of a legal status brings with it ever more significant repercussions, such as the consequences for children's social mobility or power differences within families.

The social consequences described by the families I met occurred between 1,500 and 2,000 miles away from the US-Mexican border. And although some of the social impacts differed in Ohio and New Jersey, most familial-level effects remained constant across these two different new destination sites for Mexican migration. Past restrictive immigration poli-cies may have had similar social impacts on a specific group of people, but today immigration policies affect many more families living in all parts of the United States. When unauthorized individuals in the United States number eleven million, and so many daily life activities require proof of legal status, the social consequences of illegality intensify considerably.

A MOVING TARGET

Documenting the impacts of legal status on the lives of families at times feels like trying to capture a moving target. By the time these words are printed and read, certain practices and policies will probably have changed, espe-cially at the local level. During the course of this project, they already have; for some, prospects have become slightly more hopeful. Others have experi-enced the opposite. Considering how some more recent changes have shaped children's lives suggests the even greater need for national-level reforms.

In 2012, after I had completed all of my interviews with children, the Obama administration announced the Deferred Action for Childhood Arrivals program (DACA). DACA allows unauthorized youth ages fifteen to thirty-one relief from deportation and temporary employment authorization if they have arrived prior to 2007 (and before they turned sixteen), have no felony records, and have completed school in the United States. Many of the unauthorized children I interviewed will be eligible for DACA; it is a welcomed improvement with the potential to radically alter their prospects. One young woman I first interviewed in Ohio when she was twelve, for example, proudly posted a picture of her new driver's permit in 2013 with the caption "It's about time!" And a mother from New Jersey called in November 2013 to deliver the good news.

"*¿Sabe quién es?*" She asked if I knew who was calling as I scrambled to get out from the diner booth where I was eating brunch to take the call in private.

"*¡Hola Verónica!*" I answered. I had not spoken to her for more than a year.

"I won't keep you," she continued, "I can hear that you are busy. But I wanted to tell you the good news. The children's papers arrived! You cannot imagine how happy we are. My son is a new person." I could not stop grinning after we disconnected; her son was the fourteen-year-old who had told me two years earlier that he wanted to be a chef but that he worried every day because he could not pursue this career in the United States. Now it seems his dream may be possible.

DACA has had positive impacts on the approximately half a million young people who have applied for the program. A nationwide survey of DACA recipients found that 61 percent of those surveyed obtained a new job and a driver's license and 54 percent opened their first bank account.[41] However, the same study finds that recipients do not necessarily get better jobs or higher pay.[42] The penalties of having previously lived out of status prove to be a disadvantage.

Marjorie, whom I first interviewed in New Jersey when she was fourteen, exemplifies the ways DACA is not necessarily a panacea for children whose lives have been permanently altered by restrictive immigration policy. Marjorie's mother Gladys moved eight times after her husband was deported when Marjorie was eleven and her younger brother was four (as described in chapter 2). Prior to his deportation the couple had lived apart, but Marjorie's father had supported the family financially. After he returned to Mexico, Gladys lost all support from him, so she began to work full time and Marjorie began to watch her brother every day after school until 9:00 p.m. when her mother got home. In the ninth grade Marjorie slept over at her friends' homes whenever possible; she told me that Hispanic children "grew up too quickly" because they had to help their parents. Four years later, a senior in high school, Marjorie had applied for and received DACA and worked part time after school. At the beginning of the school year, Gladys asked me to talk to her about college options; she had a high GPA and might have been eligible for scholarships. By the spring, plans had changed. Gladys explained, "It's that I don't know about her going to college anymore. You see, now she can work, and I need her help with expenses." Although Marjorie is the perfect example of a bright young woman that the DACA legislation promises to help, the cost of her father's deportation has had a long-standing financial impact on the family. His deportation has had cascading effects, ultimately curtailing her pursuit of a college education. At the end of her senior year, Marjorie decided it would be better to take a few classes at community college, "to save some money."

While DACA has offered some relief, it also does not ease the fears of deportation young people have for their family members and friends. Of the DACA recipients surveyed, 68 percent knew someone who had been deported and 14 percent had had a parent or sibling deported.[43] Indeed, immigration enforcement efforts have simultaneously continued to escalate, with a recent New York Times investigation showing that two-thirds of those deported under the Obama administration either had no criminal backgrounds or had committed minor crimes such as traffic violations.[44] The administration has favored Secure Communities as a way to target dangerous criminal offenders: under this program anyone arrested has his or her immigration status systematically checked. Secure Communities had not been put into place at the time of my interviews in either site, suggesting that this program alone is not responsible for the negative social outcomes I describe here. However, it has since been adopted. The harrowing experience of one family I interviewed illustrates how this program often fails to identify criminal offenders and instead risks separating from their family members unauthorized individuals with no criminal backgrounds.[45]

True stories are so often stranger than fiction; "You can't make this stuff up," an English professor told me once in class.[46] And so I return now where I started, to Inés. Despite her anxiety attack in 2011 after the police investigated her husband Adrián, nothing came of that incident, as explained in chapter 2. Adrián had done nothing wrong. Yet things have since changed. One of the fathers I interviewed, for example, messaged me to report that he had been detained for a week for driving without a license and had been recently released. He was now fighting a deportation order. His ten-year-old son, during our interview two years earlier, had said he worried that his parents were immigrants because other kids had their parents taken away, but that his parents had told him, "that it's not gonna happen, to not worry about it."

And so I learned from Inés on a visit in 2014 that the unimaginable had happened. Two weeks after Inés gave birth to the couple's second US citizen child, the family went out to eat on a Sunday afternoon. Entering the restaurant, Adrián noticed an unclaimed cell phone out on a bench. He picked it up. As they accommodated nine-year-old Lesly and their two-week-old baby at the table, Inés reminded him they had left the baby's blanket back in the car. Adrián hurried out to get it. Back inside, Adrián asked a staff person if someone had lost a cell phone. She said yes, but then he realized he had accidently left the cell phone in the car and went back to retrieve it. In the parking lot the police arrested him. Apparently, the teenager who had lost the phone noticed it in Adrián's car while he was inside and called the police. "You cannot imagine, Joanna . . . all the lights outside the restaurant. . . . Lesly was so scared. She was in tears."

Later that week, the case against Adrián was dropped. The teenager did not press charges, as clearly there had been a mix-up. However, once arrested and his status checked, Adrián was detained for immigration violations. When I last saw Inés, Adrián had been released and was awaiting the deportation hearing. "The lawyer is going to fight it on the grounds that we have two US citizen children who need his support," Inés explained.

"But, Joanna," she continued. "I never expected this to happen. You know Sandra, well, that scared me. But her husband was doing something wrong. He was speeding and the children weren't in their car seats. But Adrián has never done anything wrong. And he was trying to do the right thing. I still cannot believe it." Neither can I; Inés's dream had proved to be a premonition. Her nightmare had come true.

I offer the stories of families in this book as a baseline.[47] Nationwide immigration laws will surely, at some point, change; reform is badly needed. And at the local level, different practices will be adopted; hopefully some will ameliorate the problems I outline here, preventing the nightmarish cases like Adrian's arrest from happening.[48] Yet these stories instruct on the worst-case scenarios of what has happened, can happen, and will happen to children and families under restrictive immigration policies when pathways to legalization are nonexistent and enforcement prevails as the primary tactic to regulate US immigration.

IMPROVING POLICY IN THE TWENTY-FIRST CENTURY

To date comprehensive reform has been proposed in Congress multiple times, to no avail.[49] Smaller measures have also been proposed but not passed.[50] Reform feels perpetually on the horizon. In the meantime, we have seen the devastating social consequences of a tightening regulatory system. Restrictive immigration policies like those in place in 2014 are particularly bad for families. How might immigration policy be crafted to reduce the social costs and negative impacts for families? What features of policy have promoted legal status into a crucial feature of the social hierarchy? Alternately, what types of policies have the potential to transform immigration status into what—I optimistically still think—it is really intended to be, an administrative category?

Enforcement practices harm families more acutely than nearly any other characteristic of current immigration policy. An emphasis on enforcement, however, has increased rather than decreased over the past twenty to thirty years. Funding for ICE in 2012 was fifteen times that spent on INS operations in 1986.[51] In fact, this is the one area of comprehensive immigration reform proposals in the twenty-first century consistently receiving bipartisan support, with those supporting immigration reform—including President Obama—favoring reforms under the stipulation that the United States remain tough on enforcement.[52] If we care about the social consequences of immigration policy, and its impact on public health, this is a misguided approach.

Why is enforcement so popular? Simultaneous with the increase in enforcement has been a trend toward the criminalization of the immigrant population.[53] In fact, the comments of children I interviewed equating immigration with illegality mirror popular discourse in the United States, which has begun to equate those noncompliant with immigration regulations with criminal offenders. "While immigrants may be decent people, they have broken the law and should be punished for doing so," the opinion goes. This popular perspective completely ignores the fact that fluctuations in immigration law, rather than individuals' actions, determine who and what is considered illegal.

The conflation of illegal immigration with criminal behavior is far-reaching, evident even in American pop culture. Take for example *Border Wars*, a spin-off show from the long-standing reality TV show *Cops*, which follows police officers around on patrol. Although suspects in the show *Cops* are assumed innocent until proven guilty, the show clearly contrasts law enforcement officials with the "criminals" they seek to apprehend.[54] Similarly, *Border Wars* follows Department of Homeland Security officials' interactions with "illegal immigrants," and many episodes conflate immigration with drug-smuggling operations and other criminal activity.[55]

No immigration policy, except for an entirely open system of immigration, can completely remove unauthorized individuals. From this perspective, the question is not how to eliminate the number of unauthorized but what approach to use in dealing with this population. If we shift the frame from considering unauthorized immigrants to be criminals to considering them to be, as Hiroshi Motomura suggests, "Americans in waiting," then the priorities for a pathway forward with immigration policy become clear.[56] Policies that emphasize enforcement and criminalize this group will have long-standing social impacts not only on "Americans in waiting" but also on all US citizens: the ramifications will be felt well beyond those living out of status, like the US citizen children and spouses I interviewed who had unauthorized family members. Policies that seek to criminalize immigrants, like Secure Communities, should cease.

Aside from the decoupling of immigration and criminality and de-emphasizing of enforcement, legalization pathways must enable the regularization of those living out of status. A rise in mixed-status families results directly from the decrease in opportunities for legalization. In fact, although families with members of different legal statuses clearly existed in the twentieth century, not until the year 2000 does the term *mixed-status family* appear frequently in the scholarly literature.[57] The negative experiences of those living in mixed-status families have arisen as an acute social problem only in the twenty-first century, during the time in which legislation has blocked legalization. Parents' unauthorized legal status, for example, deprives their US citizen children of resources by limiting access to social services, curtailing informal social support, and magnifying economic stressors associated with parenting. These in turn shape children's learning, socioemotional well-being, and physical health.[58] Similarly, the hardships faced by unauthorized members of the 1.5 generation (those who were born abroad but have grown up in the United States) who cannot legalize are particular to the current era, in which they are experiencing blocked educational pathways, increased fear and stigma, and feelings of exclusion, with wide-reaching impacts not only on social mobility and integration but also on more personal matters, such as their dating practices and their family formation experiences.[59]

Reform that reduces these social impacts must allow for legalization so that the unauthorized siblings and parents of US citizens can share equal rights under the law. Reforms that reduce social impacts also must allow for immediate family members to legalize simultaneously so that illegality cannot complicate the intersecting gender and generational inequalities in families. Legal status becomes the source of significant family-level inequalities when the system creates differential pathways toward legalization for each family member and includes various schedules of wait times for visas and residency applications. Concurrent applications for all family members are likely to diminish some of the adverse social impacts of existing legislation.

An equally important feature of policy that will reduce undesirable social repercussions is the institution of speedy mechanisms for regularization. Children's and families' experiences suggest that the longer individuals wait to regularize their status, the greater the social impact their being out of status will have on their children's lives. A US citizen child whose father lacks legal status for a two-year period has very different experiences from a child whose mother remains unauthorized for all of her childhood in that she faces many years of economic marginalization and poor health care access.[60] A child in Mexico blocked from living with a father in the United States for two years who gets to see his father during this time period experiences less trauma and fewer negative impacts on schooling and the parent-child relationship than a child separated from his parents for four or five years whose parents cannot visit while they await regularization.[61] The longer period of time required for regularization to occur, the greater the possibility for negative outcomes for families.

Recent proposed reforms support simultaneous applications of family members, yet they do not seek to reduce the period of time immigrants remain out of status. To the contrary, the 2013 Senate bill S. 744, the Border Security, Economic Opportunity, and Immigration Modernization Act, proposed a new category of Registered Provisional Immigrants (RPI) status prior to legal permanent residency. Someone with RPI status, under the proposed legislation, would face a minimal thirteen-year waiting period before becoming eligible for citizenship.[62] This type of proposal, which includes lengthy periods of time out of status, will only increase the social impacts of legal status on children and families.

Why such lengthy waiting periods if they have clear penalties for families? A preference for a system that includes wait times derives directly from the discourse of immigrant criminality. As long as we view unauthorized immigrants as lawbreakers, then making these migrants "pay" for their time out of status and "wait in the back of the line" seems rational. However, it is exactly this perspective that has severe social repercussions for children and families. When we view immigrants as undeserving criminals, requiring them to repent and prove their worthiness in order to stay in the United States, the social impacts of immigration will inevitably multiply. When those who seek admission into the United States can do so relatively quickly and seamlessly, the social costs of immigration will lessen.

"HEY, MR. OBAMA"

"I don't know President Obama, and I don't think I'll ever meet him," I tell ninth grader Lizbeth at the conclusion of our interview. Lizbeth lives in central New Jersey and attends a vocational-technical school. "But I'm writing about what it is like to be a kid growing up in New Jersey from what you guys tell me. If you could tell anything to President Obama or someone else important like him, what would you say?"

"Not all immigrants are bad people. Just because they want to work," she says after taking a moment to think about it. "I would say that I think this country would not be the same as it is right now without immigrants: Mexicans and everybody. I think Americans should be happy that they are here. Basically, they're taking jobs that don't get paid that well. Americans get the good jobs. I think immigrants help a lot of people. Probably most of the criminals are not immigrants. It would be fair that everybody could be here. USA is supposed to be about opportunities."

Lizbeth acutely identifies key issues: immigrants are not criminals, immigrants play an important role in the US employment structure, and therefore immigrants need to be given the opportunity to stay. I would add the following: if we do not allow immigrants to stay and if we continue to criminalize international migration, children and families will continue to suffer great hardships, and legality will continue to amass the power of social exclusion in ways similar to race, class, and gender.

Not all children had such pointed, on-topic messages for President Obama. Two wanted to tell him that it was great being a Mexican kid, that they felt proud for who they were, and good about themselves; a seven-year old passed on the message, "My life is going good, and we are having fun." A couple of boys asked Obama to fix the economy, a girl asked that he do something about the gang violence in her school, and another wanted him to know that being a kid was hard, "because I don't like homework."

Most children—of both genders and all ages—who answered this question, however, expressed feelings of frustration related to immigration, as Lizbeth had. A fourteen-year-old ninth grader answered, "It's kind of, um, how would I say it, like it's kind of unfair for us because, for example, I want to become a doctor. But I probably can't do college here because first of all, it's so expensive and you need to like have papers." A twelve-year-old boy explained, "First he said he was gonna help us. . . . Obama on the news, he said he was gonna help us and everything. He never helped us." And a ten-year-old who attended PS 13 told me, "I would tell him that other people also have dreams of traveling and stuff and they won't be able to because they don't have papers or anything."

Some children spoke directly about their fears related to current enforcement practices. A ten-year-old girl said she wanted to tell President Obama that "sometimes kids like us are scared about our families being taken away. . . . Sometimes they trap people just because, like to get them, and take them back to their country because they did, just because they're immigrants, but I think they should just take the people that do stuff wrong." And a boy added his message: "to get a better economy and to not have the, to not have them to take our parents away and take them back to [another] country."

Others ended our interviews imploring President Obama for change. Miguel, age ten, said, "I would tell him, Hey, Mr. Obama, could you change the law of immigrants?" Moisés, also ten, suggested, "Take away the papers for immigrants so that we can live in peace, be friends and live together." Third grader Preciliano asked President Obama "to change the laws. To let the people come and work here." And Osvelia, a sixth-grader, stated,

> Quisiera que sepa que los inmigrantes también tienen derechos . . . Porque no es fair que los americanos tengan más derechos que los hispanos. Porque están viviendo acá. Quisiera decirle que los que están acá que les den papeles. [Que les den] derechos. Para que ya no sean inmigrantes.
>
> [I would like him to know that immigrants also have rights . . . because it isn't fair that Americans have more rights than Hispanics. Because they [Hispanics] are living here. I want to tell him to give papers to those who are living here, and give them rights, so that they no longer have to be immigrants.]

Children, experts in identifying what is fair and what is not fair, expressed their concerns quite clearly. Immigration law is not fair, creating disadvantages in their everyday lives. This is the meaning legal status has accrued in the United States in the twenty-first century. As we face these difficult policy issues, perhaps it is time to listen to children and create legislation that diminishes these inequalities that they so accurately describe and identify, rather than heightening them. Perhaps it is time to reframe immigrant illegality.

Talking to Kids

METHODOLOGICAL ISSUES

When I present my work, colleagues—usually sociologists—ask me how I interview children. Qualitative researchers, and especially those working in the tradition of grounded theory, emphasize open-ended questions that elicit long, narrative responses from those we interview, allowing them to introduce and elaborate on important themes from their perspectives.[1] But most recognize, and those who are parents just know, that children do not usually talk this way. When children do become absorbed in narratives, their stories usually wander, at times nonsensical, veering away from the specific topics of interest to a social scientist, the types of themes one hopes an interview will get at, things like social meaning and social practices. So how does a sociologist, especially when working in the ethnographic tradition, manage to elicit useful and valuable information from young children in interviews?

The other day, I posed this question to undergraduates enrolled in my upper-division writing seminar "Children's Social Worlds," at the University at Albany. I had slowly learned how to talk to children through trial and error, and I struggled to explain my techniques to professional colleagues.

Opposite: Photograph by Bob Anderson

But these students, many of whom had multiple siblings or nieces or nephews whom they had helped to raise, or who had had some experience with children through current or past employment, as camp counselors, youth outreach workers, coaches, lifeguards, and so on, just knew instinctively. "Short sentences that are easy to answer," one student offered. Another said you had to start with questions that made children comfortable and ease slowly into anything deeper. "And you have to ask simple questions, ones they understand." "And you have to really listen to them."

"This is harder than it seems," I added. "I mean, who wants to hear about all the details of the video game they mastered. I usually blank out when my kids start on this."

We laughed, but the advice holds. Essentially, the praxis is not all that different from how qualitative researchers train to interview adults. One must make the interview setting comfortable, listen, ask questions that can be answered, and contextualize the interview. Although these tenets apply no matter whom you interview, with younger interviewees strategies to accomplish these goals can differ.

Additionally, ethical concerns—and current protocols for human subjects research by universities' Institutional Review Boards (IRBs)—require extra consideration in research with children. Parental consent is required for all research with minor children. I would not have been able to observe children in their classrooms without parents' first agreeing to my visiting their children's school. The attitudes of the administrators I approached about the project changed from reluctant to willing when they learned that parents' permission would be required first. Although important, requirements for parental consent mean that a child who does not want to be interviewed may feel pressured by the adults in his or her life to participate once a parent agrees to the research. Similarly, children who want to participate in a study will not be able to unless they get the consent of their parents. Children do not hold the same rights as research participants as do adults, making qualitative research on the lives of children even more challenging.

This project, focusing on both children and families with members without legal status, posed many methodological challenges. Although the text provides many examples of my process, here I provide some reflections, and a few more details, about my strategy. I also include interview schedules for both parents and children, as I think the contrast is instructive.

SAMPLING

Like adults, children need to feel comfortable in interviews. Comfort starts with introductions and the invitation to participate in the research project. For children in this project, parents were the gatekeepers, and my entry into children's worlds was framed by my access to their parents.

My strategy to meet parents varied in Ohio and in New Jersey, as my social position in these two communities differed. In Ohio, I met many families through my participation in a church-run youth program. Although I attended the program with my children for a year before I started research, I felt like an outsider in the community. Funding for the project allowed me to hire a research assistant, someone who had participated in the church program for years, to help identify potential interviewees. She recruited a little over half of the families I interviewed in Ohio; the others I found as my own ties in the Latino community developed over the course of the project. Families trusted this person. She contacted parents on my behalf, explaining my goals and asking if they were willing to be interviewed. Some of the parents, I later learned, then contacted another member of the church to check me out. I met a few parents at church events, but most often I called them directly. Most children I interviewed saw me at one or more community activities—before the interview or often after. Usually I was accompanied by my children. I imagine they viewed me as someone who knew their mothers and who was also the mother of two children around their same ages.

In Ohio research unfolded slowly. I started interviewing families referred to me by the research assistant and ended with those I met through my own contacts. Not until a year into the project did I approach the six families whose children I wanted to observe in school and home settings. I deliberated over the smaller group of families to focus on: Which ones represented the patterns in the larger sample that I wanted to learn more about, and who did I think would be receptive? I selected families with whom I had fairly good rapport and whose experiences spanned the range of mixed-status households I had seen in my interviews. In one family all members had US citizenship, in one family all members had obtained a legal status, and in one family all members were undocumented. I also selected a range of mixed-status families: one with unauthorized parents and US-born children, one with legal-status parents and both legal migrant and unauthorized children, and one with unauthorized parents and both unauthorized and US-born children. I carefully considered the age of the children, deciding to focus on seven- and eight-year-olds, and this eventually brought me into first-, second-, and a few third-grade classrooms.

The process hit hurdles; two families I originally selected declined when the research assistant contacted them about further participation. Also, because families in Ohio lived quite scattered, I needed to select children who attended different schools—one private and five public, meaning I had to get permission from each school separately (and from a school district) for these visits. Because I had already obtained parents' permission, most schools let me in, although one did not. And so I had to recruit a different family. The whole process took time; I worked on data collection in Ohio for two years.

In New Jersey I had only six months, although I made trips in advance to set up the work, drawing on contacts I already had in the area. Given my experiences in Ohio, I knew that access to schools would be the most difficult. Before I arrived to begin collecting interviews, I approached school officials. Already familiar with the area, I wanted to be sure to include students attending a charter school, one of the city schools with a high concentration of Mexican families, and a more diverse school in the suburbs where a clustering of Mexican families lived. I talked to principals and a district superintendent ahead of time in order to obtain permission to visit three schools. Upon arrival to New Jersey, I aimed to interview forty families and crossed my fingers that I would be able to find at least six of them with children attending those three schools.

Because the research in New Jersey was more condensed, I felt sure I needed to hire someone to help me identify families as I had done in Ohio. Despite having many contacts and a few people in mind to whom I offered the job, no one wanted it. My friends and acquaintances felt too busy with work and other obligations. They offered, instead, a couple of recommendations to families, so I resigned to recruit myself. About a fourth of the sample included families I had known in the past, and then they—as well as other friends and acquaintances—recommended me to the others. In Ohio I spent more time developing networks, yet in New Jersey I felt greater trust from the families I interviewed, perhaps because we so often had mutual friends. In New Jersey, I began school and home visits with a smaller group of families immediately after interviewing a family that met the profile I sought, a seven- or eight-year-old child who attended the schools I had permission to visit and who matched the profile of the families I had already observed in Ohio. I began these visits while I continued to collect interviews. Although I may not have spent as much time at community events in New Jersey, many of the children I ended up interviewing had seen me at their schools or with their families and friends.

The biggest hurdle I faced in New Jersey was identifying families with the variety of legal-status configurations I had been able to find in Ohio. Ultimately, the clean comparison I sought was impossible. While in Ohio some families had arrived on visas, recruited to work for a major employer in the region, I could not find any families in New Jersey on professional work visas during my short stint there. Instead, I found families who had eventually been able to legalize through family-based petitions. In Ohio I also had a wide range of class backgrounds in my sample, interviewing families with much higher incomes than my own, along with those who lived in quite impoverished conditions. Finding a similar range in New Jersey proved difficult; to find variety I recruited some families that lived outside the main metropolitan area. I interviewed a few with an economic background similar to my own, but the vast majority had lower incomes than my own family.

In New Jersey, I purposively sought out interviews for specific formations of mixed-status families and especially families in which children had been born in Mexico. In fact, I decided not to follow up on quite a few recommendations for families with US-born children and unauthorized parents. If I had, the entire sample would have consisted of these families. In the end, the six families I focused on in New Jersey included one in which the father and child were US citizens and the mother had legalized, one in which all members were unauthorized, and four mixed-status families. Of the mixed-status families, in one parents were unauthorized and the children US citizens, and in another the father had been deported while the mother was unauthorized and had one US-born and one unauthorized child who lived with her. In the third the parents were unauthorized and the unauthorized children had experienced separation while the

US-born child had not. In the final family the parents and youngest children were unauthorized but the oldest children had gained legal status.

Sampling those who are unauthorized can be difficult. I believe that I was able to do so successfully only because I had lived, worked, and or participated in both communities prior to starting the research project. Even so, families would not have talked to me without having been personally introduced or recommended to me by a mutual acquaintance.

THE INTERVIEW SETTING

Initial contacts framed the way children perceived me and may have shaped their comfort level with me. Beyond the initial introduction, I sought to make children and families comfortable by allowing them to decide when and where the interview occurred. I suggested that I could come to their home, at times that they could come to mine, or we that could meet at a mutually convenient location. From the researcher perspective, I preferred interviewing families in their homes, as this gave me so much information about the rhythms of children's daily lives, evident in simple things like the layout and condition of their apartment or house, or the type of neighborhood where children lived. I could not require these invaluable slices of life, but I got lucky. When presented with different options, parents typically invited me to their homes, citing this to be most convenient and hassle free, especially given the often hectic work and school schedules we arranged our meetings around. Of eighty-one families, I met just two families in a public park, one at the family-owned store where the mother worked, and one at the house of a friend.

Children, however, did not get to choose where they met me for interviews; their parents did. After interviewing parents, I asked parents if I could interview as many of their children as were willing to participate. If parents agreed—and almost all did, although a few recommended me to only one or two of their children—either they brought their children to me to be interviewed in the same place where we had spoken or, in about half of the cases, I returned on a different day to interview children, sometimes visiting families multiple times to complete the interviews. This procedure alone, I suspect, actually helped children feel more comfortable.

Comments like "Oh yeah, I remember you, you came to talk to my mom the other day" suggested the importance, for children, of knowing that their parents endorsed our conversation.

As per IRB protocol, I of course asked all children for assent to interview them, but the children I met never refused, perhaps because their parents had already consented and had already filtered access on behalf of their children. In both New Jersey and in Ohio, quite a few families chose not to be interviewed: I'll never know if parents themselves did not want to be interviewed or refused for the sake of their children. I do know that some children I met—friends of children I interviewed—wanted to participate but that their parents did not consent, an awkward situation. Parents' prerogative to silence children while children cannot do the same troubles me, endorsing unequal power in families. Most parents, however, seemed to sincerely want their children to express themselves and went out of their way to enable our conversations.

Aside from letting families decide if, when, or where an interview took place, I tried to increase children's comfort by being flexible about the interview setting in the home. Some researchers control the research setting, asking parents to leave so that children can disclose information they might hide from their parents. Others ask parents to remain present, offering children support throughout. I allowed parents and children to dictate, deciding that what was comfortable would vary depending on the specific nature of that parent-child relationship.

Nearly all parents chose public settings in the home, in the kitchen or living room, occasionally outside on a porch or in the yard: I did not interview any children in their bedrooms. Most parents chose to leave us alone during the interview. A small group of parents chose to sit with their children, usually the youngest ones. At first I worried that children might filter the information they shared. The children I interviewed in this manner, however, seemed to need their parents, looking to them when they felt stuck by a question or were frozen in discomfort. I suspect parents chose to sit with their children because they knew it would ease them. None seemed to look over at their parents to seek approval for their answers (as I have occasionally seen women do with their husbands in joint interviews with couples); rather, they asked for help when they couldn't remember a fact, like the name of a relative living in Mexico.

Another small group of parents moved into another part of the house where they could hear what was going on in the interview but gave us some semblance of privacy. I, and their children, knew their parents were listening because, unprompted, parents at times called out or offered information after one of the questions I posed. In these cases, more than when parents sat with children, I noticed children monitor their responses. Any time a parent intervened, I cringed. But I decided to trust that this practice itself reflected valuable information, demonstrating parents' and children's typical interactions. And sometimes parents' encouragement led to rich information from children, like the time one ten-year-old told me his border-crossing story only after his mother reminded him, calling in from the kitchen, "Tell her the story about when you came here."

In general, most comments from the children I interviewed with their parents physically present—especially about immigration—did not seem to differ remarkably from those of children I interviewed whose parents purposefully left the room so we could talk privately. Ultimately, my interviews did not seek highly private information, information that children might want to hide from their parents, with just a few exceptions. For example, I did ask older children about whether they had boyfriends or girlfriends, and I chose not to ask this question if I suspected it might be an issue if the parent stood nearby.

Of course, differences in the micro-setting possibly affected the information children told me. But I believe that discomfort in the interview setting would have had a much larger impact. Families' minicultures vary, and what may be normal and natural for children in one family might not be the same in the next. To make children comfortable I tried to be sure that they knew of my rapport with their parents, and I gave them as much control over the interview setting as possible within the constraints of the parent-child relationship.

LISTENING TO CHILDREN

Informed consent presents an inevitable problem; when researchers are adults, and the only people who give legal consent are adults, children may feel pressured to participate in an interview if the other adults in their lives have already consented. Some strong-willed children may say no, of course. But most will cede to their parents, because dependence characterizes the social relations between parents and children. And if children change their minds about participation during the study, they may not know how to back out because their parents have already told them they should do this. Although such a power differential cannot be entirely avoided, I believe researchers can seek ethical practice in interviewing children by listening carefully to children. Children may not be as verbal as adults, especially in formal interview settings, so one has to listen to both verbal and nonverbal cues.

I have cut interviews short even when parents wanted me to interview their children and told me to keep going but the children seemed uncomfortable, shifting repeatedly in their chairs or finding something to continually distract them. I did so by skimming through the questions, just asking one or two more, and stopping, saying, "Those are all my questions," thanking them for my time, and saying they had done a great job. I also prefaced all my interviews telling children that if they did not know the answer, or did not want to answer, to just say "I don't know." A few children whom I interviewed begin with all one-word answers or answered "I don't know" to a series of questions. This indicated that the children were done, so I stopped the interview.

Some children grew uncomfortable just about certain questions, or a line of questioning, something they communicated by putting their heads down or avoiding eye contact. In these instances, I always skipped the question, even when a nearby parent probed the child to get him or her to answer. Although I carefully selected questions that would not seem too personal, it was difficult to know what might bother or bore a particular child. Even if I might be personally interested in the topic—and might push an adult to answer a similar question—with children I moved to different questions anytime a child seemed disquieted by a line of questioning. Doing so meant I certainly lost interesting information from interviews. A colleague recently asked, for example, how children felt about the inequalities between siblings that I write about in chapter 4 when asked directly about them. Looking through my transcripts, I realized I did not know more except that it was uncomfortable for them, because when I broached the topic, children—and sometimes parents—grew uncomfortable and I dropped the line of questioning. Ultimately I must leave that topic for interviews with older children reflecting back on past experiences. I may have missed some things by being so attentive to children's small cues, but I wanted to allow them power over the interview process in a world that does not give them much.

I tried to listen carefully to children in other ways as well. With my own children, I grow bored at the long stories they sometimes tell me, especially about different video games. I am simply not interested in these details. With children I interviewed, though, I listened. The listening helped increase our comfort with each other even when children went on tangents that had nothing to do with the interview question I asked. So we ended up talking about favorite video games, or TV shows, and I got play-by-plays, which I could barely follow—"I hit the last goomba with a koopa shell and then Bowser comes out of nowhere! He throws a fiery breath at me, but I jump out of the way." The strategy paid off, because then when I tossed in something a bit more serious, as in this case when I followed up by asking the young boy how often he talked to his father on the phone, the father he didn't live with, the one who had been deported to Mexico, he answered.

Not all children had relevant things to say in interviews, but I tried to listen to them anyway. Rarely did children ask whether they had given me the type of information I was looking for, as sometimes happened in adult interviews. They did not worry about relating their comments back to my overall goals. So by really listening, and engaging in what interested them, we built rapport. Then, when I least expected it, some children seemed to feel comfortable enough to throw in a golden nugget, a comment directly relevant to my purposes.

I also learned that just like adults, children shut down when asked questions that were hard for them to answer. With adults, I have trained myself to avoid yes/no questions, as these tend to be conversation stoppers and lead to dry, one-dimensional interviews. With children, however, straightforward yes/no questions were the easiest ones to answer. Children liked the affirmation involved in being able to answer such questions. So I actually built frequent easy-to-answer questions purposefully into the interview schedule. As a sociologist, I also wanted to ask about topics like legal status and identity, things that might be more difficult for children to reflect upon. I asked these questions mostly after having already gone through a number of routine questions. I also used a strategy of varying the pace of the interview, moving from light questions to more sociologically relevant questions, and then back again to easier topics.

Doing so required flexibility with the interview questionnaire, something also required in adult interviews. At times, I lingered on a topic that was heavy when children had something to say. And I also learned to let go more than I had previously been comfortable doing in adult interviews. Some children at six amazed me with how verbal and thoughtful they were; others were not nearly so articulate. Many of the children I interviewed did not answer all the questions I had prepared to ask them. I took what I could get. While missing data might frustrate a survey researcher, from a qualitative perspective silences sometimes said as much about a child and his or her family as the answers.

CONTEXTUALIZING THE INTERVIEW

Despite these strategies, the information children gave to me in interviews was undeniably limited. I wanted to hear children's voices; interviews were essential to this end. But interviews with children had many missing pieces. They would be void without more information about the context of children's lives. I set up a research design to contextualize children's comments in their interviews by triangulating their accounts with information from observations and from the accounts of the adults in their lives.

First, with all those I interviewed, I observed before, during, and after the interview and took detailed field notes after every interview. I observed the setting where the interview occurred, including in my field notes things like the furnishings of the child's home, the types of toys the child had access to, whether there were books around, and the types of foods parents offered children. When reviewing a child's interview transcript, I often found this information invaluable, as it helped me to understand something a child had mentioned in the interview that I might not understand without that physical setting etched into my mind.

Second, I interviewed parents. I told parents when I met with them that the study focused on the lives of children but that to understand children's experiences I had to know something about the family background and the family's story of migration. Parent interviews proved to be the most important for contextualizing children's interviews. At times, children told me something I would not have understood had I not first spoken to parents, about a family member in Mexico, for example. Because I had interviewed parents, I did not have to ask children to clarify who specifically they were talking about when they said they spoke to "Mama Lupe" on the phone; this was something I could piece together later. At times children said something I did not quite understand during an interview, like Preciliano's statement that he had no friends at school, and I asked parents later for help with interpretation. More often I found myself cross-checking accounts on mundane topics, like numbers of extended relatives and time lines of family migration. For example, some of the children told me that they had been born in Mexico and that they had come to live in the United States at a certain age, but they reported a time line that seemed improbable or even impossible; parents' accounts clarified. Other children spoke of returns to Mexico but did not know the details of these trips. Of course, interviews with children also corrected parents' accounts at times, whether mistakes or omissions. For example, I had not known that Camilo's father was not the biological father to Rebecca and Silvio until Rebecca repeatedly referred to him as her stepfather in our interview. Later, he spoke quite candidly about this.

Aside from triangulating interviews with children and their various family members, especially parents, I designed the study to enable observations of children in their home and school settings. Repeated home visits proved fruitful, not only because they allowed me to observe children, but also because they allowed me to have repeated casual conversations with parents and children. This sometimes led to more in-depth conversations about the family's migratory experiences. More often I learned about how families dealt with more minor events, especially related to access to health care and other social services. Once, for example, I visited Kevin and saw his arm in a cast. I knew that Kevin did not have health insurance, so I spoke with his mother Elizabeth about how she had navigated services to get care for her son after this incident.

Repeated contact with families also gave insight into changes in children's experiences. Two formal interviews with the children in the twelve families I focused on were especially revealing about how children's identity or their school experiences, for example, altered over the course of a year's time. Relationships I developed with families in order to do the observations also led to ongoing communication with some, even after I stopped collecting data officially. In the book I have drawn sparingly on these updates and have brought them in only when not doing so would misrepresent a story.

Visits to children's schools proved equally important for providing insight into children's relationships in the broader communities in which they lived. Ethics related to access made the expansion of the research, starting in the home and then moving into the schools, necessary. However, this mirrors how children experience their own lives: starting at home in the morning and then going out into the school environment. My attempts to mimic this process yielded invaluable insights into how children took their understandings of their own families' legal situation into their interactions in the broader communities in which they lived.

Finally, in order to triangulate data from multiple family members I used an unexpected, but quite fruitful, analytical strategy. Given the large number of interviews, I decided early on to organize the data using not only Excel but also SPSS. I thought it was the only way to stay on top of the information from various family members and multiple families in two locations. The strategy proved more valuable than I anticipated. After starting the laborious coding process, I realized that while I had formally interviewed at least two members of each family (although usually more), I actually had information on all members of the nuclear family ,including spouses and those children that I could not interview. Together with research assistants, we coded the information on all of these individuals into SPSS. The analytical power of this strategy became clear only as I later began to sift through the file, looking for patterns among the unauthorized and US-born members of families. Acknowledgment of the differences in distribution of housework, for example, did not always come up in interviews. In fact, children talked so often about how legal-status differences within their families did not matter to them that I found it hard to push them in interviews about apparent inequalities. Parents too admitted to these differences but often did not want to talk about them (unless they had experienced a conflict with a partner). By putting information from children and parent interviews about the entire family unit's experiences into a data set, I was able to get a much more comprehensive picture of the daily patterns—in language usage, extracurricular activities, and more—that most certainly shaped children's lives.

INTERVIEW SCHEDULE—CHILDREN

Background

How old are you?

What grade are you in?

Who do you live with?

    If not with parents, where does your (mother, father) live?

Do you have family here in (Ohio/New Jersey)?

Who lives here?

Do you have family in (Mexico, other relevant country)?

Who lives there?

Do you talk to them on the phone?

    If yes, what do you tell them?

    What do they tell you?

Have you ever been to (Mexico, other mentioned country)?

    If yes, can you tell me about what it is like there?

    What was your favorite thing to do there?

    Is there anything you did not like about it? What?

    Which do you like better, (Mexico, other country) or (New Jersey/Ohio)?

        How come?

Is your mom from (Mexico)?

How about your dad?

Are any of your family from there?

And you, where are you from?

Would you want your friends or the kids in your class to know what country

    (you *or*) your parents come from? How come?

Language

Do you speak English?

Do you speak Spanish?

Which language do you like better?

What language do you most like to speak with your mother? How come?

    And your father? How come?

    And your siblings? How come?

What language do you like to speak with your friends? How come?

What language do you like to speak at school? How come?

Do you watch TV in Spanish or English? Which do you like better? How come?

Does your (mom, dad) read books to you in Spanish or English? Which do you like better? How come?

Do you listen to music in Spanish or English? Which do you like better? Why?

Would you want your friends or the kids in your class to know that you speak Spanish? How come?

School

What grade did you say you are in?

Do you like school?

What do you like about school?

What do you not like about school?

What is your teacher like?

Tell me about the kids in your class.

Are there kids that you don't like in your class? Why don't you like them?

Are there kids you like a lot in your class? Why do you like them?

And your friends, can you tell me about them?

    Are they girls/boys?

    What do you play with them?

    Do they speak Spanish/English?

    What do they look like?

Who are your best friends?

Peer Groups

Do you have other friends who are not in your class?

    Are they girls/boys?

How old are they?

Do they speak Spanish /English too?

What do they look like?

Where do you play with them?

What is your favorite thing to play with your friends?

Have your friends ever been to (Mexico)?

Are your mom or dad friends with your friends' parents?

Daily Routines

So can you tell me about what you do on (typical) school days (summer days)?

What time do you wake up?

Who wakes you up?

What do you do at school?

Who picks you up from school?

What do you do after school?

What time is bed?

Who cooks dinner in your house? What foods do you like to eat the best?
What foods do you not like to eat?

Who makes your lunch? What do you like to eat for lunch? Is there anything you don't like?

Do you like to eat Mexican foods? Which ones?

How about on the weekends, what do you do days you don't have school?

Do you take any classes or play any sports outside of school?

If yes, what classes?

Which one do you like best? Why?

Are there any classes you don't like? Why don't you like them?

Do you go to church?

If yes, what do you like about it?

Is there anything you don't like about it? What?

Do you speak Spanish or English there?

Do you ever go to (ethnic festivals; parties where they speak Spanish) with your parents?

If yes, what do you like about it?

Is there anything you don't like about it? What?

Do you speak Spanish or English there?

Awareness of Class

Does your mom work? What does she do?

Do you know if your mom went to school? For how long?

Does your father work? What does he do?

Do you know if your dad went to school? For how long?

Do you work?

Do your sisters/brothers work?

Who do you think earns more money, your mom or your dad (sister, brother, etc.)? How do you know?

Do you think your mom and dad make more money than (friends') parents? What gives you this idea?

Who do you think has more money, people in (Mexico) or people here in (New Jersey/Ohio)? How do you know this?

Awareness of Race/Ethnic Background

What color skin do people have in (Mexico)?

Is it the same as the color of people skin here in (New Jersey/Ohio)? If no, how come?

What color skin does your mom have?

And your dad?

How about your brothers/sisters?

And you?

Do your friends have the same color skin as you?

Now I am going to read off a list of names. If you think this applies to you, tell me yes, if no, no. Okay? Do you get it?

Mexican, Peruvian, Hispanic, Latino, White, American, Spanish, Black, Spanish-American, Mexican-American, Peruvian-American, (comprehensive list) etc. . . .

Which one of these words about you makes you feel the most happy? How come?

Does it make you feel proud to think you are (_____)? What makes you feel proud?

Have you ever been teased for being (_____)? Can you tell me about that?

Which one of these words best describes your mom?

How about your dad?

 Other members of the family?

Awareness of Gender

Are most of your friends girls or boys?

Who do you like to play with more, boys or girls? How come?

What kinds of things do you like to play with your mom?

 What kinds of things do you like to play with your dad?

 And your sisters?

 And brothers?

What kinds of chores does your mom do when you get home from school?

And your dad, what does he do when you get home from school?

Are there any kinds of chores that you do to help your mom or dad around

 the house? What?

Do your sisters/brothers do chores too? What do they do?

Do you ever translate for your family?

 If yes, when and where? Examples?

 If, yes, do you like to translate or not? What do you like about it? What

 don't you like about it?

Awareness of Immigration Issues

Do you know what an immigrant is? (If no, explain that an immigrant is

 someone who is born in another country but lives here.)

Do you know anyone who is an immigrant?

 Who?

 Where is s/he from?

 What do you do with them?

What do you think it is like to be an immigrant?

Is anyone in your family an immigrant?

Are you an immigrant?

Would you want your friends or people in to class to know you (or your

 parents) are an immigrant? How come?

Does it make you feel proud that you (or your parents) are an immigrant?

 How come?

Have you ever been teased because you or your parent is an immigrant? Tell me about that.

Thank you, those are almost all the questions I have for you right now. I just have two more. But first, is there anything else you would like to tell me about yourself?

So, I don't know President Obama, but if I could tell him something about what it is like to be a kid in (New Jersey/Ohio), what would you tell him?

What do you want to be when you grow up?

THANKS!

INTERVIEW SCHEDULE—PARENTS

Family Background

Can you tell me a little bit about your family and who you live with?
  (Include information on number of children, ages, sexes.)
  Include information on age of parents, their marital status, how old they were when children were born, where they were born.
  If married, ask about how met partner.
  If parent is a step-parent to any children or has children living in another household, ask for information on these children.
  If not a parent, ask about how this person came to live with this family and their relationship with them.)

How long have you lived here in New Jersey/Ohio? In what country/state/town did you live before you moved here?

Have you ever lived apart from any of your children? Can you tell me about that?

Can you tell me a little bit about why you (or husband/wife) came to the United States?
  (Be sure to ask about age of migration, reasons for migration, goals with migration.)

Transnational Ties

Can you tell me a little bit about your family back in (country of origin)?

How often do you talk to them? Who specifically do you talk to? How long and often?

Do you communicate with them via e-mail or Internet or text messaging? With who?

How often do you visit? Who do you stay with when you go?

How often do you send money or gifts back to them? Who do you send this to?

Do you have family members in any other countries? (If yes), can you tell me about them?

How about your partner? Does he or she have family in (country of origin)?

How often do you talk to them? Who specifically do you talk to?

How often do you visit? Who do you stay with when you go?

How often do you send money or gifts back to them? Who do you send this to?

Do you have family members in any other countries? (If yes), can you tell me about them? ·

Do you have friends from your country here in the United States? From your town or state? Where do they live? How often do you see them? What do you do together?

Employment

Can you tell me about your current job?

   (Include information on job description, how long been there, how close to home, work schedule.)

Can you tell me about any jobs you had before you migrated?

How long did you go to school for? Where?

What does your partner do? Can you tell me about his or her job?

Can you tell me about any jobs your partner had before migration?

How long did he or she go to school for? Where?

Language

How well do you speak English? And Spanish? Have you ever taken lessons?

Which language do you prefer for watching TV? Listening to music? Reading? Why?

Which language do you use most of the time at work?

How about at home? Which family members do you speak English with?
Who do you speak Spanish with?
Do you speak any other languages? Can you tell me about that?

Child-Rearing Ideas

Can you tell me about what are some of the good things about raising children here in New Jersey/Ohio?
What are some of the bad things?
How does life here compare to other places you have lived before?
What things would you change about New Jersey/Ohio to make it a better place to raise children?

Daily Routines

Can you tell me about a typical weekday in this home?
(Probe, who gets children up, makes breakfast, gets them to school, etc. Who picks up from school, makes dinner, does chores, etc.)
Can you tell me about how the family spends a typical weekend?
Who does the chores in this home?
(Probe on who does which chores, including cleaning, cooking, maintenance, etc.
Probe on any responsibilities children have in the home.)
What kinds of foods do you typically eat together as a family? Who cooks? Who does the shopping? What foods do your children like the best? Is there anything that they don't like? Why?
Does this family attend church? If so, who in the family goes? Which church?
Does this family typically participate in other community activities together? Please tell me about them.
Are there other families that you socialize with on a regular basis as a family? Can you tell me about them?
Who usually takes care of the children if you are going out somewhere? Who else can you call on? Who do you prefer and why? Who does your child prefer and why?

Children (Ask about Each Child Separately)

Can you tell me about the child's (NAME) experiences in school? How are
they doing?

What do you think they like most about school?

What do you think they don't like about school?

How well does he or she do academically?

Do you have any concerns about your child's performance at school?

What child care arrangements have you had in the past for this child?
Describe each one.

What did you like about this arrangement?

What did you dislike?

What did your child like/dislike?

What kinds of extracurricular activities does this child do?

Who decided she or he would do this?

Which does she or he like the best? Why?

Anything the child doesn't like to do?

Can you tell me about this child's closest friends?

Which ones do you like the best? Why?

Which ones do you not like so much? Why?

Can you tell me about this child's language skills? Which language is stronger?

Who in the family does she or he speak English with?

Who does she or he speak Spanish with?

How about TV? Music? Reading?

At school?

Has your child ever taken formal lessons?

What do you do to support his or her language skills?

Who does this child get along best with in your family?

How would you describe your relationship with this child?

Do you have any concerns about this child?

Race/Ethnicity

How would you describe your race or ethnicity?

How about that of your partner?

And your children?

How do you think your child would describe your race or ethnicity?

Has he or she ever asked you anything about this?

What race or ethnicity are your children's closest friends?

How about your friends? What are their ethnic/racial backgrounds?

Have you ever felt discriminated against at work because of your ethnic or racial background? Can you tell me about that?

Immigration

Have you ever felt discriminated against because of your immigrant background? Can you tell me about that?

How about because of your race or ethnicity? Or because of your gender?

Is your child aware of your immigrant background? How do you know? Is he or she proud of this?

Do you think your child feels different because you are an immigrant? Has he or she ever been teased about this?

Does your child have other friends who are immigrants?

How about you? Do you have many friends who are also immigrants?

Have you ever had any legal difficulties because of your immigrant background?

To the best of your knowledge, is your child aware of these problems?

Has your child ever talked to you about being afraid of losing a parent? How did this topic come up?

So those are all the questions I have for now. Is there anything you would like to add about what it is like to raise your child here in New Jersey/ Ohio or about your family's experiences with immigration?

Thank you so very much for your time.

Notes

1. INTRODUCTION

1. The forty million figure is from Grieco et al. (2012).

2. The *Merriam-Webster Dictionary* definition of *illegality* is "the quality or state of being illegal." However, I draw my working definition from both De Genova (2002), who defines illegality as a political identity, and Menjívar (2011), who argues that the concept of illegality does not fully account for "many in-between and ambiguous legal categories that the law creates nor the fluidity with which individuals sometimes move from one category to another, often to a realm of legal uncertainty" (379). I hope to show that a consciousness of this spectrum of political identity—of the range between legal and illegal—has become the basis by which individuals and families experience social differentiation. This is related to but somewhat distinct from the broader definition of citizenship used by some scholars that encompasses legal status, rights, participation, and belonging (Bloemraad, Korteweg, and Yurdakul 2008; Bosniak 2000). I use the term *illegality* to capture the way individuals come to terms with the dichotomous states of being allowed or unallowed, legitimate or illegitimate, during their daily lives.

3. For just some examples of scholarship around the world exploring the lived experiences of illegality, see Willen (2007, 2012) and the accompanying special issues dedicated to this topic in the journals *International Migration* and *Social Science and Medicine*. For a review of recent literature on unauthorized migration in the United States, see Donato and Armenta (2011).

4. See De Genova (2004) for a description of how the legal system in the United States has had a particularly negative impact on Mexicans.

5. Passel, Cohn, and Gonzalez-Barerra (2013) and Pew Hispanic Center (2013b). The estimate for the percentage of the unauthorized who are Mexican is based on 2010 data.

6. I published the principal findings from the study in Dreby (2006, 2007, 2009, 2010).

7. For a good description of the militarization process, see Andreas (2009). For more on the suffering that militarization has caused for families, see Michalowski (2007). For an explanation of the unintended consequences of US immigration policy, see Massey and Pren (2012).

8. Hondagneu-Sotelo (1994); Massey et al. (1987).

9. On the stress of spousal separations on couples, see Dreby (2009); Marroni (2000); Mummert (1988); Pribilsky (2004).

10. See González-López (2005) and Hirsch (2003) for more on the changing expectations of marriage and courtship that underlie these migratory decisions.

11. On the demographics of Mexican women's migration to the United States, see Cerrutti and Massey (2001); S. Curran and Rivero-Fuentes (2003); Donato (1993); Greenlees and Saenz (1999). On some of Mexican women's reasons for migration, see Dreby (2010); Hondagneu-Sotelo (1994); Malkin (2004).

12. On the increase in deaths at the border, see Cornelius (2001); Eschbach et al. (1999). On families' view of the risks of women's border crossing, see Marquardt et al. (2011).

13. For more on the sacrifices of family separation, see Abrego (2014); Dreby (2010); Hondagneu-Sotelo and Avila (1997); Parreñas (2001, 2005).

14. This change took place starting on March 2, 2003. See US Citizenship and Immigration Services (2013).

15. IRCA included a 50 percent increase in border enforcement staffing, and border enforcement efforts have only continued to grow ever since. See B. Cooper and O'Neil (2005); Massey and Pren (2012). For more on the cooperation between local police departments nationwide and ICE, see Armenta (2012); M. Coleman (2007); Decker et al. (2009); Wishnie (2004).

16. For more on the strange bedfellows involved in immigration policy decisions, see Tichenor (2008). For a comprehensive account of US immigration policy, see Zolberg (2006).

17. Examples are the ABC Settlement Act of 1991 and the Nicaraguan Adjustment and Central American Relief Act (NACARA) of 2003.

18. See Kim (2013); Motomura (2013); Olivas (2010).

19. During the summer of 2013, bipartisan support for a major increase in spending on the border was passed by the Senate. See Parker (2013). For a look at how recent proposed legislation continues to prioritize border security, see Migration Policy Institute (2013).

20. Meissner et al. (2013).

21. Estimates suggest nearly four hundred thousand deported every year since 2009. See US Department of Homeland Security (2014); Wessler (2011b). There have been some recent debates about these numbers because of changes in the ways removals have been counted. However, these numbers account for returns and removals that result from the actions of the US government. Estimates of the earlier repatriation of Mexicans fluctuate between 350,000 and 600,000. See Fox (2012: 187); Ngai (2004: 72).

22. Although Congress is committed to border security, opinions among the electorate are more mixed. See Pew Hispanic Center (2013a).

23. Slack and Whiteford (2011).

24. Massey, Durand, and Malone (2002).

25. Passel, Cohn, and González-Barerra (2012).

26. For data on the growth of the Mexican American population, see Pew Hispanic Center (2011); Taylor et al. (2011).

27. I describe some of the specific barriers to legalization that Mexicans face in the subsequent chapters. For an overview, see Bergeron (2013).

28. Chavez (1992).

29. Taylor et al. (2011).

30. Taylor et al. (2011).

31. Kreider and Ellis (2011).

32. See the Appendix for more details on the methodology.

33. This information comes from American Fact Finder and is census data from 2010.

34. Again, statistics are from American Fact Finder's 2010 census data.

35. Menjívar (2011) theorizes that immigration policy makes the Central Americans living in Arizona she studied hyperaware of the law. Here I apply this concept to children. An emerging body of scholarship documents the specific ways legal status accrues meaning as young people transition into adulthood, especially when they consider college. See Abrego (2006, 2011); Abrego and Gonzales (2010); Gonzales (2011); Gonzales and Chavez (2012). I suggest that as the policy environment tightens, the social impacts of immigration policy extend downward, with heightened meaning for children at even younger ages.

36. My evidence supports a growing literature on the indirect impacts of deportation policies. See De Genova (2002, 2010); Hagan, Castro, and Rodríguez (2010); Hagan, Rodríguez, and Castro (2011); Talavera, Núñez-Mchiri, and Heyman (2010).

37. Research indicates that local contexts matter very much in shaping the daily lives of unauthorized migrants. See, for example, Marrow (2011); Schmalzbauer (2014); Zúñiga and Hernández-León (2005). My findings suggest that as national policy tightens, local differences in the experiences of the unauthorized across the country may become less pronounced.

38. I suppose this is my response to the ethical problem endemic to ethnographic research that Stacey (1988) identifies: ethnographic approaches involve inherently unequal power relationships between the researcher and the participants in the study.

39. Menjívar (2006).

40. Menjívar (2011).

41. Gonzales (2011) shows this to be the case for undocumented youth coming of age in California in the late 1990s and early 2000s.

42. On "domestic ethnography," see Dreby (2010). For just a few examples of classical and contemporary neighborhood-based approaches to ethnographic research, see Duneier (2000); Horowitz (1983); Kornblum (1975); Liebow (1967); Patillo-McCoy (2000); Stack (1974).

43. Dreby (2010: 229).

44. I felt this was somewhat compensated for by the prior research with families I had done for *Divided by Borders* at this site.

45. See Smith (2014) for a similar use of quantitative analyses with case study data.

46. This is because no list of the unauthorized exists from which to derive a sample. For examples of qualitative research designs with the unauthorized prior to the current political environment, see Chavez (1991, 1992); Cornelius (1982); Rodríguez (1987). For examples of qualitative research techniques with contemporary unauthorized populations, see Dreby (2012); Gonzales and Chavez (2012); Marrow (2011); Menjívar and Abrego (2012); Schmalzbauer (2009).

47. I tried to identify Mexican migrants in New Jersey who came as legal migrants. The combined criteria of being a legal migrant and having children in the United States, however, were hard to meet: I couldn't find anyone. The only legal migrants I found came as students and typically did not have family with them.

48. Ragin (2009) describes the problems with positivistic focused quantitative analyses as the limitations of net-effects thinking.

49. Given ethical concerns, questions about legal status are not included in the US Census or in most nationally representative surveys. Most demographic estimates for the unauthorized population use proxy measures (e.g., foreign-born, noncitizen Mexicans with less than high school educations). For more on demographers' estimates of the unauthorized, see Massey (2013). Some recent surveys have attempted to capture the experiences of the unauthorized: see, for example, Amuedo-Dorantes, Puttitanun, and Martinez-Donate (2013).

50. There is a significant body of literature theorizing the differences in the experiences of immigrants in new destinations in the United States from those in more traditional settlement regions. See Hernández-León and Zúñiga (2003); Fink (1998); L. Jensen (2006); Marrow (2011); Massey (2008); Schmalzbauer (2009); Singer (2004); Terrazas (2011); Zúñiga and Hernández-León (2005).

51. See all of the sources in the previous note for descriptions of different settlement patterns in "new destination" sites.

2. NERVIOS

1. Social scientists' use of key informants in research is long-standing. For examples of key informants in ethnographic studies, see Duneier (2000); Liebow (1967); Stack (1974). For some of the complications of reliance on key informants, see Soucy (2000).

2. See Bassuk, Perloff, and García Coll (1998); Dura-Vila and Hodes (2012); Guarnaccia (1993); Guarnaccia, De La Cancela, and Carrillo (1989); Weller et al. (2008).

3. For a sociological analysis of the increases in enforcement activities since 9/11, see Golash-Boza (2012). For more on the economics of enforcement, see Meissner et al. (2013).

4. For more stories on deportation, see Brotherton and Barrios (2011); Golash-Boza (2012).

5. Massey, Durand, and Malone (2002: 34). Estimates on the numbers of earlier deportations vary. See also Balderrama and Rodríguez (2006); Fox (2012); Guerin-Gonzales (1994); Hernández (2009); Hoffman (1974); Ngai (2004).

6. US Department of Homeland Security (2014). See also Simanski and Sapp (2012), U.S. Department of Homeland Security (2011a, 2011b).

7. There has been a change in the way these statistics are reported. Nonetheless, taken together, returns and removals have risen.

8. De Genova (2004). See also Chavez (2008).

9. Passel and Cohn (2011).

10. US Department of Homeland Security (2011b).

11. Kohli, Markowitz, and Chavez (2011).

12. No More Deaths/No Mas Muertes (2011).

13. Brotherton and Barrios (2011).

14. Berumen, Ramos, and Ureta (2011).

15. Golash-Boza and Hondagneu-Sotelo (2013: 272).

16. Armenta (2012); M. Coleman (2007); Decker et al. (2009); Wishnie (2004).

17. For more on 287g agreements, see Armenta (2012).

18. For more on Secure Communities, see Kohli, Markowitz, and Chavez (2011); Pedroza (2013); Strunk and Leitner (2013).

19. De Genova (2002: 438).

20. De Genova (2002, 2010). For more on the rippling impacts of deportation on families and communities, see also Hagan, Castro, and Rodríguez (2010); Hagan Rodríguez, and Castro (2011); Thronson (2008); Talavera, Núñez-Mchiri, and Heyman (2010).

21. Hagan, Castro, and Rodríguez (2010: 1815–16).

22. Yoshikawa (2011).

23. Križ and Skivenes (2012).

24. Menjívar (2011).

25. Mark López and Minushkin (2008).

26. Majumdar and Martínez-Ramos (2012).

27. Cavazos-Rehg, Zayas, and Spitznagel (2007).

28. Arbona et al. (2010).

29. See Golash-Boza and Hondagneu-Sotelo (2013) on the racialized nature of enforcement practices. For more on the racial overtones of US immigration policy, see Fitzgerald and Cook-Martin (2014).

30. See Chavez (1992), for example, about the risks for those living in shanty-towns in Southern California.

31. Gottlieb (2012).

32. Raúl legalized through the 245i provision, which I discuss further in the next chapter. The provision is no longer available. See also Golash-Boza (2012) for more on 245i.

33. Talavera, Núñez-Mchiri, and Heyman (2010).

34. Capps et al. (2003).

35. De Casanova (2012).

36. Immigrant women often link their families to social services. See Hondagneu-Sotelo (1994).

37. Dreby (2012, 2014). For more on how these gendered enforcement practices affect children's schooling, see Gallo (2014).

38. On the targeting of men for deportation, see Golash-Boza and Hondagneu-Sotelo (2013). Note that local districts do not release data on these gendered practices. However, among those I interviewed, women were regularly released on home arrest whereas men remained in detention centers. On suddenly single mothers, see also Dreby (2012, 2014).

39. For more on the experiences of children of the incarcerated, see Hanlon, Carswell, and Rose (2007); Roy and Dyson (2005).

40. Yoshikawa (2011).

41. Yoshikawa (2011).

42. There is a vast literature on fathers' involvement with children after divorce and a wide spectrum of involvement. See, for just a few examples, Amato (2000); Pryor and Rodgers (2001); Stone (2006); Troilo and Coleman (2012); Wade and Smart (2003).

43. See Megan Comfort's (2008) book *Doing Time Together* for more on the ways women stay connected with their incarcerated partners.

44. Dreby (2006, 2010); Parreñas (2005).

45. On factors, financial and others, that affect nonresidential fathers' contact with children after divorce, see Amato and Gilbreth (1999); Braver et al.

(1993); King and Sobolewski (2006); Seltzer (1991); Stone (2006); Troilo and Coleman (2012).

46. See also Golash-Boza (2013).

47. Brotherton and Barrios (2011); Golash-Boza (2013).

48. Confraternity of Christian Doctrine classes, a religious education program of the Catholic Church.

49. Brabeck and Xu (2010); Capps et al. (2007); Chaudry et al. (2010).

50. Gonzales and Chavez (2012).

51. Gonzales (2011).

52. While other studies focus on the impacts of a threat of deportation on communities and families, my research suggests that these impacts differ depending on each member's position within the family. See also Dreby (2014) for more on the different ways immigration policies specifically affect children.

53. There is a vast literature on gender and power in immigrant families. See Pessar (1999) for a review of just some of this literature.

54. As an example of the vilification of deadbeat fathers, the US Department of Health and Human Services publishes on their fraud website a "Deadbeat Dad of the Month." See http://oig.hhs.gov/fraud/child-support-enforcement/. For scholarship on the phenomenon, see Bartfeld and Meyer (1994); Bartfeld (2003); L. Curran and Abrams (2000); Presbury et al. (1997).

55. Amato (2000) finds that discord, breaches in parent-child relationships, and economic instability with divorce lead to negative outcomes among children (and adults).

56. Santos, Menjívar, and Godfrey (2013).

57. Abrego (2011); Dreby (2012).

3. STUCK

1. The information on Isabel's neighborhood comes from American Fact Finder of the U.S. Census Bureau. Upon meeting with families, I looked up information on the census tract they lived in and recorded the information on key neighborhood variables. To maintain confidentiality, I do not reveal the census tracts of study participants.

2. Because of her specific circumstances, Isabel cannot apply for VAWA: she is a repeat EWI (enter without inspection), and she also does not qualify for 245(i) because she married *el güero* after 245(i) had been rescinded.

3. On children's lack of power vis-à-vis adults, see A. Jensen and McKee (2003); Wrigley and Dreby (2005). On the similarities in the power imbalances due to generation and gender, see Thorne (1987).

4. Taylor et al. (2011). See also Fix and Zimmerman (2001); Menjívar and Abrego (2009) on mixed-status families.

5. Taylor et al. (2011).

6. I am referring to heterosexual relationships because only one of the mothers I interviewed spoke openly about being in a same-sex relationship (and this person did not parent her child). That illegality may influence relationships in non-gender-conforming relationships in different ways seems a particularly informative topic for future research but not one I can address. Steinbugler (2012) looks at racial boundary work among same-sex and heterosexual partners and finds little difference in how couples negotiate race-based inequalities. For the role of sexual regimes in constructing the distinction between legal and illegal status, see Luibheid (2008).

7. A significant body of work on immigrant families has explored nuances of gender relationships within families. For examples, see Boehm (2012); George (2005); Glick (2010); González-López (2005); Hirsch (2003); Hondagneu-Sotelo (1994, 2003); Kibria (1994); Menjívar (2000). In this chapter I draw on these contributions to the field to further explore the intimate negotiations within families under a period of time in which illegality is likely to highly affect these relationship negotiations.

8. Banerjee (2013); George (2005); Salcido and Menjívar (2012).

9. Boehm (2012: 62).

10. See Ingram et al. (2010) for the barriers women still face applying through the program. In fact, one mother I interviewed had left her emotionally abusive husband but remained married to him in order to obtain her papers through their marriage. She consulted a lawyer and determined that the pathway to legalization would be much easier through the spousal petition than a VAWA petition. Luckily, her husband agreed to this; after their separation he had already met another woman and, unlike *el güero,* left her alone.

11. Raj and Silverman (2002). For critiques of the success of VAWA for women, see Salcido and Menjívar (2012); Villalón (2010).

12. Marquardt et al. (2011).

13. B. Cooper and O'Neil (2005).

14. Immigration law is complex. This is my interpretation of the law. For a much more detailed description of the provisions of the changes to the law in 1996 that implemented the bars to readmission, see Fragomen (1997).

15. For more on 245(i), see Golash-Boza (2012).

16. Note this does not apply to visa overstayers. So someone who arrived on a visa and fell out of status can still apply for adjustment of status through a marriage-based petition.

17. For more on the relationship between immigration policy, illegality, and domestic violence, see Salcido and Adelman (2004).

18. There is an extensive literature on this topic. For a review of intimate partner violence among immigrant women, see Raj and Silverman (2002). For just a few examples of case studies with different immigrant groups, see Abraham

(1998, 1999); Ayyub (2000); Bui and Morash (1999); Morash, Bui, and Santiago (2000); and Rhee (1997).

19. Raj and Silverman (2002).

20. Raj and Silverman (2002).

21. See Anderson (2010) for a discussion of power structures and family violence.

22. For more on the informal networks Mexican women—and immigrant women more broadly—may rely on, see Hondagneu-Sotelo (1994); Kibria (1993); Schmalzbauer (2014).

23. De Genova (2002).

24. Wessler (2011a).

25. For more on patterns of violence in Mexican American families, see Sugihara and Warner (2002).

26. On men's accounts of violence as related to threats to their masculinity, see Anderson and Umberson (2001). For more on domestic violence more broadly, see Anderson (2010); Perilla, Bakeman, and Norris (1994); Schaefer, Caetano, and Clark (1998).

27. Bianchi et al. (2000); Coltrane (2000); Kroska (2004); Shelton and John (1996); South and Spitze (1994).

28. Coltrane (2000); DeVault (1991); South and Spitze (1994).

29. I triangulated accounts from parents and children in analysis.

30. In the eighty-one families, three women were single mothers, three had divorced, and five had separated. Four mothers shared custody with their children's fathers. I include single mothers without male partners in table 2 because this accurately reflects the reality of women's greater responsibility to child-rearing activities.

31. I counted contributions of women's male partners and also those of non-custodial fathers of single mothers; some of the latter helped with the children, and others made no contributions. Tellingly, I did not find any men to interview who were caring for their children without female partners. Although this may skew men toward never helping with household tasks, it accurately reflects the reality faced by mothers in raising their children.

32. On housework across the population, see Bittman et al. (2003); Coltrane (2000); South and Spitze (1994). On the distribution of housework among immigrant groups, see George (2005); Hondagneu-Sotelo (1994); Kibria (1993); Pinto and Coltrane (2009).

33. See the references in the previous note.

34. For the income of and taxes paid by immigrants and their adaptation, see Passel and Clark (1998). For the experience of poverty among Mexican American and Mexican immigrants, see García (2011). For statistics on poverty among unauthorized migrants, see Passel and Cohn (2009).

35. Research suggests that differences between spouses due to race, class, and other cultural differences may influence negotiations between partners. For more on these types of negotiations, see Bystydzienski (2011); Steinbugler (2012).

36. Describing the class backgrounds of migrants is complex, as migrants' class backgrounds and work experience often differ before and after migration. See Portes and Rumbaut (2006). Additionally, educational expectations in Mexico differ from those in the United States. In the United States, schooling is mandatory through the ninth grade. However, I interviewed some from rural parts of Mexico who had not studied past the second or third grade. Regardless, I interviewed parents with a range of class backgrounds, from those with little formal education to those who were college graduates.

37. Pinto and Coltrane (2009) find that Mexican-origin women's employment hours are inversely related to time spent on housework.

38. Konrad and Lommerud (2000); Lundberg and Pollak (1996); McElroy and Horney (1981); Manser and Brown (1980).

39. A. Hochschild (1990).

40. While these concepts were first articulated by Bourdieu, for definitions of social and cultural capital see J. Coleman (1988); Lareau (2003).

41. Some previous research indicates that immigrant women compensate with household chores when their partners have lower-status or lower-paid jobs in the United States. See George (2005); Kibria (1993); Menjívar (2003).

42. Donato and Sisk (2012).

43. Rivera-Batiz (1999).

44. There is a vast literature on care work. See the webpage of the Carework Network at www.carework-network.org/index.cfm?nodeid=2 for the network of researchers working in the area of care work and care work policy. See also England (2005).

45. See DeVault (1991) on the centrality of food to women's roles in families.

46. Mills (1959).

47. Yoshikawa (2011). Terriquez (2012), however, finds that legal status is not a significant indicator of maternal involvement in schools in Los Angeles.

48. There is a vast literature on children's brokering activities. A complete bibliography is available at Education and Social Research Institute, Manchester Metropolitan University, "Children and Adolescents as Language Brokers: Bibliography" (under "Research Projects"), www.esri.mmu.ac.uk/resprojects/brokering/biblio.php. For some examples, see Buriel et al. (1998); C. Cooper, Denner, and López (1999); Dorner, Orellana, and Li–Grining (2007); Jones and Trickett (2005); Katz (2014); C. Martínez, McClure, and Eddy (2009); Morales and Hanson (2005); Orellana (2001, 2009); Orellana, Dorner, and Pulido (2003); Phinney et al. (2001); Trickett and Jones (2007); Tse (1995); Valenzuela (1999); Weisskirch and Alva (2002).

49. For children's roles specifically as paraphrasers or translators, see Orellana (2009); Orellana, Dorner, and Pulido (2003); Katz (2014).

50. Orellana, Dorner, and Pulido (2003) describe these different domains in which children work as translators for their families, as does Valenzuela (1999).

51. On school outcomes, see Buriel et al. (1998); Tse (1995). On brokering and acculturation, see Katz (2014); Weisskirch and Alva (2002).

52. See Katz (2014).

53. Menjívar (2000) describes these types of tensions in El Salvadoran families as well. For more on power in intergenerational relations, see Foner (2009); Foner and Dreby (2011); Wrigley and Dreby (2005).

54. Katz (2014); Valenzuela (1999).

55. Foner (2009); Umaña-Taylor (2003).

56. See also Kibria (1993); Stepick and Stepick (2003); Suárez-Orozco and Suárez-Orozco (2001); Waters (1999); Waters and Sykes (2009); Zephir (2001). In the early twentieth century, reports to child protection by children of their immigrant parents were also common. See Gordon (1988); Pleck (1983, 1987).

57. For an example, see Menjívar (2000).

58. Corsaro (2003).

59. Buriel et al. (1998); Tse (1995).

60. See Lareau (2002, 2003) and Ferguson (2000) on the ways race and class shape parenting.

61. For some work that does define children's work in the home as an expression of power in the household, see Orellana (2001, 2009); Valenzuela (1999).

62. Although I do have information from families on the housework contributions of all children in the families I interviewed, here I report just on the experiences of interviewed children. These reports may be more reliable, since I determined contributions by triangulating more than one family member. Additionally, doing so excludes the youngest—and the oldest—children in families, which skew the reports of child's contributions significantly, with young children doing no work in families. Also for purposes here, I am excluding the nine children I interviewed who were legal migrants or naturalized citizens.

63. This pattern contradicts Katz's (2014) findings in interviews with twenty child-brokering families that most brokers are US citizen children to unauthorized parents. Given that my sample is not generalizable to all Mexican immigrant populations—or US immigrant populations more broadly—more large-scale quantitative data are needed to determine patterns in brokering activities by child and parent legal status.

64. The expectation is expressed by Katz (2014).

65. Raley and Bianchi (2006); Valenzuela (1999).

66. Valenzuela (1999). On familism or *familismo,* see Sabogal et al. (1987); Steidel and Contreras (2003); Tienda (1980); Valenzuela and Dornbush (1994).

67. On the second shift, see A. Hochschild (1990).

68. Boehm (2012: 80).

69. Weisskirch and Alva (2002).

70. While Lareau (2003) finds that child-rearing practices vary significantly by class backgrounds, the work children are expected to do in the contemporary United States is fairly minimal. See, for example, Kolbert (2012).

4. IT'S NOT FAIR

The chapter epigraph is from Conley (2004: 8).

1. Lareau (2003); Levey (2013).

2. Information on the neighborhood where Camilo lived with his family is available via American Factfinder. However, because I am keeping the location confidential I do not cite the specific website here.

3. See the previous note.

4. This is true among both legal and undocumented migrants. See Akresh (2008); Chriswick and Hurst (1998); Segura (1989); Sullivan (1984).

5. Information on the schools in this city and statewide is available on the New Jersey Department of Education website. Because I am keeping the site confidential, I do not cite the specific website here.

6. See the previous note.

7. See note 5.

8. Extensive scholarship outlines the extent to which the concept of the American dream shapes US society. For an interesting treatment of this shared dream, see J. Hochschild (1996).

9. Abowd and Killingsworth (1985); Danziger and Gottschalk (1993); Farley and Allen (1987); Keister and Moller (2000); Kirschenman and Neckerman (1991); Oliver and Shapiro (2006); Reimers (1985); Waters and Eschbach (1995).

10. Smith (2008). For general information on the intergenerational transmission of social inequality, see Bowles and Gintis (2001, 2002). For intergenerational inequality among immigrant groups, see Portes and Zhou (1993); Zhou (1997b).

11. Alexander, Entwisle, and Olson (2014); Huston (1991); Lareau (2002).

12. See, for example, Beller and Hout (2006).

13. Meir, Slone, and Lavi (2012); Ortega et al. (2009); Suárez-Orozco et al. (2011); Yoshikawa (2011); Yoshikawa and Kalil (2011).

14. Maria López (2005).

15. For more on the controversy in Alabama, see Fox News Latino (2012). For general attendance issues faced by immigrant students, see Driscoll (1999); Suárez-Orozco and Suárez-Orozco (2001); Zhou (1997b).

16. Abrego (2006); Eckstein (2009); Gonzales (2011); Ruge and Iza (2004); Seo (2011); Vandenhole et al. (2011).

17. Nandi et al. (2008); Yoshikawa (2011); Yoshikawa and Kalil (2011).

18. Gonzales, Suárez-Orozco, and Dedios-Sanguineti (2013); Potochnick and Perreira (2010).

19. See Chilton et al. (2009); Hadley et al. (2008); Van Hook and Balistreri (2006).

20. Yoshikawa (2011). See also Yoshikawa and Kalil (2011).

21. Passel and Cohn (2009).

22. Flippen (2001); Keister and Moller (2000); Krivo and Kaufman (2004); Rosenbaum and Friedman (2007).

23. Conley (2004).

24. Dahan and Gaviria (2003); Rosenzweig (1986); Yamauchi (2006).

25. Of course, Messi has sported various hairstyles over the years.

26. For more on code switching, see Portes and Schauffler (1994); Reyes (2004); Vu, Bailey, and Howes (2010).

27. See Waters and Jiménez (2005).

28. The pattern did not hold among fourteen- and fifteen-year-olds, as all of the US-born children had had friends over but only four of the six unauthorized children had.

29. Lareau (2003).

30. Bianchi and Robinson (1997); Cogle and Tasker (1982); Hofferth and Sandberg (2001).

31. Cogle and Tasker (1982); Gager, Sanchez, and DeMaris (2009).

32. Hofferth and Sandberg (2001).

33. Katz (2014); Orellana (2001); Song (1999).

34. Some research suggests that the experience of immigration makes men more open to helping out with domestic tasks. See DeBiaggi (2002); Hondagneu-Sotelo (1994); Pribilsky (2004).

35. Cogle and Tasker (1982).

36. Legal permanent residents can petition for their minor children, but they are put on a waiting list. Citizens who petition for minor children avoid the waiting list, although it still can take one to two years for an application to process.

37. Cerrutti and Massey (2001); Dreby (2010); Kanaiapuni (2000).

38. Note that the great majority of the men I met accepted their nonbiologically children seamlessly, at least in public.

39. Dreby (2006, 2010).

40. See Dreby (2010) on the ways children and parents experience time differently while living apart. Also see Bernhard, Landolt, and Goldring (2005) on mothers' experiences of reunification with their children.

41. Research suggests hardship during periods of separation for children. See Aguilera-Guzmán et al. (2004); Dreby (2007); Parreñas (2005). Some research suggests long-term impacts of separation after reunification. See Artico (2003); Gindling and Poggio (2009); Suárez-Orozco, Todovora, and Louie (2002). For

some children in other cultural contexts, separations may not be nearly so devastating. See Olwig (1999).

42. Suárez-Orozco, Todorova, and Louie (2002).

43. Lareau (2003).

44. Gans (1992); Smith (2006); Portes and Zhou (1993); Waldinger and Feliciano (2004); Waters et al. (2010); Zhou (1997b).

45. To be eligible for deferred action, youth must be between the ages of fifteen and thirty-one and be in school or have graduated from high school. See US Citizenship and Immigration Services, "Consideration of Deferred Action for Childhood Arrivals," www.uscis.gov/portal/site/uscis/menuitem.eb1d4c2a3e5b9ac892 43c6a7543f6d1a/?vgnextoid=f2ef2f19470f7310VgnVCM100000082ca60aRCRD &vgnextchannel=f2ef2f19470f7310VgnVCM100000082ca60aRCRD#guidelines (accessed August 29, 2014). For more on how deferred action has affected children, see Gonzales and Terriquez (2013).

46. Conley (2004).

47. Research by Bernal et al. (1990) suggests that ethnic identity formation corresponds to developmental stage, with Mexican American children developing an understanding of ethnic identity before they reach the age of seven or eight.

48. Bernal et al. (1990); Brown and Chu (2012); Phinney et al. (2001); Portes and Schauffler (1994); Umaña-Taylor and Fine (2004).

49. On children's development of a sense of ethnicity, see Gans (1979). On teenagers' development of a pan-ethnic identity, see D. López and Espiritu (1990). On Mexican American adolescents' ethnic identity formation, see Umaña-Taylor and Fine (2004).

50. Most literature on identity formation focuses on the adolescent years. For example, Phinney (1989) suggests three stages in children's identity development and states that for minorities ethnic identity develops most strongly in adolescence. Some sociologists have suggested that children develop understandings of race and ethnicity at earlier ages. See, for example, Van Ausdale and Feagin (1996).

51. For a fascinating study of children's preoccupation with fairness during divorce, see Wade and Smart (2003). Children's preoccupation with fairness has also been extensively studied in psychological and economic literatures. For example, see Almas et al. (2010); Evans et al. (1994).

52. Conley (2004).

53. Smith (2006).

54. Artico (2003). For more on transnational family reunions, see Ramirez, Skrbis, and Emmison (2007). For more on the emotions involved in the maintenance of transnational families, see Baldassar (2007, 2008); Svasek (2008).

55. Gindling and Poggio (2009).

56. Gleeson and Gonzales (2012).

57. On the marginality of undocumented youth, see Silver (2012). On activism among undocumented youth, see Gonzales, Heredia, and Negrón-Gonzales (2013); Negrón-Gonzales (2013).

58. Greenman and Hall (2013).

5. STIGMA

The chapter epigraph is from Goffman (1963: 3).

1. Sociologists have long considered the family as a primary site for children's socialization. Parsons and Bales (1955) analyzed the functional imperatives of nuclear families, for example, arguing that families socialized children into stable adult personalities. For symbolic interractionalists, the family also plays a critical role in the development of what Cooley ([1902] 1922) called "the looking glass self" and, for Mead (1934) the development of self-identity through social interaction and the understanding of a generalized others. See Handel (1988, 2011).

2. On the early forging of group hierarchies, see P. Adler and Adler (1998). On race, see Lewis (2003a, 2003b). On gender, see Hey (1997), Pascoe (2007); Thorne (1993). On class, see Willis (1977). On the interactions of race, class, and gender, see Bettie (2003).

3. On the formation of ties in extracurricular activities, see Levey (2013); Medrich et al. (1992). On the development of identities through these activities, see Fine (1987); Grasmuck (2005); Messner (2000).

4. Much of immigration scholarship falls within assimilation paradigms, considering to what extent adults—and by extension children over time—adjust to life in the United States. See, for example, Alba and Nee (2003); Portes and Zhou (2003); Rumbaut and Portes (2001); Waters and Jiménez (2005); Zhou (1997a).

5. On downward assimilation, see Fernández-Kelly and Schauffler (1994); Rumbaut (1994); Waldinger and Feliciano (2004); Zhou (1997b). On the relationship between acculturation and delinquent behavior, see Fridrich and Flannery (1995).

6. See, for example, Chinn (2009); Thomas and Znaniecki ([1918] 1958); Ware ([1963] 1994).

7. Zhou and Bankston (1998).

8. Most research suggests that it isn't until the college years that coethnic peer group relationships have positive impacts on children's identity and self-esteem. See Min and Kim (2000); Zhou and Lee (2004).

9. Warikoo (2011).

10. What scholars term the new sociology of childhood perspective challenges the socialization processes underlying assimilation paradigms. See James, Jenks, and Prout (1998); Qvortrup (1999); Thorne (1987). Scholars like Willis (1977) and Corsaro (2003) argue that children actively create peer group cultures that,

although in ways representing reactions to adult-based culture, form unique cultural perspectives.

11. Corsaro and Eder (1990: 200).

12. Thorne (1993).

13. Lewis (2003a).

14. For more on cliques in high schools, and their consequences, see Bettie (2003); Clasen and Brown (1985); Kinney (1993).

15. P. Adler and Adler (1998, 1996).

16. P. Adler and Adler (1998, 1996).

17. P. Adler and Adler (1998, 1996). Although stories about outcasts or loners abound in studies of children in schools, research specifically on the topic surged only recently with the concern for school shootings. See, for example, Newman et al. (2004); Newman and Fox (2009).

18. Terrazas (2011). For more on Mexican migration to new destination sites, see Durand, Massey, and Capoferro (2005); Marrow (2011); Millard and Chapa (2004); Schmalzbauer (2009, 2011).

19. Thorne (1993) wrote about cross-gender chasing games being typical in the schools she studied in the early 1930s. Remarkably, I observed similar games at recess at all nine schools I visited thirty years later. Cross-gender chasing seems to be a distinctive component of kids' culture. See Corsaro (2003).

20. Information on the demographics and performance of students at this school is available on the New Jersey Department of Education website school report cards. For confidentiality purposes, I cannot cite the specific report card data for the school here.

21. In interacting with families, I often used the approach of full engagement, cooking and even cleaning with women on my visits when appropriate. At schools, however, I decided the best role would be that of disengaged observer. After all, I did not want to embarrass the children I was observing by letting on that I knew them outside school. So I told children who asked when I visited classrooms that I was simply there to learn about what it was like in the third, or first or second, grade. The only people who knew I was there to learn about the experiences of a specific child was the child's parent, the child as per his or her parent's explanation, and the student's teachers. While I explicitly told the schools I was there to watch the focal child, I avoided disclosing this information in all my interactions with children in schools.

22. For more on patterns of Oaxacan migration, see Besserer and Kearney (2006); Cohen (2004); Kearney (2000); Méndez Morales (2000); Rivera-Salgado (1999); Stephen (2002, 2007).

23. For more on the history of Mexican migration to the greater New York metropolitan region, see Cortés Sánchez (2003); Smith (2006).

24. For more on overcrowded housing among immigrants, see Myers and Lee (1996).

25. For an example of the level of statewide organization of Latinos in the state of New Jersey, see the website of the Latino Leadership Alliance of New Jersey at http://llanj.org/.

26. For more on the ways infrastructure matters for immigrant women, see Dreby and Schmalzbauer (2013).

27. For more on Mexican youth gangs in the greater New York City region, see Cortés (2012); Smith (2006). New Jersey has a higher rate of gang per capita than New York State. See National Gang Intelligence Center (2011).

28. Information on the demographics and performance of students at this school is available on the New Jersey Department of Education website school report cards. For confidentiality purposes, I cannot cite the specific report card data for the school here.

29. See previous note.

30. See note 28.

31. Rotheram-Borus and Phinney (2008); Way et al. (2001).

32. P. Adler and Adler (1996, 1998).

33. See Dreby (2010); Dreby and Stutz (2012).

34. Perhaps I should not have been surprised, since ethnic minority students report more discrimination than majority groups; see Seaton et al. (2013). They especially report discrimination from adults; see Rosenbloom and Way (2004).

35. See also Edwards and Romero (2008) on how fears of immigration may be linked to the experiences of discrimination that Mexican children report and on the consequences for some of youths' coping mechanisms.

36. Bettie (2003) argues that there are specific expressions of femininity among girls of different racial and class backgrounds. The same is likely true among boys in school.

37. Information on the demographics and performance of students at this school is available on the Ohio Department of Education website school report cards. For confidentiality purposes, I cannot cite the specific report card data for the school here.

38. See Felix and You (2011) and S. Graham (2006) on how nondiverse school contexts are associated with higher reports of discrimination from nonmajority youth. Hanish and Guerra (2000) find, however, that Hispanic children have lower victimization scores than do white and African American children.

39. Crosnoe (2005).

40. This does not necessarily lead to poor academic outcomes. A body of research recently suggests that there is an immigrant advantage in educational attainment. See García Coll and Marks (2012); Fuligni (1997); Feliciano (2012).

41. For more on problem behaviors among Mexican-origin youth, see Marsiglia, Parsai, and Kulis (2009).

42. In my experience, often teachers blame children's misbehavior on parents' lack of involvement. Indeed, there is a large literature linking parental involvement

to school outcomes. For examples, see Fehrmann, Keith, and Reimers (1987); Ho Sui-Chu and Willms (1996); Jeynes (2007); Sheldon and Epstein (2005); Steinberg et al. (1992).

43. I write more on the dynamics between Elizabeth and her husband in Dreby and Schmalzbauer (2013).

44. Larson and Richards (1991) look at reports of boredom and find that students bored in school also often report being bored at home, and thus that boredom may be an individual disposition. While this may be the case, Kevin rarely reported boredom at home and easily entertained himself even though he participated in few extracurricular activities, suggesting that he did not tend toward boredom in his personality.

45. Kozol (1991).

46. Kozol (1991). See also Berner (1993) and Uline and Tschannen-Moran (2008) on physical aspects of school facilities and student achievement.

47. Stanton-Salazar and Spina (2005); Updegraff et al. (2006); Way et al. (2001).

48. See Stanton-Salazar and Spina (2005); Updegraff (2006); and Way et. al (2001) for the social support that peer groups provide for youth and the potential negative consequences for youth without such peer group support.

49. Nansel et al. (2001: 2094).

50. That Mexican parents in Ohio reported more discrimination from white Americans than from African Americans is interesting, given that in a new destination site in the South Marrow (2011) reports many more tensions between African American and Mexican communities than between Mexican and white American communities.

51. On theories of racialization, see Omi and Winant (1986).

52. Lewis (2003a: 297).

53. For more on minority youths' problems with discrimination from teachers in schools, see Rosenbloom and Way (2004).

54. Research suggests that hostile school environments—for LBGTQ-identified youth especially—can be extremely detrimental to children's school experiences and academic success and that school intervention in bullying incidents has a large positive outcome for children experiencing harassment. See Birkett, Espelage, and Koenig (2009); Kosciw (2004); Pearson, Muller, and Wilkinson (2007). For the impact of discrimination in school on minority youth, see Flores et al. (2010) and Rosenbloom and Way (2004).

55. Lamont and Molnar (2002: 168) define symbolic boundaries as "the conceptual distinctions made by social actors to categorize objects, people, practices and even time and space."

56. See also Gonzales, Heredia, and Negrón-Gonzales (2013).

57. Goffman (1963: 42).

58. Lamont and Molnár (2002: 168).

59. I don't think this was a daily occurrence or a typical feature of the game. Later I asked another girl I interviewed who played the "girls chase the boys" game about the incident and she didn't recall it. However, as Corsaro argues, one central theme in children's peer group culture involves children's attempts to deal with confusions, concerns, fears, and conflicts in their daily lives through play (Corsaro and Eder 1990: 214). As this example indicates, at least for one child on the blacktop that day, immigration featured in play perhaps in order to reconcile his concerns or fears about the topic.

60. Corsaro (2003: 37).

61. Corsaro (2003: 115).

6. CONCLUSION

1. Grieco et al. (2012).

2. In 1990, one in five foreign-born US residents were estimated to be unauthorized (Passel, Cohn, and González-Barrera 2013).

3. For more on the DREAMers, see Kim (2013); Olivas (2010); Nicholls (2009); Seif (2011).

4. Wessler (2011a).

5. For more information on the Center for American Progress's work in immigration, see the Immigration Archives on their website at www.americanprogress .org/issues/immigration/view/page/2/. For more on First Focus's work, see Children of Immigrants," under "Our Work," www.firstfocus.net/our-work/children-of-immigrants. For more on the work of the Domestic Workers' Alliance We Belong Together Campaign, see "We Belong Together," www.domesticworkers .org/we-belong-together.

6. Legal status is now the focal point of much social science research on immigration. See, for example, Abrego (2011, 2006); Arbona et al. (2010); Armenta (2012); Brabeck and Xu (2010); Cavazos-Rehg, Zayas, and Spitznagel (2007); Coutin (2001); De Genova (2002, 2004, 2010); De Genova and Peutz (2010); Donato and Armenta (2011); Enriquez (2011); Fix and Zimmerman (2001); Gleeson and Gonzales (2012); Gonzales (2011); Gonzales, Heredia and Negrón-Gonzales (2013); Kanstroom (2007); Majumdar and Martínez-Ramos (2012); Marrow (2011); Menjívar (2006, 2011); Menjívar and Abrego (2012); Menjívar and Kanstroom (2013); Ngai (2004); Pedroza (2013); Suárez-Orozco et al. (2011); Talavera, Núñez-Mchiri, and Heyman (2010); Willen (2007, 2012); Yoshikawa and Kalil (2011); Yoshikawa (2011).

7. De Genova (2002).

8. Bloemraad, Korteweg, and Yurdakul (2008).

9. Gonzales (2011).

10. Menjívar (2011: 379).

11. See Gonzales, Suárez-Orozco, and Dedios-Sanguineti (2013); O. Martínez et al. (2013); Willen (2012).

12. See Ngai (2004) and Zolberg (2006) for more on changes in the meaning of legality and illegality at different points in US history.

13. See Foner (2000) for a comparison of life in New York City at the beginning and end of the twentieth century.

14. E-Verify is a program that employers can participate in voluntarily, allowing them to check the immigration status of potential employees. Reform measures have considered making E-Verify mandatory. See Rosenblum (2011).

15. See Pinkerton (2008) for a media report on the market for false documents.

16. Bettie (2003); Lewis (2003a, 2003b); Pascoe (2007); Thorne (1993); Van Ausdale and Feagin (1996).

17. Lamont and Molnár (2002). See also Alba (2005) as this applies to immigrants.

18. Lareau (2002, 2003).

19. On class distinctions and social mobility, see Abowd and Killingsworth (1985); Danziger and Gottschalk (1993); Farley and Allen (1987); Keister and Moller (2000); Kirschenman and Neckerman (1991); Oliver and Shapiro (2006); Reimers (1985); Waters and Eschbach (1995).

20. For more on the complexities of power related to gender and generation specifically in immigrant households, see Foner (2009); Foner and Dreby (2011); George (2005); Hondagneu-Sotelo (1994); Kibria (1993); Menjívar (2000); Wrigley and Dreby (2005).

21. For more on the demographic composition of mixed-status families, see Fix and Zimmerman (2001).

22. For more on intersectionality and family relationships, see Berg (2010); Bratter and Zuberi (2008); Brewer (1999); Hancock (2007); Hill (2004); Hill and Sprague (1999); Luttrell (1989).

23. Romero (2008).

24. N. Adler and Rehkopf (2008: 237).

25. For more on health outcomes, see Cavazos-Rehg, Zayas, and Spitznagel (2007); Flores et al. (2010); Fountain and Bearman (2011); Gonzales, Suárez-Orozco, and Dedios-Sanguineti (2013); Križ and Skivenes (2012); O. Martínez et al. (2013); Meir, Sloane, and Lavi (2012); Nandi et al. (2008); Willen (2012).

26. See Acevedo-García et al. (2003); Williams and Collins (2001); Williams, Neighbors, and Jackson (2003).

27. See Gray (2013). Also see Smith (2006) on changing patterns of Mexican migration to the East Coast in the 1990s.

28. For more on the specific ways political upheaval in Central America has shaped migratory patterns, see Menjívar (2000).

29. I had to call my father and stepmother to clarify the details of this event. Paz was the name she used while in sanctuary, meaning "peace" in Spanish, although this was not her real name.

30. Leo Chavez's (1992) book accurately depicts undocumented individuals in the 1980s as living "shadowed lives."

31. For more on the Sanctuary Movement, see Coutin (1993); Davidson (1988); Wiltfang and McAdam (1991).

32. Leaders of the Sanctuary Movement had been targeted, resulting in over twenty indictments of Sanctuary Movement volunteers. In retrospect I believe that those known to be living in sanctuary had at times been identified by local border patrol agents and had experienced harassment because of this.

33. For more on new destinations, see Durand, Massey, and Capoferro (2005); Marrow (2011); Millard and Chapa (2004), Schmalzbauer (2009, 2011); Smith (2006).

34. For more on Secure Communities, see Kohli, Markowitz, and Chavez (2011); Pedroza (2013); Strunk and Leitner (2013). For more on the changes brought on by 9/11 to current immigration enforcement practices, see M. Coleman (2007); De Genova (2010).

35. I write about Dylan's experiences in understanding immigration in Dreby (2013).

36. Balderrama and Rodríguez (2006); Kanstroom (2007); Ngai (2004); Zolberg (2006).

37. Nakano Glenn (1983).

38. Golash-Boza and Hondagneu-Sotelo (2013).

39. Foner (2000).

40. For a good description of changes in border funding and policy, see Marquardt et al. (2011).

41. Gonzales and Terriquez (2013).

42. Clozel (2014).

43. Gonzales and Terriquez (2013).

44. Thompson and Cohn (2014).

45. For an excellent investigative report on the failure of Secure Communities in Maryland, see Fritze (2014).

46. Thank you to Mary Valentis.

47. Thank you to Hiroshi Motomura for the idea of describing these experiences as a baseline.

48. In some places they already have. In 2014 California passed the Trust Act, leading to a drop in immigration holds. See Spagat and Taxin (2014).

49. See Migration Policy Institute (2013) for a comparison of the Senate bills proposed in 2006, 2007, and 2013. None made it through the House of Representatives.

50. The DREAM Act, for example, has not passed when proposed at the federal level. See Galassi (2003); Olivas (2010). For more on the DREAM Act, see Motomura (2013).

51. Meissner et al. (2013).

52. Migration Policy Institute (2013).

53. See Coutin (2001, 2011); Marquardt et al. (2011).

54. For more on *Cops*, see www.cops.com/. See Curry (2001); Prosise and Johnson (2004) for analyses of the *Cops* TV show.

55. For more on the show, see the show overview provided on the National Geographic Channel's website: http://channel.nationalgeographic.com/channel /border-wars/. For a critique of the show, see Caramanica (2010).

56. Motomura (2012).

57. A Google Scholar search of the term for the years up to 1999 yields 21 hits, with only 13 being related to immigrant families. The same search for the years 2000–2013 yields 706 results, all of which appear to refer to immigrant families.

58. Yoshikawa (2011).

59. For scholarly work on the impacts of illegality on the 1.5 generation, see Abrego (2006, 2011); Abrego and Gonzales (2010); Enriquez (2011); Gonzales (2011); Gonzales and Chavez (2012); Gurrola, Ayón, and Salas (2013); Sigona (2012); Zhou et al. (2008).

60. Yoshikawa (2011).

61. For more on the impacts of lengthy family separations on child well-being, see Abrego (2014); E. Graham and Jordan (2011); Heymann et al. (2009); Lahaie et al. (2009); Landolt and Da (2005); Nobles (2011); Parreñas (2005).

62. Migration Policy Institute (2013).

APPENDIX

1. For more on grounded theory, see Charmaz (2006); Glaser and Strauss (1967).

References

Abowd, John M., and Mark R. Killingsworth. 1985. "Employment, Wages, and Earnings of Hispanics in the Federal and Non-federal Sectors: Methodological Issues and Their Empirical Consequences." In *Hispanics in the U.S. Economy*, edited by George J. Borjas and Marta Tienda, 77–126. Orlando, FL: Academic Press.

Abraham, Margaret. 1998. "Speaking the Unspeakable: Marital Violence against South Asian Immigrant Women in the United States." *Indian Journal of Gender Studies* 5 (2): 215–41.

———. 1999. "Sexual Abuse in South Asian Immigrant Marriages." *Violence against Women* 5 (6): 591–618.

Abrego, Leisy. 2006. "'I Can't Go to College Because I Don't Have Papers': Incorporation Patterns of Latino Undocumented Youth." *Latino Studies* 4:212–31.

———. 2011. "Legal Consciousness of Undocumented Latinos: Fear and Stigma as Barriers to Claims-Making for First and 1.5 Generation Immigrants." *Law and Society Review* 45 (2): 337–69.

———. 2014. *Sacrificing Families: Navigating Laws, Labor, and Love across Borders.* Stanford, CA: Stanford University Press.

Abrego, Leisy, and Roberto Gonzales. 2010. "Blocked Paths, Uncertain Futures: The Postsecondary Education and Labor Market Prospects of Undocumented Latino Youth." *Journal of Education for Students Placed at Risk* 15:144–57.

Acevedo-García, Dolores, Kimberly A. Lochner, Theresa L. Osypuk, and S. V. Subramanian. 2003. "Future Directions in Residential Segregation and Health Research: A Multilevel Approach." *American Journal of Public Health* 93 (2): 215–21.

Adler, Nancy E., and David H. Rehkopf. 2008. "U.S. Disparities in Health: Descriptions, Causes, and Mechanisms." *Annual Review of Public Health* 29:235–52.

Adler, Patricia A., and Peter Adler. 1996. "Preadolescent Clique Stratification and the Hierarchy of Identity." *Sociological Inquiry* 66 (2): 111–42.

———. 1998. *Peer Power*. New Brunswick, NJ: Rutgers University Press.

Aguilera-Guzmán, Rosa María, V. Nelly Salgado de Snyder, Martha Romero, and María Elena Medina-Mora. 2004. "Paternal Absence and International Migration: Stressors and Compensators Associated with the Mental Health of Mexican Teenagers of Rural Origin." *Adolescence* 39:711–23.

Akresh, Ilana R. 2008. "Occupational Trajectories of Legal U.S. Immigrants: Downgrading and Recovery." *Population and Development Review* 34 (3): 435–56.

Alba, Richard D. 2005. "Bright vs. Blurred Boundaries: Second-Generation Assimilation and Exclusion in France, Germany, and the United States." *Ethnic and Racial Studies* 28 (1): 20–49.

Alba, Richard, and Victor Nee. 2003. *Remaking the American Mainstream: Assimilation and Contemporary Immigration*. Cambridge, MA: Harvard University Press.

Alexander, Karl, Doris Entwisle, and Linda Olson. 2014. *The Long Shadow: Family Background, Disadvantaged Urban Youth and the Transition to Adulthood*. New York: Russell Sage.

Almas, Ingvild, Alexander W. Cappelen, Erik Sorensen, and Bertil Tungodden. 2010. "Fairness and the Development of Inequality Acceptance." *Science* 328 (5982): 1176–78.

Amato, Paul R. 2000. "The Consequences of Divorce for Adults and Children." *Journal of Marriage and Family* 62:1269–87.

Amato, Paul R., and Joan G. Gilbreth. 1999. "Nonresident Fathers and Children's Well-Being: A Meta-analysis." *Journal of Marriage and the Family* 61:557–73.

Amuedo-Dorantes, Catalina, Thitima Puttitanun, and Ana P. Martinez-Donate. 2013. "How Do Tougher Immigration Measures Affect Unauthorized Immigrants?" *Demography* 50:1067–91.

Anderson, Kristin L. 2010. "Conflict, Power, and Violence in Families." *Journal of Marriage and Family* 72 (3): 726–42.

Anderson, Kristin L., and Debra Umberson. 2001. "Gendering Violence: Masculinity and Power in Men's Accounts of Domestic Violence." *Gender and Society* 15 (3): 358–80.

Andreas, Peter. 2009. *Border Games: Policing the US-Mexico Divide*. Ithaca, NY: Cornell University Press.

Arbona, Consuela, Norma Olvera, Nestor Rodríguez, Jacqueline Hagan, Adriana Linares, and Margit Wiesner. 2010. "Acculturative Stress among Documented and Undocumented Latino Immigrants in the United States." *Hispanic Journal of Behavioral Sciences* 32:362–84.

Armenta, Amada. 2012. "From Sheriff's Deputies to Immigration Officers: Screening Immigrant Status in a Tennessee Jail." *Law and Policy* 34 (2): 191–220.

Artico, Ceres I. 2003. *Latino Families Broken by Immigration: The Adolescents' Perceptions*. New York: LFB Scholarly Publishing.

Ayyub, Ruksana. 2000. "Domestic Violence in the South Asian Muslim Immigrant Population in the United States." *Journal of Social Distress and the Homeless* 9 (3): 237–48.

Baldassar, Loretta. 2007. "Transnational Families and the Provision of Moral and Emotional Support: The Relationship between Truth and Distance." *Identities* 14 (4): 385–409.

———. 2008. "Missing Kin and Longing to Be Together: Emotions and the Construction of Co-presence in Transnational Relationship." *Journal of Intercultural Studies* 29 (3): 247–66.

Balderrama, Francisco, and Raymond Rodríguez. 2006. *Decade of Betrayal: Mexican Repatriation in the 1930s*. Santa Fe: University of New Mexico Press.

Banerjee, Pallavi. 2013. "Not Valid for Identification: Gendered Migrations, Visa Structures and Invisible Webs of Dependence." Paper presented at the annual meeting of the American Sociological Association, New York. http://citation.allacademic.com/meta/p_mla_apa_research_citation/6/4/8/7/0/p648709_index.html.

Bartfeld, Judi. 2003. "Falling through the Cracks: Gaps in Child Support among Welfare Recipients." *Journal of Marriage and Family* 65 (1): 72–89.

Bartfeld, Judi, and Daniel Meyer. 1994. "Are There Really Deadbeat Dads? The Relationship between Ability to Pay, Enforcement, and Compliance in Nonmarital Child Support Cases." *Social Service Review* 68 (2): 219–35.

Bassuk, Ellen., Jennifer N. Perloff, and Cynthia García Coll. 1998. "The Plight of Extremely Poor Puerto Rican and Non-Hispanic White Single Mothers." *Social Psychiatry and Psychiatric Epidemiology* 33 (7): 326–36.

Beller, Emily, and Michael Hout. 2006. "Intergenerational Social Mobility: The United States in Comparative Perspective." *Future of Children* 16:19–36.

Berg, Justin Allen. 2010. "Race, Class, Gender, and Social Space: Using an Intersectional Approach to Study Immigration Attitudes." *Sociological Quarterly* 51 (2): 278–302.

Bergeron, Claire. 2013. *Going to the Back of the Line: A Primer on Lines, Visa Categories and Wait Times*. Migration Policy Institute Issue Brief 1.

Washington, DC: Migration Policy Institute. www.migrationpolicy.org/pubs /CIRbrief-BackofLine.pdf.

Bernal, Martha E., George P. Knight, Camille A. Garza, Katheryn A. Ocampo, and Marya K. Cota. 1990. "The Development of Ethnic Identity in Mexican-American Children." *Hispanic Journal of Behavioral Sciences* 12:3–24.

Berner, Maureen M. 1993. "Building Conditions, Parental Involvement, and Student Achievement in the District of Columbia Public School System." *Urban Education* 28 (1): 6–29.

Bernhard, Judith, Patricia Landolt, and Luin Goldring. 2005. "Transnational, Multi-local Motherhood: Experiences of Separation and Reunification among Latin American Families in Canada." CERIS Working Paper 40, Joint Center of Excellence for Research on Immigration and Settlement, Toronto. July. www.yorku.ca/cohesion/LARG/PDF/Families_Bernhard_ final_sep_12_05.pdf.

Berumen, Salvador, Luis Felipe Ramos, and Isabel Ureta. 2011. "Migrantes mexicanos aprehendidos y devueltos por Estados Unidos: Estimaciones y características generales." In *Apuntes sobre migración*, Migratorios del INM 2. Mexico City: Centro de Estudios.

Besserer, Federico, and Michael Kearney. 2006. *San Juan Mixtepec: Una comunidad transnacional ante el poder filtrador y clasificador de las fronteras*. Mexico City: Juan Pablos.

Bettie, Julie. 2003. *Women without Class: Girls, Race and Identity*. Berkeley: University of California Press.

Bianchi, Suzanne M., Melissa A. Milkie, Liana C. Sayer, and John P. Robinson. 2000. "Is Anyone Doing the Housework? Trends in the Gender Division of Household Labor." *Social Forces* 79:191–228.

Bianchi, Suzanne M., and John Robinson. 1997. "What Did You Do Today? Children's Use of Time, Family Composition, and the Acquisition of Social Capital." *Journal of Marriage and Family* 59:332–44.

Birkett, Michelle, Dorothy L. Espelage, and Brian Koenig. 2009. "LGB and Questioning Students in Schools: The Moderating Effects of Homophobic Bullying and School Climate on Negative Outcomes." *Journal of Youth and Adolescence* 38 (7): 989–1000.

Bittman, Michael, Paula England, Liana Sayer, Nancy Folbre, and George Matheson. 2003. "When Does Gender Trump Money? Bargaining and Time in Household Work." *American Journal of Sociology* 109:186–214.

Bloemraad, Irene, Anna Korteweg, and Gökçe Yurdakul. 2008. "Citizenship and Immigration: Multiculturalism, Assimilation, and Challenges to the Nation-State." *Annual Review of Sociology* 34 (1): 153–79.

Boehm, Deborah. 2012. *Intimate Migrations: Gender, Family, and Illegality among Transnational Mexicans*. New York: New York University Press.

Bosniak, Linda. 2000. "Universal Citizenship and the Problem of Alienage." *Immigration and Nationality Law Review* 21:373.

Bowles, Samuel, and Herbert Gintis. 2001. "The Inheritance of Economic Status: Education, Class and Genetics." *International Encyclopedia of the Social and Behavioral Sciences: Genetics, Behavior and Society* 6:4132–41.

———. 2002. "Inter-generational Inequality." *Journal of Economic Perspectives* 16 (3): 1–28.

Brabeck, Kalina, and Qingwen Xu. 2010. "The Impact of Detention and Deportation on Latino Immigrant Children and Families: A Quantitative Exploration." *Hispanic Journal of Behavioral Sciences* 32:341–61.

Bratter, Jennifer L., and Tukufu Zuberi 2008. "As Racial Boundaries Fade: Racial Stratification and Interracial Marriage." In *White Logic, White Methods: Racism and Methodology*, edited by T. Zuberi and E. Bonilla-Silva, 251–67. Lanham, MD: Rowman and Littlefield.

Braver, Sanford L., Sharlene A. Wolchik, Irwin N. Sandler, Virgil L. Sheets, Bruce Fogas, and R. Curtis Bay. 1993. "A Longitudinal Study of Noncustodial Parents: Parents without Children." *Journal of Family Psychology* 7 (1): 9–23.

Brewer, Rose M. 1999. "Theorizing Race, Class and Gender: The New Scholarship of Black Feminist Intellectuals and Black Women's Labor." *Race, Gender and Class* 6 (2): 29–47.

Brotherton, David, and Luís Barrios. 2011. *Banished to the Homeland: Dominican Deportees and Their Stories of Exile.* New York: Columbia University Press.

Brown, Christina S., and Hui Chu. 2012. "Discrimination, Ethnic Identity, and Academic Outcomes of Mexican Immigrant Children: The Importance of School Context." *Child Development* 83 (5): 1477–85.

Bui, Hoan N., and Merry Morash. 1999. "Domestic Violence in the Vietnamese Immigrant Community: An Exploratory Study." *Violence against Women* 5 (7): 769–95.

Buriel, Raymond, William Perez, Terri L. DeMent, David V. Chávez, and Virginia R. Moran. 1998. "The Relationship of Language Brokering to Academic Performance, Biculturalism, and Self-Efficacy among Latino Adolescents." *Hispanic Journal of Behavioral Sciences* 20:283–97.

Bystydzienski, Jill. 2011. *Intercultural Couples: Crossing Boundaries, Negotiating Difference.* New York: New York University Press.

Capps, Randy, Rosa Maria Castañeda, Ajay Chaudry, and Robert Santos. 2007. *Paying the Price: The Impact of Immigration Raids on America's Children.* Washington, DC: Urban Institute and National Council of La Raza. www.urban.org/UploadedPDF/411566_immigration_raids.pdf.

Capps, Randy, Michael Fix, Jeffrey S. Passel, Jason Ost, and Dan Pérez-López. 2003. *A Profile of the Low-Wage Immigrant Workforce.* Immigrant Families

and Workers Brief 4. Washington, DC: Urban Institute. www.urban.org
/UploadedPDF/310880_lowwage_immig_wkfc.pdf.

Caramanica, Jose. 2010. "Monitor: 'Border Wars' Looks at Illegal Immigration
and Efforts to Stop It." *Los Angeles Times*, September 5. http://articles.
latimes.com/2010/sep/05/entertainment/la-ca-monitor-20100905.

Cavazos-Rehg, Patricia A., Luís H. Zayas, and Edward L. Spitznagel. 2007.
"Legal Status, Emotional Well-Being and Subjective Health Status of
Latino Immigrants." *Journal of the National Medical Association*
99:1126–32.

Cerrutti, Marcela, and Douglas Massey. 2001. "On the Auspices of Female
Migration from Mexico to the United States." *Demography* 38:187–200.

Charmaz, Kathy. 2006. *Constructing Grounded Theory: A Practical Guide
through Qualitative Analysis*. Thousand Oaks, CA: Sage Publications.

Chaudry, Ajay, Randy Capps, Juan Manuel Pedroza, Rosa Maria Castañeda,
Robert Santos, and Molly M. Scott. 2010. *Facing Our Future: Children in the
Aftermath of Immigration Enforcement*. Washington, DC: Urban Institute.
http://carnegie.org/fileadmin/Media/Publications/facing_our_future.pdf.

Chavez, Leo. 1991. "Outside the Imagined Community: Undocumented Settlers
and Experiences of Incorporation." *American Ethnologist* 18 (2): 257–78.

———. 1992. *Shadowed Lives: Undocumented Immigrants in American Society*.
Fort Worth, TX: Harcourt Brace Jovanovich.

———. 2008. *The Latino Threat: Constructing Immigrants, Citizens and the
Nation*. Stanford, CA: Stanford University Press.

Chilton, Mariana, Maureen M. Black, Carol Berkowitz, Patrick H. Casey, John
Cook, Diana Cutts, Ruth Rose Jacobs, Timothy Heeren, Stephanie Ettinger
de Cuba, Sharon Coleman, Alan Meyers, and Deborah A. Frank. 2009. "Food
Insecurity and Risk of Poor Health among US-Born Children of Immigrants." *American Journal of Public Health* 99 (3): 556–62.

Chinn, Sarah. 2009. *Inventing Modern Adolescence: The Children of Immigrants in Turn-of-the-Century America*. New Brunswick, NJ: Rutgers
University Press.

Chriswick, Barry R., and Michael E. Hurst. 1998. "The Labor Market Status of
Immigrants: A Synthesis." In *Immigration, Citizenship and the Welfare
State in Germany and the United States: Immigrant Incorporation*, edited
by H. Kurthen, J. Fijalkowski, and G. G. Wagner, 73–94. Stamford, CT: JAI
Press.

Clasen, Donna Rae, and Bradford Brown. 1985. "The Multidimensionality of
Peer Pressure in Adolescence." *Journal of Youth and Adolescence* 14 (6):
451–68.

Clozel, Lalita. 2014. "Harsh Immigration Realities Set in for Many 'Dreamers.'"
Los Angeles Times, March 24. www.latimes.com/nation/la-na-immigration-
dreamers-20140325,0,7318302.story#ixzz2yVQyREoG.

Cogle, Frances L., and Grace E. Tasker. 1982. "Children and Housework."
Family Relations 31 (3): 395–99.

Cohen, Jeffrey H. 2004. *The Culture of Migration in Southern Mexico.* Austin:
University of Texas Press.

Coleman, James S. 1988. "Social Capital in the Creation of Human Capital."
American Journal of Sociology 94 (Suppl.): S95–S121.

Coleman, Matthew. 2007. "Immigration Geopolitics beyond the Mexico-US
Border." *Antipode* 39:54–76.

Coltrane, Scott. 2000. "Research on Household Labor: Modeling and Measur-
ing the Social Embeddedness of Routine Family Work." *Journal of Marriage
and Family* 62:1208–33.

Comfort, Megan. 2008. *Doing Time Together: Love and Family in the Shadow
of the Prison.* Chicago: University of Chicago Press.

Conley, Dalton. 2004. *The Pecking Order: Which Siblings Succeed and Why.*
New York: Vintage Books.

Cooley, Charles Horton. [1902] 1922. *Human Nature and the Social Order.* New
York: Scribner.

Cooper, Betsy, and Kevin O'Neil. 2005. *Lessons from the Immigration Reform
and Control Act of 1986.* Migration Policy Institute Brief 3. Washington, DC:
Migration Policy Institute. www.migrationpolicy.org/pubs/PolicyBrief_
No3_Aug05.pdf.

Cooper, Catherine R., Jill Denner, and Edward M. López. 1999. "Cultural
Brokers: Helping Latino Children on Pathways toward Success." *Future of
Children* 9 (2): 51–57.

Cornelius, Wayne. 1982. "Undocumented Immigrants: Methodological Reflections Based on Fieldwork in Mexico and the U.S." *International Migration
Review* 16:378–411.

———. 2001. "Death at the Border: Efficacy and Unintended Consequences of
U.S. Immigration Control Policy." *Population and Development Review*
27:661–85.

Corsaro, William. 2003. *"We're Friends, Right?": Inside Kids' Cultures.* Washington, DC: Joseph Henry Press.

Corsaro, William, and Donna Eder. 1990. "Children's Peer Cultures." *Annual
Review of Sociology* 16:197–220.

Cortés, Zaira. 2012. "Pandillas Mexicanas son el Azote de Brooklyn." *El Diario,*
August 14. www.eldiariony.com/article/20120814/LOCALES20/308149973.

Cortés Sánchez, Sergio. 2003. "Migration by Residents of the State of Puebla in
the Decade of the 1990s." In *Immigrants and Schooling: Mexicans in New
York,* edited by R. Cortina and M. Gendreau, 182–202. New York: Center for
Migration Studies.

Coutin, Susan Bibler. 1993. *The Culture of Protest: Religious Activism and the
U.S. Sanctuary Movement.* Boulder, CO: Westview Press.

———. 2001. "Questionable Transactions as Grounds for Legalization: Immigration, Illegality and Law." *Crime, Law and Social Change* 37:19–36.

———. 2011. "Legal Exclusion and Dislocated Subjectivities: The Deportation of Salvadoran Youth from the United States." In *The Contested Politics of Mobility: Borderzones and Irregularity*, edited by V. J. Squire, 169–83. London: Routledge.

Crosnoe, Robert. 2005. "Double Disadvantage or Signs of Resilience: The Elementary School Contexts of Children from Mexican Immigrant Families." *American Educational Research Journal* 42:269–303.

Curran, Laura, and Laura S. Abrams. 2000. "Making Men into Dads: Fatherhood, the State, and Welfare Reform." *Gender and Society* 14 (5): 662–78.

Curran, Sara R., and Estela Rivero-Fuentes. 2003. "Engendering Migrant Networks: The Case of Mexican Migration." *Demography* 40:289–307.

Curry, Kathleen. 2001. "Mediating Cops: An Analysis of Viewer Reaction to Reality TV." *Journal of Criminal Justice and Popular Culture* 8:169–85.

Dahan, Momi, and Alejandro Gaviria. 2003. "Parental Actions and Sibling Inequality." *Journal of Development Economics* 72:281–97.

Danziger, Sheldon, and Peter Gottschalk. 1993. *Uneven Tides: Rising Inequality in America*. New York: Russell Sage Foundation.

Davidson, Miriam. 1988. *Convictions of the Heart: Jim Corbett and the Sanctuary Movement*. Tucson: University of Arizona Press.

DeBiaggi, Sylvia Duarte Dantas. 2002. *Changing Gender Roles: Brazilian Immigrant Families in the U.S.* New York: LFB Scholarly Publishing.

De Casanova, Erynn Masi. 2012. *Making Up the Difference: Women, Beauty, and Direct Selling in Ecuador*. Austin: University of Texas Press.

Decker, Scott, Paul G. Lewis, Doris M. Provine, and Monica W. Varsanyi. 2009. "On the Frontier of Local Law Enforcement: Local Police and Federal Immigration Law." *Sociology of Crime, Law and Deviance* 13:261–76.

De Genova, Nicholas. 2002. "Migrant 'Illegality' and Deportability in Everyday Life." *Annual Review of Anthropology* 31:419–47.

———. 2004. "The Legal Production of Mexican/Migrant 'Illegality.'" *Latino Studies* 2:160–85.

———. 2010. "The Deportation Regime: Sovereignty, Space and the Freedom of Movement." In *The Deportation Regime*, edited by Nicholas De Genova and Nathalie Peutz, 33–65. Durham, NC: Duke University Press.

De Genova, Nicholas, and Nathalie Peutz, eds. 2010. *The Deportation Regime*. Durham, NC: Duke University Press.

DeVault, Marjorie. 1991. *Feeding the Family: The Social Organization of Caring as Gendered Work*. Chicago: University of Chicago Press.

Donato, Catherine M. 1993. "Current Trends and Patterns of Female Migration: Evidence from Mexico." *International Migration Review* 27 (4): 748–68.

Donato, Catherine, and Amada Armenta. 2011. "What We Know about Unauthorized Migration." *Annual Review of Sociology* 37:529–43.

Donato, Catherine, and Blake Sisk. 2012. "Shifts in the Employment Outcomes among Mexican Migrants to the United States, 1976–2009." *Research in Social Stratification and Mobility* 30 (1): 63–77.

Dorner, Lisa, Marjorie Faulstich Orellana, and Christine P. Li-Grining. 2007. "I Helped My Mom, and It Helped Me: Translating the Skills of Language Brokers into Improved Standardized Test Scores." *American Journal of Education* 113 (3): 451–78.

Dreby, Joanna. 2006. "Honor and Virtue: Mexican Parenting in the Transnational Context." *Gender and Society* 20:32–59.

———. 2007. "Children and Power in Mexican Transnational Families." *Journal of Marriage and Family* 69:1050–64.

———. 2009. "Transnational Gossip." *Qualitative Sociology* 32:33–52.

———. 2010. *Divided by Borders: Mexican Migrants and Their Children.* Berkeley: University of California Press.

———. 2012. "The Burden of Deportation on Children in Mexican Immigrant Families." *Journal of Marriage and Family* 74 (4): 829–45.

———. 2013. "The Intimate Ties between Work and Home." In *Family and Work in Everyday Ethnography,* edited by T. Mose-Brown and J. Dreby, 63–79. Philadelphia: Temple University Press.

———. 2014. "U.S. Immigration Policy and Family Separation: The Consequences for Children's Well-Being. *Social Science and Medicine.* Prepublished August 30. doi: 10.1016/j.socscimed.2014.08.041.

Dreby, Joanna, and Leah Schmalzbauer. 2013. "The Relational Contexts of Migration: Mexican Women in New Destination Sites." *Sociological Forum* 28 (1): 1–26.

Dreby, Joanna, and Lindsay Stutz. 2012. "Making Something of Sacrifice: Gender, Migration and Mexican Children's Educational Aspirations." *Global Networks* 12 (1): 71–90.

Driscoll, Anne K. 1999. "Risk of High School Dropout among Immigrant and Native Hispanic Youth." *International Migration Review* 33 (4): 857–75.

Duneier, Mitchell. 2000. *Sidewalk.* New York: Farrar, Straus and Giroux.

Durand, Jorge, Douglas S. Massey, and Chiara Capoferro. 2005. "The New Geography of Mexican Immigration." In *New Destinations: Mexican Immigration in the United States,* edited by Victor Zúñiga and Rubén Hernández-León, 1–20. New York: Russell Sage Foundation.

Dura-Vila, Gloria, and Matthew Hodes. 2012. "Cross-Cultural Study of Idioms of Distress among Spanish Nationals and Hispanic American Migrants: *Susto, Nervios* and *Ataque de Nervios.*" *Social Psychiatry and Psychiatric Epidemiology* 47 (10): 1627–37.

Eckstein, Megan. 2009. "In-State Tuition for Undocumented Students: Not Quite Yet." *Chronicle of Higher Education* 55 (35). http://chronicle.com /article/In-State-Tuition-for-Undocu/44298/.

Edwards, Lisa, and Andrea J. Romero. 2008. "Coping with Discrimination among Mexican Descent Adolescents." *Hispanic Journal of Behavioral Sciences* 30:24–39.

England, Paula. 2005. "Emerging Theories of Care Work." *Annual Review of Sociology* 31:381–99.

Enriquez, Laura E. 2011. "'Because We Feel the Pressure and We Also Feel the Support': Examining the Educational Success of Undocumented Immigrant Latina/o Students." *Harvard Educational Review* 81:476–500.

Eschbach, Karl, Jacqueline Hagan, Nestor Rodríguez, Rubén Hernández-León, and Stanley Bailey. 1999. "Death at the Border." *International Migration Review* 33:430–54.

Evans, Ian M., Christine Salisbury, Mary Palombaro, and Jill S. Goldberg. 1994. "Children's Perception of Fairness in Classroom and Interpersonal Situations Involving Peers with Severe Disabilities." *Journal of the Association for Persons with Severe Handicaps* 19:326–32.

Farley, Reynolds, and Walter R. Allen. 1987. *The Color Line and the Quality of Life in America.* New York: Russell Sage Foundation.

Fehrmann, Paul G., Timothy Z. Keith, and Thomas M. Reimers. 1987. "Home Influence on School Learning: Direct and Indirect Effects of Parental Involvement on High School Grades." *Journal of Educational Research* 806:330–37.

Feliciano, Cynthia. 2012. "The Female Educational Advantage among Adolescent Children of Immigrants." *Youth and Society* 44 (3): 431–49.

Felix, Erika D., and Sukkyung You. 2011. "Peer Victimization within the Ethnic Context of High School." *Journal of Community Psychology* 39:860–75.

Ferguson, Ann Arnett. 2000. *Bad Boys: Public Schools in the Making of Black Masculinity.* Ann Arbor: University of Michigan Press.

Fernández-Kelly, Patricia, and Richard Schauffler. 1994. "Divided Fates: Immigrant Children in a Restructured U.S. Economy." *International Migration Review* 28 (4): 662–89.

Fine, Gary Alan. 1987. *With the Boys: Little League Baseball and Preadolescent Culture.* Chicago: University of Chicago Press.

Fink, Deborah. 1998. *Cutting into the Meatpacking Line: Workers and Change in the Rural Midwest.* Chapel Hill: University of North Carolina Press.

Fitzgerald, David, and David Cook-Martin. 2014. *Culling the Masses: The Democratic Origins of Racist Immigration Policy in the Americas.* Cambridge, MA: Harvard University Press.

Fix, Michael, and Wendy Zimmerman. 2001. "All under One Roof: Mixed-Status Families in an Era of Reform." *International Migration Review* 35 (2): 397–419.

Flippen, Chenoa A. 2001. "Racial and Ethnic Inequality in Homeownership and Housing Equity." *Sociological Quarterly* 42 (2): 121–49.

Flores, Elena, Jeanne M. Tschann, Juanita M. Dimas, Lauri A. Pasch, and Cynthia L. de Groat. 2010. "Perceived Racial/Ethnic Discrimination, Posttraumatic Stress Symptoms, and Health Risk Behaviors among Mexican American Adolescents." *Journal of Counseling Psychology* 57:264–73.

Foner, Nancy. 2000. *From Ellis Island to JFK: New York's Two Great Waves of Immigration.* New Haven, CT: Yale University Press; New York: Russell Sage Foundation.

———. 2009. *Across Generations: Immigrant Families in America.* New York: New York University Press.

Foner, Nancy, and Joanna Dreby. 2011. "Relations between the Generations in Immigrant Families." *Annual Review of Sociology* 37:545–64.

Fountain, Christine, and Peter Bearman. 2011. "Risk as Social Context: Immigration Policy and Autism in California." *Sociological Forum* 26:215–40.

Fox, Cybelle. 2012. *Three Worlds of Relief: Race, Immigration and the American Welfare State from the Progressive Era to the New Deal.* Princeton, NJ: Princeton University Press.

Fox News Latino. 2012. "Alabama Public Schools Can't Check Immigration Status of Students, Court Rules." August 12. http://latino.foxnews.com/2012/08/21/alabama-cannot-check-student-immigration-status-court-rules/.

Fragomen, Austin T. 1997. "The Illegal Immigration Reform and Immigrant Responsibility Act of 1996: An Overview." *International Migration Review* 31:438–60.

Fridrich, Angela H., and Daniel J. Flannery. 1995. "The Effects of Ethnicity and Acculturation on Early Adolescent Delinquency." *Journal of Child and Family Studies* 4 (1): 69–87.

Fritze, John. 2014. "Immigration Program Aimed at Criminals Deports Many with No Record." *Baltimore Sun,* February 8. http://articles.baltimoresun.com/2014-02-08/news/bs-md-secure-communities-20140208_1_secure-communities-immigration-program-maryland.

Fuligni, Andrew J. 1997. "The Academic Achievement of Adolescents from Immigrant Families: The Role of Family Background, Attitudes, and Behavior." *Child Development* 68:351–63.

Gager, Constance T., Laura A. Sanchez, and Alfred DeMaris. 2009. "Whose Time Is It? The Effect of Employment and Work/Family Stress on Children's Housework." *Journal of Family Issues* 30:1459–85.

Galassi, Jennifer. 2003. "Dare to Dream: A Review of the Development, Relief, and Education for Alien Minors (Dream) Act." *Chicano-Latino Law Review* 24:79–94.

Gallo, Sarah. 2014. "The Effects of Gendered Immigration Enforcement on Middle Childhood and Schooling." *American Educational Research Journal* 51:473–504.

Gans, Herbert J. 1979. "Symbolic Ethnicity: The Future of Ethnic Groups and Cultures in America." *Ethnic and Racial Studies* 2 (1): 1–20.

———. 1992. "Second-Generation Decline: Scenarios for the Economic and Ethnic Future of the Post-1965 American Immigrants." *Ethnic and Racial Studies* 15 (2): 173–92.

García, Ginny. 2011. *Mexican American and Immigrant Poverty in the United States*. New York: Springer.

García Coll, Cynthia, and Amy Marks. 2012. *The Immigrant Paradox in Children and Adolescents: Is Becoming American a Developmental Risk?* Washington, DC: American Psychological Association.

George, Sheba. 2005. *When Women Come First: Gender and Class in Transnational Migration*. Berkeley: University of California Press.

Gindling, Timothy, and Sara Poggio. 2009. *Family Separation and the Educational Success of Immigrant Children*. UMBC Policy Brief No. 7. Baltimore: Department of Public Policy, University of Maryland, Baltimore County. www.umbc.edu/mipar/Documents/Immigrationbrief.pdf.

Glaser, Barney G., and Anselm L. Strauss. 1967. *The Discovery of Grounded Theory: Strategies for Qualitative Research*. Chicago: Aldine.

Gleeson, Shannon, and Roberto Gonzales. 2012. "When Do Papers Matter? An Institutional Analysis of Undocumented Life in the United States." *International Migration* 50:1–19.

Glick, Jennifer. E. 2010. "Connecting Complex Processes: A Decade of Research on Immigrant Families." *Journal of Marriage and Family* 72:498–515.

Goffman, Erving. 1963. *Stigma: Notes on the Management of Spoiled Identity*. Englewood Cliffs, NJ: Prentice-Hall.

Golash-Boza, Tanya. 2012. *Immigration Nation: Raids, Detentions and Deportations in Post-9/11 sAmerica*. Boulder, CO: Paradigm.

———. 2013. "Forced Transnationalism: Transnational Coping Strategies and Gendered Stigma among Jamaican Deportees." *Global Networks* 14 (1): 63–79.

Golash-Boza, Tanya, and Pierrette Hondagneu-Sotelo. 2013. "Latino Immigrant Men and the Deportation Crisis: A Gendered Racial Removal Program." *Latino Studies* 11:271–92.

Gonzales, Roberto. 2011. "Learning to Be Illegal." *American Sociological Review* 76 (4): 602–19.

Gonzales, Roberto, and Leo Chavez. 2012. "Awakening to a Nightmare: Abjectivity and Illegality in the Lives of Undocumented 1.5 Generation Latino Immigrants in the United States." *Current Anthropology* 53: 255–81.

Gonzales, Roberto, Luisa Laura Heredia, and Genevieve Negrón-Gonzales. 2013. "Challenging the Transition to New 'Illegalities': Undocumented Young Adults and the Shifting Boundaries of Inclusion." In *Constructing Immigrant "Illegality": Critiques, Experiences, and Responses*, edited by Cecilia Menjívar and Daniel Kanstroom, 161–80. Cambridge: Cambridge University Press.

Gonzales, Roberto, Carola Suárez-Orozco, and Maria Cecilia Dedios-Sanguineti. 2013. "No Place to Belong: Contextualizing Concepts of Mental Health among Undocumented Immigrant Youth in the United States." *American Behavioral Scientist* 57 (8): 1174–99.

Gonzales, Roberto, and Veronica Terriquez. 2013. "How DACA Is Impacting the Lives of Those Who Are Now DACAmented." Immigration Policy Center, American Immigration Council. www.immigrationpolicy.org/just-facts /how-daca-impacting-lives-those-who-are-now-dacamented.

González-López, Gloria. 2005. *Erotic Journeys: Mexican Immigrants and Their Sex Lives*. Berkeley: University of California Press.

Gordon, Linda. 1988. *Heroes of Their Own Lives: The Politics of Family Violence*. New York: Viking Penguin.

Gottlieb, Amy. 2012. "'Secure Communities' Deportation Program Breeds Mistrust among Immigrants." *Star Ledger*, March 12. http://blog.nj.com/ njv_guest_blog/2012/03/secure_communities_deportation.html.

Graham, Elspeth, and Lucy P. Jordan. 2011. "Migrant Parents and the Psychological Well-Being of Left-Behind Children in Southeast Asia." *Journal of Marriage and Family* 73:763–87.

Graham, Sandra. 2006. "Peer Victimization in School: Exploring the Ethnic Context." *Current Directions in Psychological Science* 15 (6): 317–21.

Grasmuck, Sherri. 2005. *Protecting Home: Class, Race, and Masculinity in Boys' Baseball*. New Brunswick, NJ: Rutgers University Press.

Gray, Margaret. 2013. *Labor and the Locavore: The Making of a Comprehensive Food Ethic*. Berkeley: University of California Press.

Greenlees, Clyde S., and Rogelio Saenz. 1999. "Determinants of Employment of Recently Arrived Mexican Immigrant Wives." *International Migration Review* 33 (2): 354–77.

Greenman, Emily, and Matthew Hall. 2013. "Legal Status and Educational Transitions for Mexican and Central American Immigrant Youth." *Social Forces* 91 (4): 1475–98.

Grieco, Elizabeth M, Yesenia D. Acosta, G. Patricia de la Cruz, Christine Gambino, Thomas Gryn, Luke J. Larsen, Edward N. Trevelyan, and Nathan P. Walters. 2012. *The Foreign-Born Population in the United States: 2010*. Washington, DC: US Census Bureau. www.census.gov/prod/2012pubs /acs-19.pdf.

Guarnaccia, Peter. 1993. "*Ataques de Nervios* in Puerto Rico: Culture-Bound Syndrome or Popular Illness?" *Medical Anthropology* 15:157–70.

Guarnaccia, Peter, Victor De La Cancela, and Emilio Carrillo. 1989. "The Multiple Meanings of *Ataques de Nervios* in the Latino Community." *Medical Anthropology: Cross-Cultural Studies in Health and Illness* 11:47–62.

Guerin-Gonzales, Camille. 1994. *Mexican Workers and the American Dream: Immigration, Repatriation, and California Farm Labor, 1900–1939*. New Brunswick, NJ: Rutgers University Press.

Gurrola, Maria, Cecilia Ayón, and Lorraine Moya Salas. 2013. "Mexican Adolescents' Education and Hopes in an Anti-immigrant Environment the Perspectives of First-and Second-Generation Youth and Parents." *Journal of Family Issues*, prepublished November 12. doi:10.1177/0192513X13510298.

Hadley, Craig, Sandro Galea, Vijay Nandi, Arijit Nandi, Gerald López, Stacey Strongarone, and Danielle Ompad. 2008. "Hunger and Health among Undocumented Mexican Migrants in a US Urban Area." *Public Health Nutrition* 11 (2): 151–58.

Hagan, Jacqueline, Brianna Castro, and Nestor Rodríguez. 2010. "The Effects of U.S. Deportation Policies on Immigrant Families and Communities: Cross-Border Perspectives." *North Carolina Law Review* 88:1799–1824.

Hagan, Jacqueline, Nestor Rodríguez, and Brianna Castro. 2011. "Social Effects of Mass Deportations by the United States Government, 2000–10." *Ethnic and Racial Studies* 34:1374–91.

Hancock, Ange-Marie. 2007. "When Multiplication Doesn't Equal Quick Addition: Examining Intersectionality as a Research Paradigm." *Perspectives on Politics* 5:63–79.

Handel, Gerald. 1988. *Childhood Socialization*. New York: Aldine de Gruyter.

———. 2011. "Sociological Perspectives on Social Development." In *The Wiley-Blackwell Handbook of Childhood Social Development*, edited by P. K. Smith and C. H. Hart, 119–38. Malden, MA: John Wiley and Sons.

Hanish, Laura D., and Nancy G. Guerra. 2000. "The Roles of Ethnicity and School Context in Predicting Children's Victimization by Peers." *American Journal of Community Psychology* 28 (2): 201–23.

Hanlon, Thomas, Steven Carswell, and Marc Rose. 2007. "Research on the Caretaking of Children of Incarcerated Parents: Findings and Their Service Delivery Implications." *Children and Youth Services Review* 29:348–62.

Hernández, Kelly. 2009. "'Persecuted Like Criminals': The Politics of Labor Emigration and Mexican Migration Controls in the 1920s and 1930s." *Aztlan: A Journal of Chicano Studies* 34:219–39.

Hernández-León, Rubén, and Víctor Zuñiga. 2003. "Mexican Immigrant Communities in the South and Social Capital." *Southern Rural Sociology* 19:20–45.

Hey, Valerie. 1997. *The Company She Keeps: An Ethnography of Girls' Friendships*. Buckingham: Open University Press.

Heymann, Jody, Francisco Flores-Macias, Jeffrey A. Hayes, Malinda Kennedy, Claudia Lahaie, and Alison Earle. 2009. "The Impact of Migration on the Well-Being of Transnational Families: New Data from Sending Communities in Mexico." *Community, Work and Family* 12:91–103.

Hill, Shirley A. 2004. *Black Intimacies: A Gender Perspective on Families and Relationships*. Walnut Creek, CA: Altamira Press.

Hill, Shirley A., and Joey Sprague. 1999. "Parenting in Black and White Families: The Intersection of Gender with Race and Class." *Gender and Society* 13:480–502.

Hirsch, Jennifer. 2003. *A Courtship after Marriage: Sexuality and Love in Mexican Transnational Families*. Berkeley: University of California Press.

Hochschild, Arlie. 1990. *The Second Shift: Working Parents and the Revolution at Home*. New York: Penguin Books.

Hochschild, Jennifer. 1996. *Facing Up to the American Dream: Race, Class, and the Soul of the Nation*. Princeton, NJ: Princeton University Press.

Hofferth, Sandra L., and John F. Sandberg. 2001. "How American Children Spend Their Time." *Journal of Marriage and Family* 63:295–308.

Hoffman, Abraham. 1974. *Unwanted Mexican Americans in the Great Depression: Repatriation Pressures*. Tucson: University of Arizona Press.

Hondagneu-Sotelo, Pierrette. 1994. *Gendered Transitions*. Berkeley: University of California Press.

———. 2003. *Gender and U.S. Immigration: Contemporary Trends*. Berkeley: University of California Press.

Hondagneu-Sotelo, Pierrette, and Ernestine Avila. 1997. "'I'm Here but I'm There': The Meanings of Latina Transnational Motherhood." *Gender and Society* 11:548–60.

Horowitz, Ruth. 1983. *Honor and the American Dream: Culture and Identity in a Chicano Community*. New Brunswick, NJ: Rutgers University Press.

Ho Sui-Chu, Esther, and J. Douglas Willms. 1996. "Effects of Parental Involvement on Eighth-Grade Achievement." *Sociology of Education* 69 (2): 126–41.

Huston, Aletha C. 1991. *Children in Poverty: Child Development and Public Policy*. New York: Cambridge University Press.

Ingram, Maia, Deborah Jean McClelland, Jessica Martin, Montserrat F. Caballero, Maria Theresa Mayorga, and Katie Gillespie. 2010. "Experiences of Immigrant Women Who Self-Petition under the Violence against Women Act." *Violence against Women* 16 (8): 858–80.

James, Allison, Chris Jenks, and Alan Prout. 1998. *Theorising Childhood*. Cambridge: Polity Press.

Jensen, An-Margritt, and Lorna McKee. 2003. *Children and the Changing Family: Between Transformation and Negotiation*. London: Routledge Falmer.

Jensen, Leif. 2006. *New Immigrant Settlements in Rural America: Problems, Prospects and Policies*. Durham: Carsey Institute, University of New Hampshire.

Jeynes, William H. 2007. "The Relationship between Parental Involvement and Urban Secondary School Student Academic Achievement: A Meta-analysis." *Urban Education* 42 (1): 82–110.

Jones, Curtis J., and Edison J. Trickett. 2005. "Immigrant Adolescents Behaving as Culture Brokers: A Study of Families from the Former Soviet Union." *Journal of Social Psychology* 145 (4): 405–27.

Kanaiapuni, Shawn Malia. 2000. "Reframing the Migration Question: An Analysis of Men, Women and Gender in Mexico." *Social Forces* 78:1311–42.

Kanstroom, Daniel. 2007. *Deportation Nation: Outsiders in American History*. Cambridge, MA: Harvard University Press.

Katz, Vikki. 2014. *Kids in the Middle: How Children of Immigrants Negotiate Community Interactions for Their Families*. New Brunswick, NJ: Rutgers University Press.

Kearney, Michael. 2000. "Transnational Oaxacan Indigenous Identity: The Case of Mixtecs and Zapotecs." *Identities* 7:173–95.

Keister, Lisa A., and Stephanie Moller. 2000. "Wealth Inequality in the United States." *Annual Review of Sociology* 26:63–81.

Kibria, Nazli. 1993. *Family Tightrope: The Changing Lives of Vietnamese Americans*. Princeton, NJ: Princeton University Press.

Kim, Caleb. 2013. "Lost American DREAM of Undocumented Students: Understanding the DREAM Act." *Children and Schools* 35:55–58.

King, Valerie, and Juliana M. Sobolewski. 2006. "Nonresident Fathers' Contributions to Adolescent Well-Being." *Journal of Marriage and Family* 68 (3): 537–57.

Kinney, David A. 1993. "From Nerds to Normals: The Recovery of Identity among Adolescents from Middle School to High School." *Sociology of Education* 66 (1): 21–40.

Kirschenman, Joleen, and Kathryn Neckerman. 1991. "'We'd Love to Hire Them, but . . .': The Meaning of Race for Employers." In *The Urban Underclass*, edited by Christopher Jencks and P. E. Peterson, 203–32. Washington, DC: Brookings Institute.

Kohli, Aarti, Peter L. Markowitz, and Lisa Chavez. 2011. "Secure Communities by the Numbers: An Analysis of Demographics and Due Process." Research Report, Chief Justice Earl Warren Institute on Law and Social Policy. October. www.law.berkeley.edu/files/Secure_Communities_by_the_Numbers.pdf.

Kolbert, Elizabeth. 2012. "Spoiled Rotten." *New Yorker*, July 2. www.newyorker.com/arts/critics/books/2012/07/02/120702crbo_books_kolbert?currentPage=all.

Konrad, Kai A., and Kjell Erik Lommerud. 2000. "The Bargaining Family Revisited." *Canadian Journal of Economics* 33:471–87.

Kornblum, William. 1975. *Blue Collar Community*. Chicago: University of Chicago Press.

Kosciw, Joseph G. 2004. *The 2003 National School Climate Survey: The School-Related Experiences of Our Nation's Lesbian, Gay, Bisexual and Transgender Youth*. New York: Gay, Lesbian and Straight Education Network. http://files.eric.ed.gov/fulltext/ED486412.pdf.

Kozol, Jonathan. 1991. *Savage Inequalities: Children in America's Schools*. New York: Harper Perennial.

Kreider, Rose, and Renee Ellis. 2011. "Living Arrangements of Children: 2009." *Current Population Report*, June. US Department of Commerce Economics and Statistics Administration. Washington, DC: US Census Bureau. www .census.gov/prod/2011pubs/p70-126.pdf.

Krivo, Lauren J., and Robert L. Kaufman. 2004. "Housing and Wealth Inequality: Racial-Ethnic Differences in Home Equity in the United States." *Demography* 41 (3): 585–605.

Križ, Katrin, and Marit Skivenes. 2012. "How Child Welfare Workers Perceive Their Work with Undocumented Immigrant Families: An Explorative Study of Challenges and Coping Strategies." *Children and Youth Services Review* 34 (4): 790–97.

Kroska, Amy. 2004. "Divisions of Domestic Work: Revising and Expanding the Theoretical Explanations." *Journal of Family Issues* 25:900–932.

Lahaie, Claudia, Jeffrey A. Hayes, Tinka Markham Piper, and Jody Heymann. 2009. "Work and Family Divided across Borders: The Impact of Parental Migration on Mexican Children in Transnational Families." *Community, Work and Family* 12:299–312.

Lamont, Michèle, and Virág Molnár. 2002. "The Study of Boundaries in the Social Sciences." *Annual Review of Sociology* 28:167–95.

Landolt, Patricia, and Wei Wei Da. 2005. "The Spatially Ruptured Practices of Migrant Families: A Comparison of Immigrants from El Salvador and the People's Republic of China" *Current Sociology* 53:625–53.

Lareau, Annette. 2002. "Invisible Inequality: Social Class and Childrearing in Black Families and White Families." *American Sociological Review* 67 (5): 747–76.

———. 2003. *Unequal Childhoods: Class, Race and Family Life*. Berkeley: University of California Press.

Larson, Reed W., and Maryse H. Richards. 1991. "Boredom in the Middle School Years: Blaming Schools versus Blaming Students." *American Journal of Education* 99 (4): 418–43.

Levey, Hilary. 2013. *Playing to Win: Raising Children in a Competitive Culture*. Berkeley: University of California Press.

Lewis, Amanda. 2003a. "Everyday Race-Making." *American Behavioral Scientist* 47 (3): 283–305.

———. 2003b. *Race in the Schoolyard: Negotiating Color Lines in Classrooms and the Community.* New Brunswick, NJ: Rutgers University Press.

Liebow, Elliot. 1967. *Tally's Corner.* Boston: Little, Brown.

López, David, and Yen Espiritu. 1994. "Panethnicity in the United States: A Theoretical Framework." *Ethnic and Racial Studies* 13 (2): 198–224.

López, Maria Pabon. 2005. "Reflections on Educating Latino and Latina Undocumented Children: Beyond *Plyler v. Doe.*" *Seton Hall Law Review* 35 (4): 1373–1406.

López, Mark Hugo, and Susan Minushkin. 2008. "Hispanics See Their Situation in U.S. Deteriorating: Oppose Key Immigration Enforcement Measures; 2008 National Survey of Latinos." Pew Hispanic Center. http://pewhispanic.org/reports/report.php?ReportID=93.

Luibhéid, Eithne. 2008. "Sexuality, Migration, and the Shifting Line between Legal and Illegal Status." *GLQ: A Journal of Lesbian and Gay Studies* 14 (2–3): 289–315.

Lundberg, Shelly, and Robert A. Pollak. 1996. "Bargaining and Distribution in Marriage." *Journal of Economic Perspectives* 10:139–58.

Luttrell, Wendy. 1989. "Working-Class Women's Ways of Knowing: Effects of Gender, Race, and Class." *Sociology of Education* 62:33–46.

Majumdar, Debarun, and Gloria P. Martínez-Ramos. 2012. "The Impact of Immigration-Related Challenges and Deportation Worries on the Well-Being of Latinos in the US." *Camino Real* 4 (7): 95–114.

Malkin, Victoria. 2004. "We Go to Get Ahead: Gender and Status in Two Mexican Migrant Communities." *Latin American Perspectives* 31:75–99.

Manser, Marilyn, and Murray Brown. 1980. "Marriage and Household Decision-Making: A Bargaining Analysis." *International Economic Review* 21:31–44.

Marquardt, Marie Friedmann, Timothy J. Steigenga, Phillip J. Williams, and Manuel A. Vásquez. 2011. *Living "Illegal": The Human Face of Unauthorized Migration.* New York: New Press.

Marroni, María da Gloria. 2000. "'Él siempre me ha dejado con los chiquitos y se ha llevado a los grandes . . . ': Ajustes y desbarajustes familiares de la migración." In *Migración y relaciones de género en México,* edited by D. Barrera and C. Oehmichen, 87–118. Mexico City: GIMTRAP and UNAM, Instituto de Investigaciones Antropológicas.

Marrow, Helen. 2011. *New Destination Dreaming: Immigration, Race, and Legal Status in the Rural American South.* Stanford, CA: Stanford University Press.

Marsiglia, Flavio F., Monica Parsai, and Stephen Kulis. 2009. "Effects of Familism and Family Cohesion on Problem Behaviors among Adolescents in

Mexican Immigrant Families in the Southwest United States." *Journal of Ethnic and Cultural Diversity in Social Work* 18:203–220.

Martínez, Charles, Heather McClure, and J. Mark Eddy. 2009. "Language Brokering Contexts and Behavioral and Emotional Adjustment among Latino Parents and Adolescents." *Journal of Early Adolescence* 29 (1): 71–98.

Martínez, Omar, Elwin Wu, Theo Sandfort, Brian Dodge, Alex Carballo-Dieguez, Rogeiro Pinto, Scott Rhodes, Eva Moya, and Silvia Chavez-Baray. 2013. "Evaluating the Impact of Immigration Policies on Health Status among Undocumented Immigrants: A Systematic Review." *Journal of Immigrant and Minority Health*, prepublished December 28, doi:10.1007 /s10903-013-9968-4.

Massey, Douglas. 2008. *New Faces in New Places: The Changing Geography of American Immigration*. New York: Russell Sage.

———. 2013. "Comment: Building a Better Underclass." *Demography* 50:1093–95.

Massey, Douglas, Rafael Alarcon, Jorge Durand, and Humberto González. 1987. *Return to Aztlan: The Social Process of International Migration from Western Mexico*. Berkeley: University of California Press.

Massey, Douglas, Jorge Durand, and Nolan J. Malone. 2002. *Beyond Smoke and Mirrors: Mexican Immigration in an Era of Economic Integration*. New York: Russell Sage.

Massey, Douglas, and Karen Pren. 2012. "Unintended Consequences of US Immigration Policy: Explaining the Post-1965 Surge from Latin America." *Population and Development Review* 38 (1): 1–29.

McElroy, Marjorie B., and Mary Jean Horney. 1981. "Nash-Bargained Household Decisions: Toward a Generalization of the Theory of Demand." *International Economic Review* 22:333–49.

Mead, George Herbert. 1934. *Mind, Self and Society*. Chicago: University of Chicago Press.

Medrich, Elliott, Judith Roizen, Victor Rubin and Stuart Buckley. 1992. *The Serious Business of Growing Up: A Study of Children's Lives outside School*. Berkeley: University of California Press.

Meir, Yael, Michelle Slone, and Iris Lavi. 2012. "Children of Illegal Migrant Workers: Life Circumstances and Mental Health." *Children and Youth Service Review* 34 (8): 1546–52.

Meissner, Doris, Donald Kerwin, Muzaffar Chishti, and Claire Bergeron. 2013. *Immigration Enforcement in the United States: Rise of a Formidable Machinery*. Washington, DC: Migration Policy Institute. www.migrationpolicy .org/pubs/enforcementpillars.pdf.

Méndez Morales, Sara. 2000. "Características de la migración femenina temporal en la mixteca oaxaqueña." In *Migración y relaciones de género en*

México, edited by D. Barrera and C. Oehmichen, 251–80. Mexico City: GIMTRAP and UNAM, Instituto de Investigaciones Antropológicas.

Menjívar, Cecilia. 2000. *Fragmented Ties: Salvadoran Immigrant Networks in America*. Berkeley: University of California Press.

———. 2003. "The Intersection of Work and Gender: Central American Immigrant Women and Employment in California." In *Gender and U.S. Immigration: Contemporary Trends*, edited by Pierrette Hondagneu-Sotelo, 101–26. Berkeley: University of California Press.

———. 2006. "Liminal Legality: Salvadoran and Guatemalan Immigrants' Lives in the United States." *American Journal of Sociology* 111 (4): 999–1037.

———. 2011. "The Power of the Law: Central America's Legality and Everyday Life in Phoenix, Arizona." *Latino Studies* 9:377–95.

Menjívar, Cecilia, and Leisy Abrego. 2009. "Parents and Children across Borders: Legal Instability and Intergenerational Relations in Guatemalan and Salvadoran Families." In *Across Generations: Immigrant Families in America*, edited by Nancy Foner, 160–89. New York: New York University Press.

———. 2012. "Legal Violence: Immigration Law and the Lives of Central American Immigrants." *American Journal of Sociology* 117 (5): 1380–1421.

Menjívar, Cecilia, and Daniel Kanstroom, eds. 2013. *Constructing Illegality in America: Critiques, Experiences, and Responses*. Cambridge: Cambridge University Press.

Messner, Michael A. 2000. "Barbie Girls versus Sea Monsters: Children Constructing Gender." *Gender and Society* 14:765–84.

Michalowski, Raymond. 2007. "Border Militarization and Migrant Suffering: A Case of Transnational Social Injury." *Social Justice* 34 (2): 62–77.

Migration Policy Institute. 2013. *Side-by-Side Comparison of 2013 Immigration Bill with 2006 and 2007 Senate Legislation*. Migration Policy Issue Brief 4. Washington, DC: Migration Policy Institute. www.migrationpolicy .org/pubs/CIRbrief-2013SenateBill-Side-by-Side.pdf.

Millard, Ann V., and Jorge Chapa. 2004. *Apple Pie and Enchiladas: Latino Newcomers in the Rural Midwest*. Austin: University of Texas Press.

Mills, C. Wright. 1959. "The Promise." In *The Sociological Imagination*, 3–24. New York: Oxford University Press.

Min, Pyoung Gap, and Rose Kim. 2000. "Formation of Ethnic and Racial Identities: Narratives by Young Asian-American Professionals." *Ethnic and Racial Studies* 23 (4): 735–60.

Morales, Alejandro, and William E. Hanson. 2005. "Language Brokering: An Integrative Review of the Literature." *Hispanic Journal of Behavioral Sciences* 27 (4): 471–503.

Morash, Merry, Hoan Bui, and Anna Santiago. 2000. "Cultural-Specific Gender Ideology and Wife Abuse in Mexican-Descent Families." *International Review of Victimology* 7 (1–3): 67–91.

Motomura, Hiroshi. 2012. "Who Belongs? Immigration outside the Law and the Idea of Americans in Waiting." *UC Irvine Law Review* 2:359–79.

———. 2013. "Making Legal: The Dream Act, Birthright Citizenship, and Broad-Scale Legalization." *Lewis and Clark Law Review* 16:1127–48.

Mummert, Gail. 1988. "Mujeres de migrantes y mujeres migrantes de Michoacán: Nuevos papeles para las que se quedan y las que se van." In *Movimientos de población en el occidente de México*, edited by T. Calvo and G. López, 281–95. Mexico City: Centre d'études mexicaines et centraméricaines and Colegio de México.

Myers, Dowell, and Seong Woo Lee. 1996. "Immigration Cohorts and Residential Overcrowding in Southern California." *Demography* 33:51–65.

Nakano Glenn, Evelyn. 1983. "Split Household, Small Producer and Dual Wage Earner: An Analysis of Chinese-American Family Strategies." *Journal of Marriage and Family* 45:35–46.

Nandi, Arijit, Sandra Galea, Gerald López, Vijay Nandi, Stacey Strongarone, and Danielle Ompad. 2008. "Access to and Use of Health Services among Undocumented Mexican Immigrants in a US Urban Area." *American Journal of Public Health* 98 (11): 2011–20.

Nansel, Tonya R., Mary Overpeck, Ramani S. Pilla, W. June Ruan, Bruce Simons-Morton, and Peter Scheidt. 2001. "Bullying Behaviors among US Youth: Prevalence and Association with Psychosocial Adjustment." *Journal of the American Medical Association* 285 (16): 2094–2100.

National Gang Intelligence Center. 2011. *National Gang Threat Assessment.* Washington, DC: National Gang Intelligence Center, Federal Bureau of Investigation. www.fbi.gov/stats-services/publications/2011-national-gang-threat-assessment/2011-national-gang-threat-assessment-emerging-trends.

Negrón-Gonzales, Genevieve. 2013. "Navigating "Illegality": Undocumented Youth and Oppositional Consciousness." *Children and Youth Services Review* 35 (8): 1284–90.

Newman, Katherine S., and Cybelle Fox. 2009. "Repeat Tragedy: Rampage Shootings in American High School and College Settings, 2002–2008."*American Behavioral Scientist* 52 (9): 1286–1308.

Newman, Katherine S., Cybelle Fox, David Harding, Jal Mehta, and Wendy Roth. 2004. *Rampage: The Social Roots of School Shootings.* New York: Basic Books.

Ngai, Mae. 2004. *Impossible Subjects: Illegal Aliens and the Making of Modern America.* Princeton, NJ: Princeton University Press.

Nicholls, Walter. 2013. *The DREAMers: How the Undocumented Youth Movement Transformed the Immigrant Rights Debate.* Stanford, CA: Stanford University Press.

Nobles, Jenna. 2011. "Parenting from Abroad: Migration, Nonresident Father Involvement, and Children's Education in Mexico." *Journal of Marriage and Family* 73:729–46.

No More Deaths/No Más Muertes. 2011. *A Culture of Cruelty: Abuse and Impunity in Short-Term U.S. Border Patrol Custody.* Tucson, AZ: No More Deaths/No Más Muertes. www.nomoredeathsvolunteers.org/Print %20Resources/Abuse%20Doc%20Reports/Culture%20of%20Cruelty /CultureofCrueltyFinal.pdf.

Olivas, Michael A. 2010. "The Political Economy of the Dream Act and the Legislative Process: A Case Study of Comprehensive Immigration Reform." *Wayne Law Review* 55:1757–1810. University of Houston Law Center No. 2010-A-6. http://ssrn.com/abstract=1554032.

Oliver, Melvin L., and Thomas M. Shapiro. 2006. *Black Wealth, White Wealth: A New Perspective on Racial Inequality.* New York: Routledge.

Olwig, Karen Fog. 1999. "Narratives of the Children Left Behind: Home and Identity in Globalised Caribbean Families." *Journal of Ethnic and Migration Studies* 25 (2): 267–84.

Omi, Michael, and Howard Winant. 1986. *Racial Formation in the United States: from the 1960s to the 1980s.* New York: Routledge and Kegan Paul.

Orellana, Marjorie Faulstich. 2001. "The Work Kids Do: Mexican and Central American Children's Contributions to Households and Schools in California." *Harvard Educational Review* 71:366–90.

———. 2009. *Translating Childhoods: Immigrant Youth, Language and Culture.* New Brunswick, NJ: Rutgers University Press.

Orellana, Marjorie Faulstich, Lisa Dorner, and Lucila Pulido. 2003. "Accessing Assets: Immigrant Youth as Family Interpreters." *Social Problems* 50 (5): 505–24.

Ortega, Alexander. N, Sarah M. Horwitz, Hai Fang, Alica A. Kuo, Steven P. Wallace, and Moira Inkelas. 2009. "Documentation Status and Parental Concerns about Development in Young U.S. Children of Mexican Origin." *Academic Pediatrics* 9:278–82.

Parker, Ashley. 2013. "Senate Vote on Border Gives Push to Immigration Overhaul." *New York Times,* June 24. www.nytimes.com/2013/06/25/us /politics/senate-endorses-proposal-calling-for-extra-border-security-measures.html?pagewanted=all&_r=0.

Parreñas, Rhacel Salazar. 2001. *Servants of Globalization: Women, Migration and Domestic Work.* Stanford, CA: Stanford University Press.

———. 2005. *Children of Global Migration: Transnational Families and Gender Woes.* Stanford, CA: Stanford University Press.

Parsons, Talcott, and Robert Bales. 1955. *Family, Socialization and Interaction Process.* New York: Free Press.

Pascoe, C.J. 2007. *Dude, You're a Fag: Masculinity and Sexuality in High School.* Berkeley: University of California Press.

Passel, Jeffrey S., and Rebecca Clark. 1998. *Immigrants in New York: Their Legal Status, Incomes, and Taxes*. New York: Urban Institute. www.urban.org/publications/407432.html.

Passel, Jeffrey S., and D'Vera Cohn. 2009. *A Portrait of Unauthorized Immigrants in the United States*. Washington, DC: Pew Hispanic Center. www.pewhispanic.org/2009/04/14/a-portrait-of-unauthorized-immigrants-in-the-united-states/.

———. 2011. *Unauthorized Immigrant Population: National and State Trends, 2010*. Washington, DC: Pew Hispanic Center. www.pewhispanic.org/2011/02/01/unauthorized-immigrant-population-brnational-and-state-trends-2010/.

Passel, Jeffrey, D'Vera Cohn, and Ana González-Barerra. 2012. *Net Migration from Mexico Falls to Zero—and Perhaps Less*. Washington, DC: Pew Hispanic Center. www.pewhispanic.org/files/2012/04/Mexican-migrants-report_final.pdf.

———. 2013. *Population Decline of Unauthorized Immigrants Stalls, May Have Reversed*. Washington, DC: Pew Hispanic Center. www.pewhispanic.org/files/2013/09/Unauthorized-Sept-2013-FINAL.pdf.

Patillo-McCoy, Mary. 2000. *Black Picket Fences: Privilege and Peril among the Black Middle Class*. Chicago: University of Chicago Press.

Pearson, Jennifer, Chandra Muller, and Lindsey Wilkinson. 2007. "Adolescent Same-Sex Attraction and Academic Outcomes: The Role of School Attachment and Engagement." *Social Problems* 54 (4): 523–42.

Pedroza, Juan Manuel. 2013. "Removal Roulette: Secure Communities and Immigration Enforcement in the United States (2008–2012)." In *Outside Justice: Immigration and the Criminalizing Impact of Changing Policy and Practice*, edited by D. C. Brotherton, D. L. Stageman, and S. P. Leyro, 45–65. New York: Springer.

Perilla, Julia, Roger Bakeman, and Fran Norris. 1994. "Culture and Domestic Violence: The Ecology of Abused Latinas." *Violence and Victims* 9:325–39.

Pessar, Patricia. 1999. "Engendering Migration Studies: The Case of New Immigrants in the United States." *American Behavioral Scientist* 42 (4): 577–600.

Pew Hispanic Center. 2011. *The Mexican-American Boom: Births Overtake Immigration*. Washington DC: Pew Hispanic Center. www.pewhispanic.org/files/reports/144.pdf.

———. 2013a. *"Borders First" a Dividing Line in Immigration Debate*. Washington, DC: Pew Hispanic Center. www.people-press.org/files/legacy-pdf/6-23-13%20Immigration%20Release%20Final.pdf .

———. 2013b. *A Nation of Immigrants: A Portrait of the 40 Million, Including 11 Million Unauthorized*. Washington, DC: Pew Hispanic Center. www.pewhispanic.org/files/2013/01/statistical_portrait_final_jan_29.pdf.

Phinney, Jean. 1989. "Stages of Ethnic Identity Development in Minority Group Adolescents." *Journal of Early Adolescence* 9:34–49.

Phinney, Jean. S., Irma Romero, Monica Nava, and Dan Huang. 2001. "The Role of Language, Parents, and Peers in Ethnic Identity among Adolescents in Immigrant Families." *Journal of Youth and Adolescence* 30 (2): 135–53.

Pinkerton, James. 2008. "Fake Documents for Immigrants Swamp Houston." *Houston Chronicle*, May 6. www.chron.com/news/article/Fake-documents-for-immigrants-swamp-Houston-1538235.php.

Pinto, Katy M., and Scott Coltrane. 2009. "Divisions of Labor in Mexican Origin and Anglo Families: Structure and Culture." *Sex Roles* 60:482–95.

Pleck, Elizabeth. 1983. "Traditional Authority in Immigrant Families." In *The American Family in Social-Historical Perspective*, edited by M. Gordon, 504–17. New York: St. Martin's Press.

———. 1987. *Domestic Tyranny: The Making of Social Policy against Family Violence from Colonial Times to the Present*. New York: Oxford University Press.

Portes, Alejandro, and Rubén Rumbaut. 2006. *Immigrant America: A Portrait*. Berkeley: University of California Press.

Portes, Alejandro, and Richard Schauffler. 1994. "Language and the Second Generation: Bilingualism Yesterday and Today." *International Migration Review* 28 (4): 640–61.

Portes, Alejandro, and Min Zhou. 1993. "The New Second Generation: Segmented Assimilation and Its Variants." *Annals of the American Academy of Political and Social Science* 22:217–38.

Potochnick, Stephanie, and Krista Perreira. 2010. "Depression and Anxiety among First-Generation Immigrant Latino Youth: Key Correlates and Implications for Future Research." *Journal of Nervous and Mental Disease* 198 (7): 470–77.

Presbury, Jack H., Jerry A. Benson, John E. McKee, Jon Fitch, Jon and Sherri Fitch. 1997. "How to Think about the 'Deadbeat Dad' Problem." *Journal of Humanistic Education and Development* 35 (3): 135–45.

Pribilsky, Jason. 2004. "'Aprendemos a Convivir': Conjugal Relations, Co-parenting, and Family Life among Ecuadorian Transnational Migrants in New York City and the Ecuadorian Andes." *Global Networks* 4:3–13.

Prosise, Theodore, and Ann Johnson. 2004. "Law Enforcement and Crime on Cops and World's Wildest Police Videos: Anecdotal Form and the Justification of Racial Profiling." *Western Journal of Communication* 68:72–91.

Pryor, Jan, and Bryon Rodgers. 2001. *Children in Changing Families: Life after Parental Separation*. Oxford: Wiley-Blackwell.

Qvortrup, Jens. 1999. "Childhood and Societal Macrostructures: Childhood Exclusion by Default." Working Paper 9, Department of Contemporary Cultural Studies, University of Southern Denmark, Odense. http://static.sdu

.dk/mediafiles/Files/Information_til/Studerende_ved_SDU/Din_
uddannelse/Kultur_og_formidling/WorkingPapers/09_ChildhoodAnd
SocietalMacrostructures%20pdf.pdf.

Ragin, Charles. 2009. *Redesigning Social Inquiry: Fuzzy Sets and Beyond.*
Chicago: University of Chicago Press.

Raj, Anita, and Jay Silverman. 2002. "Intimate Partner Violence against
Immigrant Women: The Roles of Immigrant Culture, Context, and Legal
Status." *Violence against Women* 8:367–98.

Raley, Sara, and Suzanne Bianchi. 2006. "Sons, Daughters, and Family Processes: Does Gender of Children Matter?" *Annual Review of Sociology*
32:401–21.

Ramirez, Marcela, Zlatko Skrbis, and Michael Emmison. 2007. "Transnational
Family Reunions as Lived Experience: Narrating a Salvadoran Autoethnog-
raphy." *Identities* 14 (4): 411–31.

Reimers, Cordelia W. 1985. "A Comparative Analysis of the Wages of Hispanics,
Blacks, and Non-Hispanic Whites." In *Hispanics in the U.S Economy,*
edited by George J. Borjas and Marta Tienda, 27–76. Orland, FL: Academic
Press.

Reyes, Iliana. 2004. "Functions of Code Switching in Schoolchildren's Conversations." *Bilingual Research Journal* 28 (1): 77–98.

Rhee, Siyon. 1997. "Domestic Violence in the Korean Immigrant Family."
Journal of Sociology and Social Welfare 24 (1): 63–77.

Rivera-Batiz, Francisco L. 1999. "Undocumented Workers in the Labor Market:
An Analysis of the Earnings of Legal and Illegal Mexican Immigrants in the
United States." *Journal of Population Economics* 12 (1): 91–116.

Rivera-Salgado, Gaspar. 1999. "Mixtec Activism in Oaxacalifornia: Transborder
Grassroots Political Strategies." *American Behavioral Scientist* 42:1439–58.

Rodríguez, Nestor. 1987. "Undocumented Central Americans in Houston:
Diverse Populations." *International Migration Review* 21 (1): 4–26.

Romero, Mary. 2008. "The Inclusion of Citizenship Status in Intersectionality:
What Immigration Raids Tell Us about Mixed-Status Families, the State
and Assimilation." *International Journal of Sociology of the Family*
34:131–52.

Rosenbaum, Emily, and Samantha Friedman. 2007. *The Housing Divide: How
Generations of Immigrants Fare in New York's Housing Market.* New York:
New York University Press.

Rosenbloom, Susan R., and Niobe Way. 2004. "Experiences of Discrimination
among African American, Asian American, and Latino Adolescents in an
Urban High School." *Youth and Society* 35 (4): 420–51.

Rosenblum, Marc. 2011. *E-Verify: Strengths, Weaknesses, and Proposals for
Reform.* Washington, DC: Migration Policy Institute. www.fosterquan.com
/news/everify0211.pdf.

Rosenzweig, Mark R. 1986. "Birth Spacing and Sibling Inequality: Asymmetric Information within the Family." *International Economic Review* 27 (1): 55–76.

Rotheram-Borus, Mary Jane, and Jean S. Phinney. 2008. "Patterns of Social Expectations among Black and Mexican-American Children." *Child Development* 61 (2): 542–56.

Roy, Kevin M., and Omari L. Dyson. 2005. "Gatekeeping in Context: Baby-mama Drama and the Involvement of Incarcerated Fathers." *Fathering: A Journal of Theory, Research, and Practice about Men as Fathers* 3:289–310.

Ruge, Thomas R., and Angela D. Iza. 2004. "Higher Education for Undocumented Students: The Case for Open Admission and In-State Tuition Rates for Students without Lawful Immigration Status." *International and Comparative Law Review* 15 (2): 1–22.

Rumbaut, Rubén. 1994. "The Crucible Within: Ethnic Identity, Self-Esteem, and Segmented Assimilation among Children of Immigrants." *International Migration Review* 28 (4): 748–94.

Rumbaut, Rubén, and Alejandro Portes. 2001. *Ethnicities: Children of Immigrants in America.* Berkeley: University of California Press.

Sabogal, Fabio, Gerardo Marín, Regina Otero-Sabogal, Barbara Vanoss Marín, and Eliseo J. Perez-Stable. 1987. "Hispanic Familism and Acculturation: What Changes and What Doesn't?" *Hispanic Journal of Behavioral Sciences* 9 (4): 397–412.

Salcido, Olivia, and Madelaine Adelman. 2004. "'He Has Me Tied with the Blessed and Damned Papers': Undocumented-Immigrant Battered Women in Phoenix, Arizona." *Human Organization* 63 (2): 162–72.

Salcido, Olivia, and Cecilia Menjívar. 2012. "Gendered Paths to Legal Citizenship." *Law and Society Review* 46 (2): 335–68.

Santos, Carlos, Cecilia Menjívar, and Erin Godfrey. 2013. "Effects of SB 1070 on Children." In *Latino Politics and Arizona's Immigration Law SB 1070*, edited by Lisa Magaña and Erik Lee, 79–92. New York: Springer.

Schaefer, John, Raul Caetano, and Catherine Clark. 1998. "Rates of Intimate Partner Violence in the United States." *American Journal of Public Health* 88:1702–4.

Schmalzbauer, Leah. 2009. "Gender on a New Frontier: Mexican Migration in the Rural Mountain West." *Gender and Society* 23 (6): 747–67.

———. 2011. "'Doing Gender,' Ensuring Survival: Mexican Migration and Economic Crisis in the Rural Mountain West." *Rural Sociology* 76 (4): 441–60.

———. 2014. *The Last Best Place? Gender, Family and Immigration in the New West.* Stanford, CA: Stanford University Press.

Seaton, Eleanor, Enrique Neblett, Daphne Cole, and Mitchell Prinstein. 2013. "Perceived Discrimination and Peer Victimization among African

American and Latino Youth." *Journal of Youth and Adolescence* 42 (3): 342–50.

Segura, Denise. A. 1989. "Chicana and Mexican Immigrant Women at Work: The Impact of Class, Race and Gender on Occupational Mobility." *Gender and Society* 3 (1): 37–52.

Seif, Hinda. 2011. "'Unapologetic and Unafraid': Immigrant Youth Come out from the Shadows." *New Directions for Child and Adolescent Development* 134:59–75.

Seltzer, Justin. 1991. "Relationships between Fathers and Children Who Live Apart: The Father's Role after Separation." *Journal of Marriage and Family* 53 (1): 79–101.

Seo, Michelle J. 2011. "Uncertainty of Access: U.S Citizen Children of Undocumented Immigrant Parents and In-State Tuition for Higher Education." *Columbia Journal of Law and Social Problems* 44 (3): 311–52.

Sheldon, Steven B., and Joyce L. Epstein. 2005. "Involvement Counts: Family and Community Partnerships and Mathematics Achievement." *Journal of Educational Research* 98 (4): 196–207.

Shelton, Beth Anne, and Daphne John. 1996. "The Division of Household Labor." *Annual Review of Sociology* 22:299–322.

Sigona, Nando. 2012. "'I Have Too Much Baggage': The Impacts of Legal Status on the Social Worlds of Irregular Migrants." *Social Anthropology* 20:50–65.

Silver, Alexis. 2012. "Aging into Exclusion and Social Transparency: Transitions to Adulthood for Undocumented Immigrant Youth." *Latino Studies* 10 (4): 499–522.

Simanski, John, and Lesley M. Sapp. 2012. "Immigration Enforcement Actions: 2011." Office of Immigration Statistics, Department of Homeland Security. www.dhs.gov/sites/default/files/publications/immigration-statistics /enforcement_ar_2011.pdf.

Singer, Audrey. 2004. *The Rise of New Immigrant Gateways*. Living Cities Census Series. Center on Urban and Metropolitan Policy. Washington, DC: Brookings Institute. www.brookings.edu/~/media/research/files/reports /2004/2/demographics%20singer/20040301_gateways.pdf.

Slack, Jeremy, and Scott Whiteford. 2011. "Violence and Migration on the Arizona-Sonora Border." *Human Organization* 70 (1): 11–21.

Smith, Robert C. 2006. *Mexican New York: Transnational Lives of New Immigrants*. Berkeley: University of California Press.

———. 2008. "Horatio Alger Lives in Brooklyn: Extrafamily Support, Intra-family Dynamics, and Socially Neutral Operating Identities in Exceptional Mobility among Children of Mexican Immigrants." *Academy of Political and Social Science* 620 (1): 270–290.

———. 2014. "Black Mexicans, Conjunctural Ethnicity, and Operating Identities: Long-Term Ethnographic Analysis." *American Sociological Review.* Prepublished April 9. doi:10.1177/0003122414529585.

Song, Miri. 1999. *Helping Out: Children's Labor in Ethnic Businesses.* New Brunswick, NJ: Rutgers University Press.

Soucy, Alexander. 2000. "The Problem with Key Informants." *Anthropological Forum* 10 (2): 179–99.

South, Scott, and Glenna Spitze. 1994. "Housework in Marital and Nonmarital Households." *American Sociological Review* 59 (3): 327–47.

Spagat, Elliot, and Amy Taxin. 2014. "AP Exclusive: California Immigration Holds Drop." *ABC News,* April 6. http://abcnews.go.com/US/wireStory /ap-exclusive-california-immigration-holds-drop-23213130.

Stacey, Judith. 1988. "Can There Be a Feminist Ethnography?" *Women's Studies International Forum* 11 (1): 21–27.

Stack, Carol. 1974. *All Our Kin: Strategies for Survival in a Black Community.* New York: Harper and Row.

Stanton-Salazar, Ricardo D., and Stephanie Urso Spina. 2005. "Adolescent Peer Networks as a Context for Social and Emotional Support." *Youth and Society* 36:379–417.

Steidel, Angel G. Lugo, and Josefina M. Contreras. 2003. "A New Familism Scale for Use with Latino Populations." *Hispanic Journal of Behavioral Sciences* 25 (3): 312–30.

Steinberg, Laurence, Susie Lamborn, Sanford Dornbusch, and Nancy Darling. 1992. "Impact of Parenting Processes on Adolescent Achievement: Authoritative Parenting, School Involvement, and Encouragement to Succeed." *Child Development* 63 (5): 1266–81.

Steinbugler, Amy C. 2012. *Beyond Loving: Intimate Racework in Lesbian, Gay, and Straight Interracial Relationships.* New York: Oxford University Press.

Stephen, Lynn. 2002. "Globalizacion, el estado y la creacion de trabajadores indiginas 'flexible': Trabajadores agricolas Mixtecos en Oregon." *Relacciones* 90:87–114.

———. 2007. *Transborder Lives: Indigenous Oaxacans in Mexico, California, and Oregon.* Durham, NC: Duke University Press.

Stepick, Alex, and Carol Dutton Stepick. 2003. "Becoming American: Immigration, Identity, Intergenerational Relations, and Academic Orientation." In *American Arrivals: Anthropology Engages the New Immigration,* edited by Nancy Foner, 229–66. Santa Fe, NM: School of American Research Press.

Stone, Glenn. 2006. "An Exploration of Factors Influencing the Quality of Children's Relationships with Their Father Following Divorce." *Journal of Divorce and Remarriage* 46 (1/2): 13–28.

Strunk, Christopher, and Helga Leitner. 2013. "Resisting Federal-Local Immigration Enforcement Partnerships: Redefining 'Secure Communities' and Public Safety." *Territory, Politics, Governance* 1 (1): 62–85.

Suárez-Orozco, Carola, and Marcelo Suárez-Orozco. 2001. *Children of Immigration*. Cambridge, MA: Harvard University Press.

Suárez-Orozco, Carola, Irina Todorova, and Josephine Louie. 2002. "Making Up for Lost Time: The Experience of Separation and Reunification among Immigrant Families." *Family Processes* 41 (4): 625–43.

Suárez-Orozco, Carola, Hirokazu Yoshikawa, Robert T. Teranishi, and Marcelo M. Suárez-Orozco. 2011. "Growing Up in the Shadows: The Developmental Implications of Unauthorized Status." *Harvard Educational Review* 81 (3): 438–72.

Sugihara, Yoko, and Judith Ann Warner. 2002. "Dominance and Domestic Abuse among Mexican Americans: Gender Differences in the Etiology of Violence in Intimate Relationships." *Journal of Family Violence* 17:315–40.

Sullivan, Teresa. 1984. "The Occupational Prestige of Women Immigrants: A Comparison of Cubans and Mexicans." *International Migration Review* 18 (4): 1045–62.

Svasek, Maruska. 2008. "Who Cares? Families and Feelings in Movement." *Journal of Intercultural Studies* 29 (3): 213–30.

Talavera, Victor, Guillermina Gina Núñez-Mchiri, and Josiah Heyman. 2010. "Deportation in the U.S.-Mexico Borderlands: Anticipation, Experience and Memory." In *The Deportation Regime*, edited by Nicholas De Genova and Nathalie Peutz, 166–95. Durham, NC: Duke University Press.

Taylor, Paul, Mark Hugo López, Jeffrey Passel, and Seth Motel. 2011. *Unauthorized Immigrants: Length of Residency, Patterns of Parenthood*. Washington, DC: Pew Hispanic Center. www.pewhispanic.org/2011/12/01/unauthorized-immigrants-length-of-residency-patterns-of-parenthood/.

Terrazas, Aaron. 2011. "Immigrants in New Destination States." Migration Policy Institute. February 8. www.migrationinformation.org/usfocus /display.cfm?ID=826.

Terriquez, Veronica. 2012. "Civic Inequalities? Immigrant Incorporation and Latina Mothers' Participation in Their Children's Schools." *Sociological Perspectives* 55:663–82.

Thomas, William I., and Florencio Znaniecki. [1918] 1958. *The Polish Peasant in Europe and America*. New York: Alfred A. Knopf.

Thompson, Ginger, and Sarah Cohn. 2014. "More Deportations Follow Minor Crimes, Records Show." *New York Times*, April 6. www.nytimes.com/2014 /04/07/us/more-deportations-follow-minor-crimes-data-shows.html.

Thorne, Barrie. 1987. "Re-visioning Women and Social Change: Where Are the Children." *Gender and Society* 1:85–109.

———. 1993. *Gender Play: Girls and Boys at School*. New Brunswick, NJ: Rutgers University Press.

Thronson, David. 2008. "Creating Crisis: Immigration Raids and the Destabilization of Immigrant Families." *Wake Forest Law Review* 43:391–418.

Tichenor, Daniel J. 2008. "Strange Bedfellows: The Politics and Pathologies of Immigration Reform." *Labor* 5 (2): 39–60.

Tienda, Marta. 1980. "Familism and Structural Assimilation of Mexican Immigrants in the United States." *International Migration Review* 14 (3): 383–408.

Trickett, Edison, and Curtis Jones. 2007. "Adolescent Culture Brokering and Family Functioning: A Study of Families from Vietnam." *Cultural Diversity and Ethnic Minority Psychology* 13 (2): 143–50.

Troilo, Jessica, and Marilyn Coleman. 2012. "Full-Time, Part-Time Full-Time, and Part-Time Fathers: Father Identities Following Divorce." *Family Relations* 61 (4): 601–14.

Tse, Lucy. 1995. "Language Brokering among Latino Adolescents: Prevalence, Attitudes, and School Performance." *Hispanic Journal of Behavioral Sciences* 17 (2): 180–93.

Uline, Cynthia, and Megan Tschannen-Moran. 2008. "The Walls Speak: the Interplay of Quality Facilities, School Climate, and Student Achievement." *Journal of Educational Administration* 46 (1): 55–73.

Umaña-Taylor, Adrianna. J. 2003. "Language Brokering as a Stressor for Immigrant Children and Their Families." In *Points and Counterpoints: Controversial Relationship and Family Issues in the Twenty-First Century*, edited by M. C. Coleman and L. H. Ganong, 157–59. Los Angeles: Roxbury.

Umaña-Taylor, Adrianna J., and Mark A. Fine. 2004. "Examining Ethnic Identity among Mexican-Origin Adolescents Living in the United States." *Hispanic Journal of Behavioral Sciences* 26:36–59.

Updegraff, Kimberly A., Shawn D. Whiteman, Ann C. Crouter, Susan M. McHale, and Shawna M. Thayer. 2006. "The Nature and Correlates of Mexican-American Adolescents' Time with Parents and Peers." *Child Development* 77 (5): 1470–86.

US Citizenship and Immigration Services. 2013. "Our History." Retrieved September 9, 2013. www.uscis.gov/portal/site/uscis/menuitem.eb1d4c2a3e5 b9ac89243c6a7543f6d1a/?vgnextoid=2f436782d3c37310VgnVCM10000008 2ca60aRCRD&vgnextchannel=2f436782d3c37310VgnVCM100000082ca60 aRCRD.

US Department of Homeland Security. 2011a. "FY 2011: ICE Announces Year-End Removal Numbers, Highlights Focus on Key Priorities Including Threats to Public Safety and National Security." News release, Office of Immigration Statistics. October 18. www.ice.gov/news/releases/1110/111018w ashingtondc.htm.

————. 2011b. *Immigration Enforcement Actions: 2010*. Annual Report, Office of Immigration Statistics. June. www.dhs.gov/xlibrary/assets/statistics /publications/enforcement-ar-2010.pdf.

————. 2014. "Table 12: Aliens Removed or Returned: Fiscal Years 1892 to 2012." *Yearbook of Immigration Statistics 2012*. Accessed September 2. www.dhs.gov/yearbook-immigration-statistics-2012-enforcement-actions.

Valenzuela, Angela. 1999. "Gender Roles and Settlement Activities among Children and Their Immigrant Families." *American Behavioral Scientist* 42 (4): 720–42.

Valenzuela, Angela, and Sanford M. Dornbusch. 1994. "Familism and Social Capital in the Academic Achievement of Mexican Origin and Anglo Adolescents." *Social Science Quarterly* 75 (1): 18–36.

Van Ausdale, Debra, and Joe Feagin. 1996. "Using Racial and Ethnic Concepts: The Critical Case of Very Young Children." *American Sociological Review* 61:779–93.

Vandenhole, Wouter, Estelle Carton De Wiart, Helene Marie-Lou De Clerck, Paul Mahieu, Julie Ryngaert, Christiane Timmerman, and Marie Verhoeven. 2011. "Undocumented Children and the Right to Education: Illusory Right or Empowering Lever?" *International Journal of Children's Rights* 9 (4): 613–39.

Van Hook, Jennifer, and Kelly Stamper Balistreri. 2006. "Ineligible Parents, Eligible Children: Food Stamps Receipt, Allotments, and Food Insecurity among Children of Immigrants." *Social Science Research* 35 (1): 228–51.

Villalón, Roberta. 2010. *Violence against Latina Immigrants: Citizenship, Inequality, and Community*. New York: New York University Press.

Vu, Jennifer A., Alison L. Bailey, and Carollee Howes. 2010. "Early Cases of Code-Switching in Mexican-Heritage Children: Linguistic and Sociopragmatic Considerations." *Bilingual Research Journal* 33 (2): 200–219.

Wade, Amanda, and Carol Smart. 2003. "As Fair as It Can Be? Childhood after Divorce." In *Children and the Changing Family: Between Transformation and Negotiation*, edited by A. M. Jensen and L. Mckee, 105–19. London: Routledge Falmer.

Waldinger, Roger, and Cynthia Feliciano. 2004. "Will the New Second Generation Experience 'Downward Assimilation'? Segmented Assimilation Reassessed." *Ethnic and Racial Studies* 27 (3): 376–402.

Ware, C. [1963] 1994. *Greenwich Village, 1920–1930*. Berkeley: University of California Press.

Warikoo, Natasha. 2011. *Balancing Acts: Youth Culture in the Global City*. Berkeley: University of California Press.

Waters, Mary C. 1999. *Black Identities: West Indian Immigrant Dreams and American Realities*. Cambridge, MA: Harvard University Press.

Waters, Mary C., and Karl Eschbach. 1995. "Immigration and Ethnic and Racial Inequality in the United States." *Annual Review of Sociology* 21:419–46.

Waters, Mary C., and Tomas R. Jiménez. 2005. "Assessing Immigrant Assimilation: New Empirical and Theoretical Challenges." *Annual Review of Sociology* 31:105–25.

Waters, Mary C., and Jennifer E. Sykes. 2009. "Spare the Rod, Ruin the Child? First- and Second-Generation West Indian Child-Rearing Practices." In *Across Generations: Immigrant Families in America*, edited by Nancy Foner, 72–97. New York: New York University Press.

Waters, Mary C., Van C. Tran, Philip Kasinitz, and John H. Mollenkopf. 2010. "Segmented Assimilation Revisited: Types of Acculturation and Socioeconomic Mobility in Young Adulthood." *Ethnic and Racial Studies* 33 (7): 1168–93.

Way, Niobe, Kirsten Cowal, Rachel Gingold, Kerstin Pahl, and Nirvani Bissenar. 2001. "Friendship Patterns among African American, Asian American, and Latino Adolescents from Low-Income Families." *Journal of Social and Personal Relationships* 18:29–53.

Weisskirch, Robert S., and Sylvia Alatorre Alva. 2002. "Language Brokering and the Acculturation of Latino Children." *Hispanic Journal of Behavioral Sciences* 24 (3): 369–78.

Weller, Susan, Roberta D. Baer, Javier García de Alba, and Ana L. Salcedo Rocha. 2008. "*Susto* and *Nervios:* Expressions for Stress and Depression." *Culture, Medicine and Psychiatry* 32:406–20.

Wessler, Seth. 2011a. *Shattered Families: The Perilous Intersection of Immigration Enforcement and the Child Welfare System*. New York: Applied Research Center.

———. 2011b. "U.S. Deports 46K Parents with Citizen Kids in Just Six Months." *Colorlines*, November. http://colorlines.com/archives/2011/11/shocking_data_on_parents_deported_with_citizen_children.html.

Willen, Sarah. 2007. "Exploring 'Illegal' and 'Irregular' Migrants' Lived Experiences of Law and State Power." *International Migration* 45 (3): 2–7.

———. 2012. "Migration, 'Illegality,' and Health: Mapping Embodied Vulnerability and Debating Health-Related Deservingness." *Social Science and Medicine* 74 (6): 805–11.

Williams, David R., and Chiquita Collins. 2001. "Racial Residential Segregation: A Fundamental Cause of Racial Disparities in Health." *Public Health Reports* 116 (5): 404–16.

Williams, David R., Harold W. Neighbors, and James S. Jackson. 2003. "Racial /Ethnic Discrimination and Health: Findings from Community Studies." *American Journal of Public Health* 93 (2): 200–208.

Willis, Paul. 1977. *Learning to Labour: How Working Class Kids Get Working Class Jobs*. New York: Columbia University Press.

Wiltfang, Gregory, and Doug McAdam. 1991. "The Costs and Risks of Social Activism: A Study of Sanctuary Movement Activism." *Social Forces* 69 (4): 987–1010.

Wishnie, Michael J. 2004. "State and Local Police Enforcement of Immigration Laws." *University of Pennsylvania Journal of Constitutional Law* 4:1084–2004.

Wrigley, Julia, and Joanna Dreby. 2005. "Children and Inequality." In *Blackwell's Companion to Social Inequality*, edited by M. Romero and E. Margolis, 213–37. Malden, MA: Oxford University Press; Victoria, Australia: Blackwell.

Yamauchi, Futoshi. 2006. *Early Childhood Nutrition, Schooling, and Sibling Inequality in a Dynamic Context: Evidence from South Africa*. Food Consumption and Nutrition Division Discussion Paper 203. Washington, DC: International Food Policy Research Institute. www.ifpri.org/sites /default/files/publications/fcndp203.pdf.

Yoshikawa, Hirokazu. 2011. *Immigrants Raising Citizens: Undocumented Parents and Their Young Children*. Russell Sage Foundation Publications.

Yoshikawa, Hirokazu, and Ariel Kalil. 2011. "The Effects of Parental Undocumented Status on the Developmental Contexts of Young Children in Immigrant Families." *Child Development Perspectives* 5 (4): 291–97.

Zephir, Flore. 2001. *Trends in Ethnic Identification among Second Generation Haitian Immigrants in New York City*. Westport, CT: Bergin and Garvey.

Zhou, Min. 1997a. "Growing Up American: The Challenge Confronting Immigrant Children and Children of Immigrants." *Annual Review of Sociology* 23:63–95.

———. 1997b. "Segmented Assimilation: Issues, Controversies, and Recent Research on the New Second Generation." *International Migration Review* 31 (4): 975–1008.

Zhou, Min, and Carl Bankston. 1998. *Growing Up American: How Vietnamese Children Adapt to Life in the United States*. New York: Russell Sage Foundation.

Zhou, Min, and Jennifer Lee. 2004. "The Making of Culture, Identity, and Ethnicity among Asian American Youth." In *Asian American Youth: Culture, Identity, and Ethnicity*, edited by J. Lee and M. Zhou, 1–30. New York: Routledge.

Zhou, Min, Jennifer Lee, Jody Agius Vallejo, Rosaura Tafoya-Estrada, and Yang Sao Xiong. 2008. "Success Attained, Deterred, and Denied: Divergent Pathways to Social Mobility in Los Angeles's New Second Generation." *Annals of the American Academy of Political and Social Science* 620 (1): 37–61.

Zolberg, Aristide. 2006. *A Nation by Design: Immigration Policy in the Fashioning of America*. New York: Russell Sage Foundation; Cambridge, MA: Harvard University Press.

Zúñiga, Víctor, and Rubén Hernández-León. 2005. *New Destinations: Mexican Immigration in the United States*. New York: Russell Sage Foundation.

Index

ABC Settlement Act (1991), 222n17
acculturation: and delinquent behavior,
235n5; Hispanic children's, 86. *See also*
assimilation
Adler, Patricia and Peter, 145
Adrián (husband of Inés), 19; arrest of, 189,
190; deportation threat against, 20–21,
24, 25, 31, 33–34, 189; relationship with
Inés, 33–34; salary of, 30
Aguascalientes (Mexico), immigrants from,
158
Alabama, citizenship requirements in, 103,
232n15
Alexa (daughter of Isabel), 58–59, 83; entry
into US, 62; household duties of, 94;
knowledge of Spanish, 84; role play by,
90; school problems of, 89–90
Amalia (immigrant woman), 37–38, 40
Amalia (schoolchild), on discrimination, 161
Amato, Paul R., 227n55
Andrea (child), fear of separation, 49
Andrés (*primo* of Inés), 41; fears of, 42–43,
45, 129; on immigrants, 42
Anita (immigrant woman): children of, 111–
12, 128; unauthorized husband of, 63–64
Applied Research Council, on deportation, 174
Arizona, S. B. 1070, 53

assimilation: downward, 135, 235n5; paradigms of, 235nn4,10. *See also* acculturation

Bales, Robert, 235n1
Barrios, Luís, 24
Bettie, Julie, 237n36
Betty (legal-status woman), unauthorized
husband of, 76–77
Boehm, Deborah, 60
Border Control, US: custody of males, 24
border security, US-Mexican: militarization
of, 2, 185; public opinion on, 223n22;
spending on, 222n19, 241n40
Border Wars (reality TV show), 191, 242n55
Bourdieu, Pierre, 230n40
brokering, children's, 85–90, 134–35; children's authority and, 88–89, 91, 95–96,
97; children's discomfort with, 86, 96–97,
176; literature of, 230n48; negotiation of,
88; translating, 85, 86–88, 93, 231nn49–
50; by unauthorized children, 93; by US
citizens, 93, 231n63. *See also* parent-child
relations
Brotherton, David, 24
bullying, 159–61, 164–65; ethnicity in, 159;
over language usage, 161; racialized, 168.
See also teasing

277

Camilo (US citizen child), 99–102; academic success of, 100–101, 102, 124; birth of, 114; effect of citizenship on, 101, 106; future prospects of, 123–24, 129, 130; gregariousness of, 106, 107; housework duties of, 111; identity formation of, 106, 124, 131; language skills of, 108; neighborhood of, 232n2; soccer scholarship of, 124; soccer skills of, 100, 106–8; on travel to Mexico, 128; unauthorized siblings of, 11, 101, 106, 113–14, 126, 176

Carlitos (US citizen child), Mexican American identity of, 125

Carlos (father of Camilo), 100, 106, 107; employment of, 101; as household role model, 111; migration of, 113; and reunification problems, 121, 122; on sibling status, 126; as stepfather, 113, 118, 208; support for Camilo, 112

Carmela (mother of Preciliano), 133–34, 138, 140; education of, 139

Carmen (unauthorized child): household duties of, 111–12; on legal status, 127

Carolina (unauthorized woman): children of, 164–65; deported brother of, 34–35

Celia (immigrant woman), on discrimination, 159–60

Center for American Progress, 174, 239n5

Central America: migratory patterns from, 240n28; refugees from, 181, 185, 241n29

Chavez, Leo, 4, 241n30

Chicharito (soccer star), 107

childhood, new sociology of, 235n10

Child Protective Services (CPS), children's invoking of, 88–89, 95, 231n56

children: appropriation of adult society, 135; creation of social knowledge, 135–36; cross-gender games of, 137, 236n19, 239n59; of divorced fathers, 226n42,45; in hostile school environments, 238n53; loner, 136, 236n17; narratives of, 197; racial/ethnic distinctions among, 136; rights during research, 198; school-based relationships of, 135; self-esteem among, 144; socialization of, 235n1

children, Hispanic: 86; awareness of immigration law, 7–8, 209; brokering work by, 85–90, 91, 93, 96–97, 134–35, 231nn49–50; bullying of, 159–61, 164–65, 168; characteristics of illegality, 137; child care duties of, 85; concept of fairness, 100, 126, 131, 195, 234n51; consciousness of legal status, 43–45, 47, 146–48, 151, 165,

168; cross-racial friendships of, 109, 158, 164; disclosure of immigrant heritage, 145–53, 161–63, 168, 169; discrimination against, 159–61, 237n35; educational experiences of, 13, 14, 103–4, 111, 130, 142–65, 237nn38,42; effect of deportability on, 53, 227n55; effect of illegality on, 8, 10–12; effect of immigration policies on, 174, 227n52; English proficiency, 108–9; ESL classes for, 121, 153, 155, 157, 183; in family decision-making, 85, 91; fear of deportation, 22, 42–49, 50, 103, 128–29, 147, 188, 189; fear of enforcement system, 194–95; feelings of difference, 167–70; in foster care, 174; friendships patterns of, 109, 233n28; and gendered enforcement policies, 226n37; home-based activities of, 109–13; in hostile school environments, 163–65; household duties of, 85–88, 90–97, 109–13, 110–13, 176, 179, 231nn61–62; immigrant versus second-generation, 146; on immigration reform, 193–95; with individualized education program, 142, 152; invoking of Child Protective Services, 88–89, 95, 231n56; isolation feelings of, 11, 157; knowledge of enforcement, 48, 49; knowledge of police, 47, 53; language usage, 106–9, 130, 142, 143, 151, 152, 166; Limited English Proficiency (LEP) students, 142, 143, 151, 152; in mixed-status families, 10–12, 59, 101–6, 109–14, 118, 122, 124–31; in new destination sites, 136; in New Jersey immigrant communities, 140–53; perceptions of immigration, 49–51, 53, 184, 190–95, 214–15, 237n35; pride in ethnicity, 51; role play by, 90; self-identification choices of, 165–66; sense of belonging, 53; separation from parents, 2, 3, 118–19, 120–21, 130, 174, 233n41; social construction of illegality, 177; on social differences, 50; social mobility of, 11; Spanish proficiency of, 108–9; stepfathers of, 113, 118, 208, 233n38; in unsafe neighborhoods, 135, 154–55. See also families; identity formation; parent-child relations; peer groups; schools; siblings

children, unauthorized: awareness of status differences, 126–27; behavioral problems of, 152–56, 237nn41–42; bullying of, 164–65; church participation of, 128, 129; deferred action for, 123, 186–88, 234n45; educational barriers facing, 103–4, 130,